AF572280

AROUND WEST FLORIDA *IN 80 YEARS*

A West Florida Pioneer Series Book

AROUND
WEST FLORIDA
IN 80 YEARS

by BRADEN LEE BALL

illustrated by LESLIE E. THOMPSON JR.

a venture of the University of West Florida Foundation
Pensacola

Printed in the United States of America

ISBN: 0-9659142-0-8

❧

Library of Congress Catalog Card Number: 97-60867

THIS BOOK IS DEDICATED TO
YOU!

I cannot be sure who you are, for I hope many will read these pages. But, very possibly we have met. How do I know that? Well... this story goes back many years, and as you will see there have been men and women, boys and girls by the hundreds who lived or ate in the hotels in which the Ball family lived... or who perhaps were students when I was at Palmer College, or the University of Florida. ☛ Perhaps you attended one of the Fall barbecues held at my Woodbine Springs farm. Or... we may have served together in Rotary, or on one of the several statewide or local boards of which I was privileged to be a part. ☛ Finally, perhaps we just met socially, for Pensacola has always been a friendly, social village, a place where it has been easy to meet people and make friends. Happily for me, those associations have been many and ever-so friendly! ☛ Yes, I may not know who is holding this book at this moment, but I hope I may consider you a friend. If we were not associates as you began to turn the pages, I hope we shall be once you have read the final paragraphs. ☛ I have enjoyed such a good life, in such wonderful and exciting times, that I wanted others to share my experiences. Thus this book is dedicated... to YOU! ☛ ☛ ☛

ACKNOWLEDGMENTS

Every community boasts a person whose keen interest in history helps keep the stories alive for future generations. In Pensacola, that person is John Appleyard. It was John who "egged me on" to write this book, and I thank him for his persistence and support.

In the course of preparing this manuscript for publication, I also made a new friend at the University of West Florida, Connie Marse. I want to thank her and Randy Williams for helping me become the first pioneer in the University of West Florida Pioneer Series.

CHAPTER ONE
Welcome to the Panhandle

In that great motion picture *Forrest Gump* the hero began the action seated on a park bench with a box beside him. One of his first lines was: LIFE IS LIKE A BOX OF CHOCOLATES . . . you never know what you're going to get."

That's pretty sound reasoning, but there's another thought that I think is almost as appropriate, and it goes like this: "LIFE IS A JOURNEY, AND HOW YOU TRAVEL FROM PLACE TO PLACE SAYS A LOT ABOUT THE UPS AND DOWNS YOU'VE EXPERIENCED."

In my own life that has surely been true. I can trace my life and that of my family by associating our good times (and less good times) with how we traveled from place to place, and the quality of the vehicles that carried us.

For example, my father, Hector Lee Ball, was slow to learn to drive. He was a very able man, with many skills; but getting behind the wheel, shifting gears, and steering the car, somehow made him nervous. He was a mature man and I was seven years old before he took the plunge and bought his first automobile, a 1917 Ford Model T (you know the kind . . . with the handsome brass radiator frame and the gas lamps beside the windscreen). We were getting ready to move once again, my father, mother and I, from an Alabama town to the village of Marianna, Florida, which was to be Dad's regional base for selling pharmaceuticals. In that somewhat remote town Dad reckoned that traveling from place to place might not be easy, thus an automobile seemed the logical answer. He ordered the car, and it arrived at a railroad siding in York, Alabama, traveling on a flat car. Dad was there to meet the train, and he had already engaged someone to be his chauffeur. They proudly drove that Model T across the state to Florala to pick up Mother and me, and with that

Dad's Model T looked just like this! It was a four door Touring Car Model, with isinglass curtains that would fold into place in bad weather. The three pedal Model T would go almost anywhere, and dad (with his chauffeur) did so. Once they were ticketed for speeding. The arresting officer said they were going seventeen miles per hour in a fifteen-mile zone.

magic carpet we made the short trip to Marianna. The Model T of that day was America's utility car; it was not a symbol of wealth or prestige . . . but it had four wheels and an engine . . . and it got us there. That's the way the transportation thread of my life's story was first spun.

How did I happen to remember that tale of so long ago? Well, the human memory is a strange thing. Many adults, when they approach advanced age, draw pleasure from being able to quietly relive events of the past. But others, of similar age or less, have problems with this. They bemoan the fact that they "just can't remember things . . . sometimes fairly recent ones at that . . ."

I'm one of the more fortunate ones. I don't know why, and certainly I can't produce any medical reason for my good fortune. But it is true that I can recall events vividly that occurred when I was quite young. Nowadays that's a handy advantage, for increasingly there are people who enjoy hearing about "the good old days." Of course, being a garrulous old man I like to tell stories of how things were . . . in those times.

An example? Let's turn back the calendar to that little Florida farm crossroads of Marianna, in 1917-1918.

My father had been married three times, my mother, Elizabeth Widgeon, twice. She was widowed, and at the time of the death of her first husband she had borne five children. I was the only child of her marriage to Hector Lee Ball. My early years had been in Virginia, and then Alabama, but in 1917, for reasons that remain somewhat obscure, my father, mother and I moved to Marianna. My half-brothers and sisters remained behind and were cared for there.

My dad was an unusual man. He was trained in the law, and in medicine, but as he reached mature years he found that he disliked both professions and he turned instead to sales . . . something he loved doing. Prior to his Florida years Dad had sold a number of things, but when we relocated into Florida's Panhandle he had become a sales representative for the National Drug Company, selling pharmaceuticals to drug stores and to country doctors. He was a very good salesman, glib of tongue, precise with facts, keen of memory. And people liked him. He was the type of salesman that customers liked to see coming. Everyone called him Doc . . . "Dr. Ball."

Dad chose Marianna as a place to settle because it was more or less centrally located in a sales territory which would carry him back and forth over much of the Panhandle and southern Alabama. These were times of great change for America, and especially for this part of Florida. The state had recently been "discovered," and destination resorts were being built up and down the peninsula. That next year—1918—was right in the midst of the first great land boom for some. But that wasn't the case in the Panhandle. This area was, you see, in the heart of the piney woods, close to former plantation sites, a part of the state's rather primitive farm country.

Marianna had about 2,000 residents. The little town was located near the Chipola River, and it was one of a series of similar villages built soon after the Louisville & Nashville (or Pensacola & Atlantic Railroad, as it was originally known) was put through in 1882. A second small line crisscrossed through the town, pushing south to Blountstown, where sturdy farmers produced excellent crops of vegetables. (This rather primitive short line, the M & B, the Marianna and Blountstown, was called "the Mud and Bump" by many locals.) Marianna, if your memory is good, was much like the mythical River City, Iowa, which Meredith Wilson created as the vehicle for his great show *The Music Man*. You'll see why shortly.

When our family arrived in Marianna my father's means were limited. Yes, he had purchased the Ford, and apartment rentals were all but unheard of there. So Dad arranged for the three of us to live at the Chipola Hotel, which stood opposite the public square. The Chipola was considered one of the three finest hotels in the Panhandle (only slightly below Pensacola's San Carlos and Tallahassee's Cherokee in service and appointments). However, if we compare the Chipola to almost any hostelry of the 1990s it would suffer badly in the study. Our rooms there were comfortable enough for that time.

The Chipola Hotel was a grand place! Of frame construction, the rambling, two-story affair had been moved to its in-town location from another site, and in the early 1920s had become the haven for many a salesman whose labors had carried him over rutted roads or aboard the not-too-comfortable coach of the Louisville & Nashville Railroad. The Chipola's dining room attracted many, for one could get a tremendous breakfast for thirty-five cents, a fine lunch for fifty, and a magnificent chicken dinner, with collards and trimmings, for seventy-five cents. No wonder people willingly traveled extra miles to stay or eat there.

A typical room at the Chipola Hotel would have looked much like this. There was a comfortable bed, a sideboard-dresser, and a single light suspended from the ceiling by a cord. Then there was a wash basin and pitcher plus a slop jar, complete with cover. In the more plush rooms there might also be some form of carpeting. Cost of such accommodations? One to two dollars per night.

The beds were soft, and each room had a single electric light bulb which hung from the ceiling. There was a neat, white slop jar beneath each bed, and on the dresser-sideboard stood a sturdy white ceramic pitcher and a companion wash bowl. If one wanted plain water, all he had to do was ring the bell one time and a porter would hurry upstairs with that water. If one wanted ice water, two rings was the proper signal. For hot water, the signaler rang three times, and so forth. The managers, Mr. and Mrs. Frank Edwards, ran a reliable establishment, thus the porters were almost always available and prompt in their deliveries. On the whole, the quarters were quite comfortable, especially when compared with housing in many local homes at that time.

The Chipola's comfort system was modeled after the nineteenth century's installations; that is, each room had its own fireplace, which fortunately worked well. Summertime brought another need. Yes . . . there were screens on many windows, but out in the country there was no such thing as mosquito control, and at night the pesky critters could make life miserable and sleep difficult. So each bed had its own large mosquito net which hung over the sleeper's head. This wasn't a perfect solution, but it helped.

Mr. and Mrs. Frank Edwards were wonderful, friendly, warm hearted folks. Mr. Frank was pencil-thin, tall, and always properly dressed, in suit, collar and string tie. His rimless spectacles were a permanent feature, and his duties included managing a large staff (large because help was plentiful and cheap) and keeping the guests happy. On some occasions, when Marianna was staging patriotic events, Mr. Edwards would portray Abraham Lincoln, and he did look the part.

The hotel's dining room was the domain of Mrs. Edwards. Now, you'll remember the nursery rhyme about Jack Sprat and his wife. He could eat no fat, she could eat no lean . . . and the illustrations always showed him look°ing like a bean pole and her with ample poundage. That description fit the Edwardses. Poor Mrs. Edwards suffered from her presence in the kitchen. I suppose she was a sampler, for she surely had a weight problem. Oh, she fought it, and tried various remedies. But I often heard her say that after she died they could wait one hundred years and then dig her up . . . and sure enough, the fat would still be there.

At any rate, she knew good food, and she made sure the guests got it. Her right-hand man we simply called Chef. He was an older man, with many years of good training and experience, and he knew how to cook. He had, of course, the benefit of quality ingredients. The hotel's chickens came from its own coop in the rear yard. These were chickens "grown on the ground," and they were always plump and tender. Quality hams and sausages came from area farmers who brought meat they had cured to the hotel, and vegetables too. Most items were purchased on a daily basis, for there was only a traditional ice box for protection. However, I will tell you that no kitchen and chef ever had access to better quality items.

The hotel's kitchen was built in the Southern tradition of that time, "out back and detached" because of the fire hazard, and the high heat of cooking. The range was a giant wood burning stove, and between top-of-the-stove cooking and the baking of biscuits and desserts, the kitchen was HOT. Chef (that's what we all called him) was not young but he bore a French look, with a thin mustache that curled upward on either side of his mouth. He was not a temperamental man, and those who worked with him liked him a lot.

The meals themselves, always overseen by Mrs. Edwards, were quite formal, really. This was no boarding house style. Each patron was carefully served by a uniformed waiter, who saw to it that each one got plenty to eat. There were many favorite meals, but the headliners were roast beef and fried chicken, and I'll have to tell you that Chef's chicken was an absolute delight. It was so

THREE FAMOUS CHEF'S RECIPES AT THE CHIPOLA HOTEL

FRIED CHICKEN

Get a young chicken, 1 1/2 to 2 pounds. Have 2 inches of lard in skillet. Salt and pepper chicken pieces, then roll in sifted flour. Place in hot grease. (Put large pieces in first into the hot part of the pan.)

When all chicken is in—cover for 5 minutes. Then open up and turn over brown bottom side. Cook for 30 minutes. Only turn once. Be sure to cover pieces with plenty of grease as it will boil up.

SMOTHERED COLLARD GREENS

Pick and wash collards good to remove grit. Take several leaves in hand, cut into bits. Fry 3 or 4 slices of salt meat in a frying pot. Leave the meat in the pot. Put the cut collards in the pork fat. Add a cup of water. Cover and cook for 40 or 50 minutes. With a cover on the pot cook rapidly for 10 minutes. Turn down heat. If water boils too low, add more water.

SOUTHERN PONE CORNBREAD

2 cups meal (water-ground best)
1 tsp. salt
1 Tbsp. lard
Cold water to make into dough

Sift meal, add salt and lard drippings—mix into dough with cold water and let stand a minute, adding more water if necessary. Shape into small pones and place on hot, greased shallow pan, leaving space so they do not touch. Press each pone with 3 middle fingers to leave imprint. Put in hot (450 degrees) oven for 10 minutes then reduce to 350 degrees, bake 30 to 40 minutes until slightly browned.

Serve with Smothered Collards.

good that those salesmen who had their own cars would drive miles out of the way to sit at the Chipola's table of an evening. The desserts were mighty good too.

And the prices? They are hard to believe today.

A wonderful breakfast, with eggs prepared just about any way in the world, plus grits, biscuits, bacon or sausage, sometimes with a gravy for the biscuits, was served daily. That word "breakfast" is inadequate. This meal was a FEAST.

The evening meal was equally sumptuous, with mounds of vegetables, and an entree that would rival in quality those served in the finest restaurants in New York or Paris (except that ours was country style).

Breakfast was priced at thirty-five cents, while dinner was seventy-five.

Of course, from my knowledge of what went on in the kitchen I will have to admit that the ingredients used were not in keeping with those used for the diet-conscious 1990s. Good old fashioned lard was used for deep frying, thus our wonderful chicken may have had a little cholesterol. On the other hand, the 40-gallon wooden barrel of Heinz pickles was as fine a food as one might pick up. Ummm . . . I can taste those gherkins yet.

The desserts were uniformly tasty . . . but one that I remember best never saw the inside of an oven. It was introduced one evening by one of the salesmen. After dinner he entered the dining room carrying a sizeable box and began handing out little rectangular packages in silver foil. They were cold. Everyone was a little skeptical, but one by one we cracked the wrappers and discovered what looked like a block of cold bittersweet chocolate. I was among the diners. "Go on, bite in." the salesman urged. And I did. That was my introduction to the Eskimo Pie . . . a treat that I will remember to my dying day.

Of course, as a boy I couldn't always stand prosperity. On school days Chef would pack me a fine lunch to carry, complete with fresh sliced white bread, sliced roast beef and fruit. Often, however, I would hurry to the school yard and trade my deluxe fare for the lunch bucket carried by one of my country dwelling peers, whose lunch might be a genuine baking powder biscuit and some salt meat or "sow belly." In such cases each felt that he had bested the other party. I still feel that way.

Living in a hotel might not seem too attractive to today's young people, but in 1918 such living held many advantages. First off, remember that was in a time prior to radio and of course television. News came to us only via newspapers, or by the stories brought into town by the sales representatives, all of whom stayed at the Chipola. These men were an education in themselves, for their routes carried them across the vast stretches of our state and usually others, and when they came to town they would have gathered all kinds of information not usually found in the print media.

Some of these salesmen drove cars, even though roads were all but nonexistent. Their Chevys and Fords were often not new, but a very few came in those great big boxy Dodge Brothers' sedans, or in one of Mr. Chrysler's fancy vehicles. Mmmm . . . those were little bits of excitement for a boy my age. That's where I learned that often the badge of success was the size and model of the car a man had. (You see . . . the thread of transportation was woven into my story even back then.) However, most "drummers" arrived by train, and would hire a drayman to haul their sample trunks to the hotel. There the salesman would unload his trunks and would position his wares in the large sample room.

Here the variety was huge, for each man was a specialist. As in *The Music Man*, if you'll remember, there was an anvil salesman, a man pitching notions and button hooks, a man whose line was "hard goods" while several sold

When World War I drew to a close just about every rural family possessed a large iron pot such as this. The pot could be suspended above a fire, and was used for everything from boiling dirty clothes to making that great traditional stew called Hoppin' John, frying fish or making lye soap.

shoes, farm tools, and best of all, fancy clothes which the ladies of Marianna and surrounding areas could not produce on their new Singer Sewing Machines. Each salesman had a target audience, one (or perhaps two) local merchants, and some from other towns too, who would come to the hotel to inspect the merchandise, dicker over prices and terms, and then often as not place an order. The salesman would spend several days in Marianna to see all his customers.

All of this took time, and during the slow periods the drummers would swap tales, or spread news for the local citizens, many of whom would drop by just to look. These visiting men all seemed to have a gift of gab, and no matter where they were there was constant conversation, often about things that a seven-year-old boy just ate up. Evenings, around the dinner table, I would stretch my ears to capture their gossip. In summer months, when these men of the road finished their meal and sat down in the large rocking chairs which lined the veranda, I would find myself a good listening post. I always learned something. During the winter the drummers gathered around the huge stove in the lobby to talk and smoke cigars.

One of the things I learned first was that these men were hungry for the

The Chipola Hotel had a large lobby with the potbellied stove as its centerpiece. There, seated in the dozen or so captain's chairs the drummers would sit after a big meal, swapping stories, giving advice, telling tall tales. Many would enjoy a good cigar today.

day's news themselves. This was the kind contained in the *Jacksonville Metropolis*, the *Pensacola Journal* or the *New Orleans Times Picayune*, which arrived in town on the morning or afternoon trains which came from east and west. Somehow the hotel had missed the opportunity to make a dollar on newspaper sales, and so I entered my own first business; I became a newspaperman.

My routine was simple, and afforded two opportunities. First, I would pick up my papers at the station, and then, later in the afternoon, as the salesmen gathered, I would go from man to man, hawking my wares. I always sold out. Then, of course, I would stand about listening to comments that might come from the salesmen's reading of events far away. Gradually the readers would take their leave, almost always leaving their papers behind. At that point I would slip in, pick up the discarded news sheets, and put them away for tomorrow . . . when I would venture down the street to where a local businessman had a sizeable chicken store. He needed lots of waste paper to keep his operation clean, and so I cashed in on both ends of the paper trade. For a seven- or eight-year-old, that was good business. One other point: these traveling men were often lonely, and company and conversation were precious to them.

Marianna was typical of ten thousand American towns of its day. It had no paved streets, and the point of focus was its square, around which most of the retail shops were located. There were a drug store, a bank, a dry goods store, a soda fountain, a dress shop, a men's clothing store, a shoe store, the livery stable, a feed store and a few others. Each was a typical small business, run by a family struggling hard to make a decent living. The stores catered to townspeople through the week, but on Saturdays they had an extra business traffic from the farmers from nearabouts. These sturdy men and their families would come into town in the farm wagon, hitch the horse to a post on the square, then enjoy their afternoon of shopping and gossiping. Some also did business at this time, bringing in fresh items from their fields for offering to the hotel and townspeople. There were good things aplenty in those wagons. Once again, my thread of life was pinned onto what I was observing. The farmer was usually a poor man, and his wagon, though sturdy, had usually seen a hard time. Most had not seen paint for years, if ever, and you could always get a bead on the affluence of the man by the state of his harness, or the state of his horse or horses. In a time when a family needed so much but had so little to buy with, transportation often enjoyed a low priority. No one ever said that to me, but by age eight I could figure that out for myself.

During our years in Marianna there were certain customs that were community wide. Some of these were pretty basic, appreciated by everyone, such as wearing overalls, going barefoot in the summer, or loving fresh fish. Then there was the asafetida bag. I suspect that almost no one of the 1990s has ever heard of such a device, let alone smelled one, or might even know what the bag was for. But . . . like Oshkosh-ByGosh overalls, this little article was considered a must in most households in certain seasons. The bags were small and homemade, usually cut out of waste cotton cloth. Inside, mothers would pack a handful of yellow-brown, bitter, offensive smelling resinous material obtained from the roots of several plants.

The asafetida bag, according to Southern mythology, was supposed to ward off childhood diseases; and so in those seasons when one was likely to contract some general malady, wise mothers prepared such bags for their children. Boys and girls alike wore them hung about their necks. Stink? My gracious, there are few things in this world that give off a more hideous odor. If the bags had any medicinal value it was in keeping the children from getting too close to one another, thus making it less possible to convey germs. I tell you that a school room where children wore such devices would never have been mistaken for a perfume factory.

I mention the asafetida bag because I was left out. And that made me very unhappy with my father. However, as a physician and the purveyor of professional medications, he forbade me to wear "the bag." Like any little boy I felt abused, left out, mistreated by my parent. But dad never relented. Alone of my classmates I did not put asafetida around my neck.

One other memory of Marianna in those times survives. The town had a volunteer fire company, and it was quite an honor for townsmen to be part of the fire brigade. The system there worked like this: If a fire broke out the word had to be flashed, by phone or messenger, to Mr. Frank Edwards, manager of the hotel. Then Mr. Edwards would rush into the town square where the fire alarm bell was located. It was Mr. Edwards' job (or someone else's from the hotel if he should be absent) to ring that bell with emphasis until the firemen could assemble, get the message as to where the blaze was, and then hurry to their duties. It was a primitive system, but not unlike what existed in many small towns at this time.

In the colder months the routine changed for some families. With their crops in and no planting due for some weeks they had little to do, so they would drive their wagons south, to the Gulf bays or inlets where shell fish were easily gathered. They would harvest a batch, then, hoping that the chilly weather would keep the oysters, salt mullet and mackerel fresh, they would hurry back to the Marianna square, where they would sell their produce. Many an oyster was sold in this way, at ten cents per dozen, opened.

One sort of hotel guest always livened things up in the town. The group (and there were several who came each season) included men who sold patent elixirs . . . you know . . . bottled remedies which they promised would cure everything from bunions to cancer. These men usually arrived in an old fashioned Conestoga wagon which had a drop down back that converted into a tiny stage. (Incidentally, most of those medicine show wagons were pretty fancy. Some were painted in bright colors, and a few had the traveling "doctor's" name lettered on the canvas side. There was a good lesson in this for my life's transportation theme: always beware of the person driving the very flashy vehicle; often there's some skullduggery somewhere. Forewarned is forearmed.) There, with wagon positioned on the square, these medicine men would begin their work by doing something to attract a crowd. Many of them had a partner, usually a man who could play the banjo. His music would ring out, and folks would gather to listen . . . after which the pitchman would regale his listeners with tales of what his nostrum would do. These men sold liquids that were probably at least 25 percent alcohol. After a good swig or two the drinker would feel a warm glow. After a day or two, such peddlers were gone.

I can still hear the chant of those medicine men. Once the crowd was assembled they would shout: "Now, LADIES and GENTLEMEN . . . step right up . . . step right up, for I have a message that every man, woman and child will want to hear. Step closer, please . . . for you'll not want to miss a single word . . . ."

A second group of hotel guests, almost one hundred strong, were the performers of THE MIGHTY HAAG BROTHERS CIRCUS. This was a genuine and legitimate small circus, complete with several elephants and other animals. Haag Brothers wintered in Marianna, and many of the cast would stay at the hotel. This was the time when they rehearsed new acts, and their band played and practiced new tunes. People from all over town would walk out to the circus campground to watch and listen. There were some mighty pretty ladies in their pink tights . . . and the strong man was mighty impressive too. Of course I got to know many of them well, since they were in town for a good many weeks before hitting the carnival trail once more. However, there was one warning signal that accompanied the circus. They traveled in trucks, some equipped with cages for the animals. During the winter quarters some of the roustabouts who were part of the show spent time repainting or fixing up the trucks, and on some quiet days I'd go out to watch. Even an eight-year-old could tell that those vehicles were not in tip-top shape. I'm sure they suffered many a breakdown on the road. There was a lesson in that for me as I continually tied my life to transportation.

Another of the salesmen who stayed at the Chipola Hotel regularly was a small, wiry guy who always seemed to be about to pop, he was that enthusiastic. This man had a line that people in town paid little attention to; his market was the farm and farm buildings. You see, he was a lightning rod salesman.

The man's stock in trade was the iron rod and all of the fittings that would direct a charge from the sky into the ground. And the way he sold his product was classic. This man would call at the farm house that obviously did not have such a device, and would say very politely: "Farmer Smith, I was just passing by and noticed that you have failed to protect yourself and your property from one of the greatest dangers we have when we live in God's wide open spaces, as you do."

Well, the average farmer would bite on that line. What did this man mean? At this point the salesman would open a portfolio of photographs and ask the farmer (and his wife if she were handy) to allow him to show some action pictures. And oh—those photos were graphic. There, in case after case were lovely farm houses and big, magnificent barns which had either been leveled or badly damaged when lightning struck. As the photos were displayed the salesman had a patter that could have accompanied a movie thriller on Saturday afternoon. Then he'd put on the clincher: "Mr. Smith, is it fair to your loved ones who have worked so hard to make this wonderful farm what it is

. . . or to the fine animals in your barn, to be without this protection? Why . . . who knows? Without a lightning rod you might be struck down this very night."

The lightning rod installation was not inexpensive, two hundred to three hundred dollars in most instances, and that was a lot of cash in those days. But after a time when we drove down the road and saw a house naked against this wrath of God, we had to surmise that this farmer was doing poorly, for surely he would have installed the lightning rod if money had been present.

Yes, this little man was a salesman.

And there was another man we'd see frequently, though he was not a patron of the hotel. This fellow was the sign painter. Now, there are sign painters and sign painters. I'm not talking about the man whose shop puts out direction signs or identifications for local businesses. No . . . this fellow painted advertising signs on the sides of barns.

You see, the automobile was really coming into its own, and as a person drove down the road he would pass many barns. Usually there would be a plain wall in sight of the drivers. This wall was the target of the painter. This era was long before outdoor advertising got to be a way of life, and what this man would do was make a deal with Farmer Brown, agreeing to pay him five dollars for the privilege of painting a big ad on his barn. The farmer could hardly lose. He was getting a new paint job on one face of his building, and he was putting five dollars in his pocket too.

I remember three messages in particular. One was a big red, white and blue sign that promoted BROWN MULE TOBACCO. The art was of the tobacco package, and the lettering suggested that HERE was the world's finest chew.

The second (and most popular sign) advertised Bull Durham smoking tobacco for roll-your-own cigarettes. This sign had REAL art. In addition to the letterings there was a lovely, demure cow, and a BIG handsome, red bull. The cow spoke the one punch line: "MY HERO," as she gazed longingly at the bull. Now . . . who could resist that?

A third barn sign was an ad for Dental Snuff. This product was around for quite some time and was a throwback to the nineteenth century. One of the boards I remember had two figures in addition to the words. A pretty girl sat on top of a rail fence and was admired by a handsome young man. The man said: "I think you have beautiful white teeth . . ." and she replied: "That's because I use Dental Snuff."

Oh, my!

One might have thought from what I've said thus far that all of the salesmen who called at the Chipola Hotel were male. Not so. One of the most memorable, and one looked forward to all through the year by the women of the region, was a lady with a German name (it may have been Helga). Helga was a professional corset fitter.

Now, in the 1990s, when the female form tends to flow quite naturally, the corset seems a device far out of the past, a device which some have described as a cross between an instrument of torture and baggage of the Victorian era. It was large. It was firm. It was designed to keep the wearer "in place" yet also to accentuate the female form in a way which few women accepted, before or after.

Now, I want you to understand that corsets were available from such emporia as Sears, Roebuck & Company, and I'm sure those garments were adequate and modestly priced. But the Custom Corset Maker's product was different, and thus became an object of desire, even though the price was far higher. These garments were custom-fitted and custom-made. They were form fitting at the most extreme. I can't speak as to their comfort, for happily men were spared such body controls. But, they were a part of life, a part to which local women looked forward.

Miss Helga (if indeed that was her name) was unusual in her own appearance. She was, as one critic described her, "mannish" in appearance. She always wore severe, long, cut dark skirts, and her shoes were low cut, almost like those men chose for dress wear in those days. Her hair was severely styled, and she had a rather deep tone to her voice. She was—well—different.

When Miss Helga arrived at the hotel she always arranged for her accommodation and also for a fitting room in which she would receive her customers. In advance word would have been sent through the proper grapevine so that Miss Helga's visit was anticipated by town dwellers and far-flung farm ladies as well. The customer would arrive and then arrange for a custom fitting. Now, I was never present for such an event, of course, but my open ears gave me a pretty good idea of what went on, for the male drummers kept up a pretty good dialogue as they discussed what they imagined might be happening behind that particular closed door. My Mother also gave me some vivid details.

Miss Helga's fitting materials included a sort of barrel shaped cloth device which was fastened around the torso of the customer. The fabric of this model was lined with what were called stays. Stays had once been made of whale bone, but by 1918 the more flexible celluloid was being substituted, for it would bend to body contours and made the garment's purposes more apparent. As Helga moved up and down the customer's body stays would be added or removed to best suit comfort and form. Stays, you see, could relocate certain body parts up or down, or even to the side in some cases. The corset thus compressed, transformed, adjusted, realigned and otherwise gave the customer the shape she desired. That often included a reduction of overall bulk, for one of the final aspects of the corset's design was that it could be drawn very tightly together. (A belle of the ball many times might appear in a gown which, through the aid of her corset, drew her dimensions to several inches less than nature had provided.)

The corset fitting might require an hour or more, and then the careful measurements had to be sent to the production house, where the corset was given its final shape and condition. Then, in the mail, the breathless customer would receive this device which, she hoped, might bring new style and beauty.

Was all of this successful in the eyes of the customer . . . and her beholders? Well, I guess for that day and time the results must have been satisfactory, for Miss Helga remained a favored visitor on a regular schedule.

I suspect that such things were natural. After all, ladies have sought assistance from beauty aids since the time of Cleopatra. Corsets were just one device. In Marianna Mrs. Edwards helped some who were her friends by providing a form of cosmetic which, for its time, became very popular. Mrs. Edwards' material was quite different. She blended bay rum with powdered talc, and then shook the mixture vigorously. This mixture was then applied lightly over the face, and it gave a bit of pleasant color and also served to conceal a blemish or two. Another point: the drug stores of those days did not provide a large range of cosmetics. Oh, they featured Lydia Pinkham's remedy, and for some this was helpful medicinally and in terms of appearance; for Lydia Pinkham's contained a hefty belt of alcohol, and one or two doses taken one right after the other could add a feeling of euphoria and also bring a dash of color to an otherwise pallid cheek. Either way, the result was a bit of the Elixir Juvinale—the elixir of youth—and what lady, regardless of age, does not seek this?

Another of the druggist's favored items was perfume, for in those days bathing was often on a once-per-week schedule at best. There was a well-used saying that if you can't come clean, at least come smelling sweet.

Not all of the sales representatives were short-stay people at the hotel. Some had a line which required a longer tenure, and usually these men would book rooms for a week or more at the hotel. Often I would get to know them well, and again, they taught me some valuable lessons in selling. When World War I came to an end and the Army began bringing home the remains of some local soldiers, there was a big short-term market in granite or marble grave markers. Salesmen for such things stayed around for quite a while to finish their work. (Tombstones are not items on which customers make up their minds quickly, thus the longer stay.)

One such man came with an allied but different purpose. This was an era when some of the Southern towns, now finally having a little hard cash after fifty-five difficult years, wished to raise a memorial to veterans of The War of Northern Aggression. This man arrived, and approached the commissioners of Jackson County with the idea of erecting such a monument in the middle

Patent medicines were often frauds, mixtures of alcohol and miscellaneous chemicals which, at best, did not harm the user. Cosmetics were also present in large variety. Mrs. Edwards, whose husband managed the Chipola Hotel, produced a whole line of cosmetics which she sold to customers who came to view the drummers' wares. BEAUTY AID claimed to clear a sallow complexion.

of the town square. This was not exactly like Professor Harold Hill selling band instruments and instructions via The Think System, but it was close. The commissioners didn't have the money, but they were easily convinced that the monument was a good idea. Now the salesman helped to set up a special company whose roles included raising the money and then formally purchasing and setting up the obelisk. Here the United Daughters of the Confederacy were active. I had to admire this salesman. The monument wasn't an easy sell, but he had the patience of Job, and one by one he overcame the obstacles. Sure enough, one day in 1921 the monument arrived and was put in place. There was a grand ceremony, and the people of Marianna felt that they had finally done right by the fallen men in grey.

I don't want to give the impression that Marianna was dull or primitive. Not so. For this time it was a very typical town, even though no one yet owned a radio. There were entertainments aplenty . . . a picture show (where I did odd jobs), picnics, parties, quilting bees, church suppers, and for boys, swimming.

My own part in the picture show is worth remembering too. In addition to helping keep the theater clean I was, on my shift, in charge of operating the player piano. The player piano looked like a standard upright, except that the front of the cabinet would open for the insertion of musical rolls. These rolls . . . one tune to the roll . . . fit into slots, and would be activated by a pedal which would turn the machine on. The roll would run across pre-set notches which set forth the melody. The operator had a second set of pedals with which he regulated the volume.

Our theater had three rolls. Each one involved a special kind of mood music . . . one for tender scenes, one for action, and one for drama. I would be given my instructions on what to play during which kinds of scenes . . . and then it was my job to watch the screen and add the appropriate musical theme at given points. The piano didn't play all the time . . . just at key moments. My only problem from time to time was that I got caught up in the action on the screen and forgot to add the underlying sound. But . . . I didn't do that often. Oh . . . and one other thing about going to that theater . . . at least for young boys. This was before the days when popcorn and candy were part of the routine. In that day the boys would go next door to the theater and buy a large dill pickle as they entered the show. Then, the careful youth would nurse that pickle all through the afternoon. I don't remember when pickles were replaced by hot buttered popcorn . . . but it was after my time as an operator.

And then there was swimming. Sometimes we would go down to splash in the river, and that was fine. But the best swimming was in Blue Spring, which was a considerable distance outside of town. For this we boys had a friend. The man's name was U. P. Hutchison, and he owned one of the first auto sales agencies in North Florida—again remembering that in 1918 there wasn't a mile of paved road outside of metropolitan areas like Tallahassee and Pensacola. This dealer owned a large, flatbed truck, with built up sides. And since he wanted to make every minute count he developed an idea for Saturday afternoons, when there was usually very little customer traffic in his business. Just after noon he would summon me and ask if I would round up a dozen or so boys and go swimming. I was thus his agent. I would scurry about and find the potential swimmers, each of whom would pay a quarter for round trip transportation. For my "work" I rode free, and was also paid fiftycents. My career in sales was definitely advancing.

One other point. The dealer was a hustler, a successful man, and he sold quality products. His truck was impressive too. It was almost new, and his mechanic kept it in fine condition. Its big engine hummed when it ran, and even with a full load of boys the vehicle could go up the fairly steep hill near town with no trouble. The dealer was successful . . . his truck was tip-top. Another lesson.

One part of life in those days (and later too, of course) was the famous yellow telegram. Arrival of that kind of missive, often brought to the family's door by a boy on a bicycle, meant a moment of hushed excitement. Who could be sending a message which commanded such importance? Often the news was good (a new baby had arrived . . . or a business deal had been successfully confirmed).

But then there was always the possibility that the telegram carried bad news, possibly reporting a death of a family member or friend. One thing we all learned in those days was that if there was a large star imprinted on the envelope of the telegram a death was involved. They don't do that anymore . . . but in the 1920s and 1930s everyone from young children on up were aware of what the star meant.

Boys had other forms of fun, especially when school was not in session.

You've heard this before, I suspect, for it was a factor in many towns of this time. Since excitement was limited, one of the Big Thrills of each day was the arrival of the L & N trains, which would come huffing and puffing into the town's depot down the hill to discharge or board passengers and mail. Freight

The Ol' Swimming Hole! In bygone days many towns had such a place, a spot where boys could swing on a rope and drop into a deep hole, or simply delight in the cool depths during a hot summer afternoon. The Ol' Swimming Hole on the Chipola River near Marianna was a delight.

trains arrived at other times. The passenger engine was a giant beast, shiny black, with a brass bell whose peal could be heard for blocks, and a whistle whose blast was so reliable that it was often used to set clocks. A train was something to admire; those who operated it were men to envy.

We boys would gather at the station, and then the game began to see which one might detect the coming of the train first. Now, that might seem like a game played on a level playing field, with each youth having a fair chance. Not so. There was one young boy who when it came to train detecting put the rest of us to shame. Each morning we would assemble, and this boy would begin placing one ear on a rail. Often his listening would be premature, but sooner or later he was able to detect the sound of the rhythm of the wheels on rails . . . and he would leap up with a big grin on his face and shout: "TRAIN'S COMIN' . . . TRAIN'S COMIN'." And sure enough, in another minute or two we would all hear the distant scream of the engine's whistle as

We boys loved to go to the railroad station in Marianna to wait for the train. Our favorite game was to see which of us would detect the train's approach first. One boy always seemed to win, for his sense of hearing was superior. He would listen, then shout "Train's coming . . . train's coming!"

the train neared a crossing, and then there would be the clickity-clack of cars over rail junctions as the cars rounded the bend and swept into the station.

Now, you may not think that was very exciting... and today, with the cold demeanor of the diesel engine as the driving force, I'll admit that a train isn't all that exciting . . . but in those days . . . well . . . I can still conjure up the sound of that whistle when a train passed in the night. About 1938 a songwriter crafted a tune which he called *Blues in the Night* . . . and some of the song's words dealt with this subject. I can hear it yet.

Trains and cars . . . a boy's interests just naturally moved in those directions.

My dad's first chauffeur for his Model T had been named Nathan, who for some time was a faithful servant. But Nathan departed for the Army and was succeeded by Dan, who proved equally capable. My dad's territory stretched over all of Panhandle Florida and beyond, and even though the roads were all but non-existent he and his car put on a lot of miles. Finally, Dad felt that the car's reliability might be coming to an end. The war had just been concluded, and automobiles were in very short supply. There had also been a significant wartime inflation. Dad had purchased the car for four hundred dollars. Now, with an estimated 150,000 miles behind it, the car still ran faithfully, but—as experience might have told me—this just might be the time to sell. Dad and his helper cleaned up the car, then put a small ad in the local paper. Sure enough, a nearby farmer was in the market for such a car, and he arrived for a demonstration ride, along with his wife. The four climbed in, the chauffeur driving, dad in the back seat, the farmer and his wife riding as passenger-observers. Before the prospect had arrived Dad had taken his helper aside and said something like this: "Now, Dan, this is important... and if we sell the car I'm going to give you five dollars."

Dan thought that was fine, and his glib tongue was working as the car and its passengers left the town limits and sped east. Things were going well when suddenly one of the back wheels came loose, and next thing Dan saw was this wheel rolling swiftly and steadily past the car, gaining as it went. The farmer stared, but Dan never lost a beat.

"Now, don't you be concerned about THAT." he began. "You know how it is with wagons. Every now 'n then a wheel comes loose and you just have to put it back on. Cars is the same. We have this happen all the time, and it don't

Many of Northwest Florida's streams and rivers were bridged with covered spans which added a picturesque quality to the landscape. The covers were built locally for two purposes; to keep bridge planking from rotting; and to shield the eyes of horses from the drop to the water. In a few places the covered bridges looked much like grist mills which also were located along streams where the current was swift enough to turn the mill wheel.

bother nuthin . . ."

The farmer, wise in the ways of wagons, nodded. Once the wheel was reattached and the ride finally ended, the prospect paid my father six hundred for the vehicle, and drove away happy.

Remember . . . I said that my father was a great salesman. That deal should prove my point.

Dad also was an outdoors man, and taught me a lot about nature. As a result, I loved fishing. A lot of what we did was with a cane pole in the Chipola River. Sometimes the results were good, sometimes not. One day old Tom Connley, a retired attorney, saw me coming home with my pole but no fish and he stopped his buggy and asked where I fished. I told him, and he smiled. "Tell you what," he said, "next week one day let's you and me go out and see if I can show you how to do better." That sounded good to me, and so a date was set and on that morning off we went, riding behind his logging horse.

We went out along the river, to a place I'd never been before. It was out of the way, and at length Mr. Tom pulled his horse off the road and behind some trees. We got out, and he went to the back of the buggy where, in a sort of trunk, he had a net. Well . . . Mr. Tom must have known that net fishing was a little illegal. As a lawyer he surely did. But that didn't matter. He showed me how to catch a mess of fish. I'd never seen so many. Now, I won't say that I ever copied Mr. Tom's technique, but I surely did put it down in my memory book.

Thinking back through the years, I like to compare modern trends with things I did back in Marianna, as a very young boy. The other day I read an account in the paper of how high school boys literally rent limousines to take dates to the prom. Well, I'll tell you they're not breaking new ground.

Back in 1920 I would do something like this, when my father happened to be in off the road and his car was not in use. I would invite two young lady friends to go with me for an ice cream soda. Then, Dad's faithful chauffeur, Dan, would drive me to their houses and we'd pick them up. The soda fountain was in a drug store on the town square, a block away, but distance had nothing to do with what we were doing. It was the principle, you see. Dan would drive us that block to the store, and the three of us would be served by the car hop and very properly enjoyed our ice cream soda. Then we would repeat the process in reverse. I tell you we were just as uptown in 1920 as these young fellows are today with their rented Town Cars. (One other point: one day when we enjoyed those sodas I discovered I had no money. Dan had to treat.)

Still another little anecdote about those good days in Marianna. We were all country people. Except for a single fancy dress that the farmer's wife might have.. and the man's one store-bought suit of clothes, most of what was worn was very basic and staple. Farm women wore long gingham dresses most of the time, sometimes with bonnets when they were outside. And of course the farm men preferred overalls . . . often from Oshkosh, Wisconsin, where Oshkosh-ByGosh was born. Those sturdy denim garments would last a long, long time, and today's styles, with their stone-washed appearance, would have been right at home back then. However, back then the manufacturers did not make the jeans designs so popular as those of today. So, young people would buy the overalls and then cut off the bib. Then they felt they were in style. I can still see myself, parading before the mirror in our rooms at the Chipola, admiring my figure in those bright blue cutoffs. At age eight I thought I was the cat's meow.

As we talk about clothing one other memory deserves reporting. In those days, as more and more dresses required dry cleaning, women had a problem. There was no dry cleaning plant nearby. The closest was The French Cleaners in Montgomery, Alabama, and that meant the cost involved two way transportation. So, many women did most of their dress cleaning by sponging spots, using a prepared liquid and a sponge which probably came from the Greek industry at Tarpon Springs. Or, they might take a chance and buy a gallon of Naphtha from the hardware store and do the cleaning—out of doors of course—by dipping the garment up and down in the solvent, contained in a bucket. Drying was done outside, so the breeze might not only dry the material but also drive away the naphtha's odor.

Step by step through those Marianna years I improved my selling skills, though of course I did this without any set plan. Things just happened. For instance, these were days before processed fertilizers became state-of-the-art on regional farms, and the farmers used imported guano from South America. Those bird droppings helped our porous soil a lot, but they lacked one specific ingredient—phosphorus—and this had to be added by the agent who sold to the farmers. That's how I was briefly a part of the fertilizer business.

In those days, you see, cattle roamed at will in North Florida. There were no range laws, and virtually no one could afford expensive fencing. So . . . the cows would drift back and forth, and they were not well cared for, either. Often, they would die, or be killed, far from "home," and the bodies would decompose where they had fallen. That left the bones. The enterprising guano merchant discovered that those bones could be ground into powder, added to the guano, and this would introduce the needed ingredient. That's where opportunity dawned for me. I would roam the countryside on foot with other boys on an afternoon, carrying a large burlap sack. I'd find those big bones and collect them, then carry them to the operator, who paid rather well for my service. By the time I was nine years old I almost always had coins jingling in my pocket.

Another point: in some of my other adventures I had traveled on some form of wheels. In the guano enterprise I rode Shank's Mare . . . I traveled on foot. Now, if one assumed that his life's theme would always lead upward, this might have seemed a step in the wrong direction. But no . . . I learned then that one has to fit the cloth to the pattern. It was easier and more practical to walk about picking up bones. Besides, what other choice did I have?

And so things proceeded through 1918 and 1919, and into the decade of the twenties. But by that year even a nine-year-old boy could see major changes beginning. Almost every day the square was crowded with new post-war motor cars. These were not well worn Model Ts but much larger, more expensive, high powered machines, Reos . . . Franklin . . . Essex . . . Packard, the kind that people of means enjoyed. Oh, my, I was impressed! Of course, many of those visitors would stay for a night or two at the hotel, and eat dinner with our regular group . . . so I got to see them up close . . . and to listen to some of their conversations. These people had money, and having money meant one could travel in luxury. Even the "look" of some people up and down the streets began to change. No, I don't mean that Farmer Jones' wife had discarded her simple frock, or that his overalls had been replaced by something fancier. Instead we could see a significant number of people we didn't know, walking up and down, peering into the stores, but most importantly, there were queues of men in and around the Jackson County courthouse, talking with the town's local lawyers, and then passing through the building's halls with large rolls of paper under their arms. At first I didn't know what they were carrying, so I asked. One of the drummers told me he thought they were building plans, or maybe property plats. We locals were interested, for these newcomers wore expressions of anxiety, and they walked with a hurried gait, unlike the slower moving farmers and townspeople.

These folks dressed differently. Their clothes were of lighter colors, in hues of tan, gray and blue, and sometimes with patterns. They wore shirts and neckties, some with fancy collars, and even their shoes were different. Most of the Marianna folks wore black shoes, many of them with high tops. Some of these visitors in the hotel wore knickerbockers (knickers), with wild plaids and long stockings. Only on Sundays were our men's shoes polished and shined. These new people had low cut shoes. Some were WHITE. A few were tan, and others still had two colors, like white and tan. The shoes had fancy toes too. And I saw one or two men that had funny things wrapped around their ankles. (One of the salesmen on the porch of the hotel told me that those coverings were called spats. I'm glad they never caught on with our people.)

What were all of those people suddenly doing in Marianna? The answer was simple, really. Earlier, when railroads were completed into the Florida peninsula, northern people with money began visiting the state during colder months. They liked what they saw, and began buying property. By 1920 they had made many such buys along the Atlantic and Gulf, and now some of them were "discovering" our part of the state. They had found that the once forested lands near Marianna had been cut over, and that the stump-filled acreage could be bought very cheap. They wanted to get their piece of land . . . and many did.

What did they do with it? Well, some seemed sure that citrus, already becoming a major crop to the South, would prosper in our area too. They cleared land and planted satsumas and a few other exotic items. Others had read literature which suggested that North Florida's climate and soil there were just right for producing mulberry trees, for silkworms to eat. And so, they began preparing silk "plantations." There were other agricultural prospects too, but like the first two, each required a genuine subtropical climate, with no intrusion by Old Man Winter. Well . . . for a few years these newcomers got their wish. I don't know why this was so, but it was. The winters in those years were exceptionally mild. There was no frost, no mornings when the temperature suddenly dipped to twenty degrees. To these new citizens it appeared that they had discovered a bonanza, low cost land and plenty of it where they only had to drop in seeds and take care of the plants. Mother Nature would do the rest. Yes . . . they thought that way, but of course in the long run their bubble burst.

Interestingly, NONE of those eager newcomers gave a minute's thought of replanting the crop which nature had placed there originally . . . the pine tree. That would have to come later. When the winter freezes finally did come, and other parts of Florida's first boom collapsed, the people wearing fancy clothes, knickerbockers and long socks packed their belongings, walked away from their plantings and departed . . . to be seen no more. Like my other adventures, this was fascinating to watch. In the watching I learned some good lessons.

Of course, not all of those who came at this time were seeking property.

Some, as has been the case in any land boom, came just to look around. They were sort of hangers-on . . . or as we might say later, tourists. One of my older friends at the time described those people like this: "They came with ten dollars in their pocket and some food in a tin can. They didn't stay long, literally ate out of the can, and when they left they still had the ten dollars in their pocket." He called 'em Tin Can Tourists.

In 1920 my father's business territory was altered, and so we left the friendly confines of the Chipola Hotel, bound for a new life that began in Bartow. That of course is another chapter, with its own special memories. But today, with more than four score years behind me, I can sit back and relive those times in the hotel, selling newspapers (twice), picking up quarters for hawking rides to the swimming hole, or collecting cow bones . . . and I think to myself: those were good times. And you know . . . they were. Times are very different for boys today, but even with their computers, adult-supervised sports leagues and fifty dollar Levi's, their experiences lack some of the flavor of what we enjoyed.

When we left Marianna and started down the road to Bartow we were riding in high cotton. My father had enjoyed a good year, and his extra earnings, added to the profits from his Model T, had enabled him to buy a fine Hudson sedan. I can't remember whether this was a new or slightly used automobile, but it was a fine piece of machinery. Hudson and Essex motor cars were made and sold by the same company, an English-based manufacturer. The Hudson was black, had a powerful Continental six-cylinder engine, and in the back seat there were soft cushions and a tie rope along the back of the driver's seat so that a blanket or "lap robe" might keep passengers warm during winter drives. As I rode along in that car I felt a sense of great pride. It told me that the Ball family was rising in the world. Happily . . . my memory seems to get better all the time. And those events and stories improve every time I bring them back to mind.

❧

CHAPTER TWO
Life in Panama City

My father's career as a pharmaceuticals salesman had centered in Marianna for some years because his assigned territory had included portions of Northwest Florida and South Alabama. During those years the Marianna location had been favorable; but as the 1920s began, his focus was directed more to the central part of Florida. This was so because that area, so long neglected, was being discovered by northerners who were venturing south on the railroad systems built by Henry Plant and Henry Flagler. Parts of Florida were in a boom which, to a degree, would one day affect the Panhandle also. My dad chose Bartow as a town which would give him a good working base, or so he thought. In that community, in the state's center, our little family repeated its housing arrangement, finding accommodations at the Commercial Hotel. Meanwhile, my father, aided by his faithful driver Dan, struck out to develop a sales territory.

I wish I could report that the move was a great success. It was not. Timing was working against my father, for while tourist visitors were coming to the state, the central part of Florida was not yet developing as a site for permanent citizens. Yes, there were hotels and boarding houses to accommodate the cold weather snow birds. But these were short-termers, and with only a modest permanent population, sales of pharmaceuticals were not outstanding. And living in that area year-round was not pleasant. At the end of the twenieth century everyone takes for granted the comforts afforded by air conditioning. But that innovation was not part of good living in 1921. Summers and even the fringe months were hot, humid, unpleasant. Even buildings with high ceilings and ceiling fans did not provide a good level of comfort. My Mother was not happy in Bartow, and this, combined with disappointing pill and potion sales, pushed my father to a decision. At the end of one year he chose to find another site for his headquarters. Thus Panama City came to be the Ball's city of residence.

Panama City is not far from Marianna. It is located on the Gulf, has marvelous natural beaches, plus numerous bays and inlets which make the region one of great beauty. By 1921 the population there was not far greater than that of Marianna. Local roads were primitive, and the humble Bay Line (the Gall Berry Special) was the only limited railroad connection. Much of the area's intercity transport came via small coastal steamers. However, my father and mother had faith in the town's future as they chose Panama City for our new home.

A quick look back in time helps provide a perspective for this region.

Early Spanish explorers had roamed the shoreline and forests, and Catholic missionaries had worked in this area briefly. During the second Spanish period (1698-1719) an outpost had been built on St. Andrew Bay by French interlopers who came from Mobile to try and by-pass the Spanish authority based in Pensacola. The little fort of Crevecour soon fell into disuse, and during the British period of ownership half a century later there were explorations of the area, but little else.

Once Florida became part of the United States American families slowly moved into the bay area. Some pursued lumbering, others developed plantations and chose the old name of St. Andrew Bay for their community. During the War Between The States the waterfront there was used by Southerners to produce salt.

In 1835 settlers had arrived and platted an eighty-acre area which they called Austerlitz (after the Napoleonic era battleground), but this location was soon eclipsed by the newly founded village of Saint Joseph.

In 1887 a group which was chartered as the St. Andrew Railroad, Land and Mining Company arrived and re-platted the land where much of downtown Panama City later developed. The new company, which neither mined nor had a railroad, sold property inexpensively, and a considerable amount was sold. However, there was only modest settlement. Then, about 1900, G. M. West of Chicago Heights, Illinois, arrived, had the land re-platted and so began what came to be called Panama City. Mr. West, a former railroad executive, invested heavily and so at last a true community began to emerge. He also founded two newspapers, with which I would one day be associated.

Nearby, other settlements were founded too . . . later to be called Lynn Haven, West Bay . . . Southport and more. Developers of these sites had dreams of growth, development and prosperity. And Panama City, like so many other villages which came into being early in this century, could be considered part of the state whose name had a magic ring to it when Northerners considered a new life. For most such villages growth would be at a snail's pace . . . but it wuld come. Panama City was such a place.

When our family arrived, Panama City had two hotels and several boarding houses. Early in the twenties, housing for the newly arrived was scarce, and my father's means remained at a level which made renting desirable. The family would have preferred rooms at the Pines Hotel, for it was posh, with finer appointments and a reputation for being upscale. But—the Pines' room and food rates were beyond our means, and so we took up lodging at the Panama Hotel. This hotel, like the Chipola in Marianna, was popular with traveling men. Its rooms were simple (the single light bulb, the wash stand and pitcher were familiar fixtures), and the food was good. There were connecting baths, which were far better than "facilities down the hall." There's little point in repeating other functions, for they largely paralleled those our family had enjoyed before. Mr. and Mrs. W. E. Hancock were managers of the Panama Hotel.

One memory that was indelibly engraved in my mind was the content of my father's sample case. In those days the pharmaceutical houses used a unique psychology to assist their physician-customers in patient relations. Dad's inventory of pills and nostrums was carried in a large leather covered case which folded out much like a fishing tackle box. The pills were kept in small vials, and the manufacturers always gave each coating a special, bright color . . . silver, red, green, yellow . . . even white. The idea, of course, was to allow the physician and patient to identify the use of the medicine by its color. However, when one worked on the inside he knew that there was more to the system than that.

Medicines then and now were packaged in different strengths, and sometimes the physician might begin his treatment of, say, a cough, by prescribing the lightest dosage. This pill might be bright green. If the patient returned saying that the first medicine hadn't worked the doctor would prescribe "a new one," this time in a red capsule. (However, this would probably be the same medication with a stronger dosage.) That way the patient would not question the doctor having given the same thing over again when the first dose had obviously failed.

In those days the medications available were limited. The three principal ailments were coughs, constipation and the itch, and the average doctor would be well prepared. The Red Devil, for example, was an explosive aid for bowel failure; two of those bright capsules and—WHAM! The other medicines were equally popular, if not so effective.

In any event, dad carried his sample case wherever he went. Sometimes he would make deliveries from his portable supply; at other times an order had to be sent to the drug house. But whatever the method, those brightly colored pills were a trademark, and Dad (or Doc as some called him) could always talk a good game about the effectiveness of the things he carried.

Economic times in Panama City early in this decade were not good. The recent war had produced a modest level of prosperity, for farmers had enjoyed strong markets, and there had been a demand for timber, lumber and naval stores. Now these products had settled into their normal income channels. There had been the anticipated recession following the war too, and that made things even worse. The country's new president, Warren Harding, was all but unknown in the South, and no one expected any kind of help from Washington anyway. (In those days that's the way Americans thought; few expected assistance from outside their own family, or perhaps from good neighbors.)

Because of the times, drummers who visited the Panama Hotel often were troubled. Their sales were soft, and they found travel across their territory more difficult, especially out of Panama City. In Bay County inland movement was almost totally by automobile, or by a taxi service which Mr. A. W. Lee provided. Mr. Lee was an adventurous soul who drove a huge ancient seven passenger touring car from Marianna to Blountstown, Wewahitchka and Chipley on a daily schedule. (I think his vehicle was a Packard, but it may have been one of those giant early Buicks. I just don't remember.) In any event Mr. Lee would start out of a morning and pass between five or six of the nearby towns. Both drummers and townspeople would take advantage of his inexpensive service.

However, whether in Mr. Lee's car or behind his own wheel, the drummer

When a man driving a horse and buggy rig came down a country road he would often find himself passing below a canopy of trees which shaded the rutted trail and brought a soft flow to even a scorching day. Under such a bower a horse might raise his ears and give a horsey sigh of relief. The driver, meanwhile might close his eyes and perhaps even nap for a moment in the comfort of that shelter.

had to travel over roads which were poor in good weather and treacherous in the rainy season. Northwest Florida's intercity trails of this period had been carved through forests and "paved" (I hate to use that term) with clay. Occasionally a mule-drawn road grader might pass over, sometimes adding a small quantity of dirt or fill, other times simply smoothing the surfaces. This equipment had large control wheels on either side to permit the operator to guide his work. Year after year, with heavy rains and runoffs occurring, the roads tended to depress. That is, instead of being at the same level as the land through which they passed, they would settle . . . a few inches at first, then after a time considerably more. Meanwhile, young trees which flanked the roadway grew to greater size, and with time they developed a sort of leafy canopy over the roads in some places. Thus travel could be almost like driving through a tunnel.

There were unique hazards too. Originally, when Florida became a U.S. Territory, its appointed county commissioners were given charge of roads, bridges and ferries. Early on this was a small task, for there were no roads, bridges or ferries. By 1921 the situation had improved, but not much. Over the larger rivers there were now narrow bridges which could handle what often had to be single lane traffic. At some large streams the old single operator ferry was still in use. But in many locations small streams were simply forded. This meant that the road's path took it to a place where a driver might cross over under his own power, his wheels swirling into water well above his hubs, his large rear wheels churning for traction. To cross such a stream the driver, of course, had to slow to a crawl.

My arrival in Panama City encouraged me to make new friends among the drummers (though of course there were some old friends from our Marianna days who simply moved from town to town as they peddled their wares). On arrival I had made a quick survey to see what kinds of odd jobs I might get, for I had become used to my side incomes from collection of animal bones or selling newspapers. However, at first Panama City offered few such opportunities. As a result I took advantage (with my mother's permission, of course) of invitations to accompany the salesmen on day trips as they drove from town to town. They would return to the hotel in time for supper, and next day would start a route in another direction. These little trips enabled me to visit the outskirts of Panama City itself, and also to move east, west and north to other settlements. There was also the chance to view conditions on the roads, and at the fordings. Which brought to mind one of the great stories which circulated about this time.

These were Prohibition days, of course, and across the Panhandle there were stills aplenty. Periodically there was news of "revenooers" making raids which often led to violence. We didn't have big city crime like they did in Chicago, but the area was not without its headline makers. One pair of these was the Blackwell Brothers.

Bob and Will Blackwell were plain old garden variety highwaymen. Sometimes they lay in wait for vehicles which they believed might be carrying cash from one place to another; or, more than likely, they would lie in wait at one of the creek crossings where the driver would be forced to slow down to inch his way through the water. As their reputation developed, the Blackwells were alleged to be killers, the perpetraters of such violence when the unwise victim chose to contest a robbery.

I can remember the stories of the Blackwells as their reputations mounted. The drummers of course were fearful; their routes forced them to pass through the danger zones, and when a new robbery (or killing) occurred these traveling men would embellish the details as they sat around the hotel stove, smoking or chewing. My ears burned with such details. My mother did not like such things at all.

At last the lawmen prevailed. I'm sorry that my memory is thin on how the capture was made, but it was . . . and the two outlaws were removed as a threat. One other tale told was of the big, black, fast car which the Blackwells drove. I never saw the car, but I heard many a story about it. I'm not sure just how that vehicle and the men who drove it fit into my life's theme of transportation and vehicles. Perhaps this was one of those little features which life provides . . . to give us a warning lest we wish for things we shouldn't have. In another case two desperadoes were caught, jailed, tried and found guilty of first degree murder. Ultimately they were hanged in the little town of Crestview. I wish I could relate that I had a front row seat for that event, but mother wouldn't let me go. However, several of the drummers were there, and their reports kept me on the edge of my seat. In memory I can still visualize the two criminals as their bodies swung back and forth on the Crestview scaffold. At such big gatherings it was not uncommon to couple a hanging with a political rally.

As my father's new routes developed he had reason to criss-cross the region. One road which he had to take with some regularity ran between Marianna and Panama City. This was lovely country, and the trail passed near several handsome bodies of water, including Round Lake and Compass Lake. Dad loved such lakes, and he came to develop a habit of slowing down for a brief rest as he and Dan drove this route. As he did so my father noticed that there was a new crop being developed in that area which offered much promise. This was the satsuma. Satsumas, of course, are a citrus product and grow on trees, and the thing that really caught Dad's eye was this handsome grove of trees which by then had grown sufficiently tall that harvesting the fruit had to be done with ladders or special long-handled fruit pickers.

Dad was impressed. Would it not make sense, he thought, to acquire some of this loamy soil which seemed so friendly to fruit, and to plant his own grove? Others were doing this, and since there was still a Recession in progress there was good property available—cheap. Dad couldn't resist. He bought 160 acres on Compass Lake . . . and then hired some help to prepare the land for planting. Within months his grove was under way.

This year was in the midst of a temperature cycle that apparently comes to North Florida with some regularity. The winters were mild . . . without frosts and certainly with no deep temperature dips. A year passed and Dad's trees looked wonderful. A second year went by, and now Dad was standing and watching his neighbors pick good cash crops of fruit. Still a third season came and went, and by now the trees were so attractive and the small satsumas so visible that casual visitors began to stop and ask to buy some. This became so troublesome that Dad even erected a sign which said OWARI NURSERY . . . NOT FOR SALE . . . or something like that.

Well, if things had continued in that vein for much longer I probably would have become the heir to a great citrus grove, but of course that was not to be. Mother Nature finally resumed her high-low temperature schedules, and one December cold winds and high humidity swept in and the entire area's growth of satsuma trees was wiped out. When that happened the value of the land plummeted, and my poor father was left a poorer and wiser man. So be it. Ultimately the property was lost for taxes, and my mother bid it in for fifty dollars on a Quit Claim Deed.

In the mid-1920s Panama City, like many other small southern towns, was casting about trying to find new sources of jobs and revenue. We were still some years away from the day when special interests arrived and built a kraft paper mill. And this was a period when the United States continued to close down World War I military operations. No hope for economic growth there. Local people hoped for an improved railroad connection, and prayed for some miracle that might provide some paved highways. At this moment such things

On September 1, 1937, the SS Tarpon and her captain, Willis Barrow, begin the slow descent into a watery grave! Tarpon sank in a storm off Panama City, with considerable loss of life. The vessel, which had been a principal source of commerce along the Gulf Coast for more than thirty years, was loaded to the gunwales with cargo… including cases of Spearman Beer.

were in the future. But there was one vital carrier who helped keep commerce flowing. He was Capt. Willis Greene Barrow with his coastal steamer, *The Tarpon.*

The *Tarpon*'s work along the coast dated from about 1906, when a group of businessmen in Pensacola got the idea of creating a service which would run between Mobile and Apalachicola, with intermediate stops, making one round trip per week. The men incorporated, gave their new company a fancy name, and then hired old-time mariner Barrow to go to New England in search of the kind of vessel they wanted. Barrow went, and found *Tarpon*, a vintage ship but with a new coal-fired engine and the kind of capacity that would make such a route profitable. Barrow, with his large mustache and a distinctive officer's cap which he seemed to wear everywhere, went into business. By the mid-1920s *Tarpon* and Barrow were a local institution.

The vessel would call at its Panama City wharf on Wednesdays heading east. Then, after its calls in Port St. Joe, Carabelle and Apalachicola, it would return, docking once more on Friday before heading on west. On the east bound run Capt. Barrow carried both freight and passengers, and I would often go there to watch the longshoremen and crew members off-load and then put new cargo on board. Capt. Barrow was a pragmatist. He also had a motto which went: "God makes the weather, and with His help I make the trip." Actually, the captain was often misquoted on this. Some people believed that he had said "GOD MAKES THE WEATHER AND I MAKE THE TRIP." Because Barrow was a religious man he didn't want the Lord to misunderstand his intentions, and so one day, when I had become associated with the *Pensacola News-Journal*, he came to the editor of the paper and asked that we print his true statement. We did. His trips seldom saw *Tarpon* run at less than 125 percent capacity. His small hold would be loaded to the fullest, and then Barrow would deckload every ounce the ship would take. Often *Tarpon* seemed in danger of foundering, so deeply was she laden. Passengers stayed in several small aft cabins. There was also a dining room stocked with goodies from Pfeiffer's Bakery in Pensacola.

Much of what Panama City's merchants used and sold came via *Tarpon*, and I would enjoy going to the dock to watch the action. This included new automobiles coming from Mobile. Then, usually, as noontime neared, the captain would walk up the street the two short blocks to The Panama Hotel, where he would eat his lunch. Everyone at the hotel loved to see him. He was both courier and news man, for his reports of what had been happening along the way were the town's best news source. Add to that that the captain was a big, friendly man, knew everyone by name and always had a word of praise for the hotel's cooking. Yes sir . . . Capt. Barrow and the *Tarpon* were really something. (Sadly, both were lost in a storm off Panama City Beach a decade later.) But . . . was it any wonder that a young boy like me would look at this seafaring pair and dream dreams? Again, the mode of transportation told me a story. Capt. Barrow was a legend in the course of the making; people along the coast who love history and stories of the past still talk about him. I was impressed.

Capt. Barrow was not the only seafarer to leave a mark on me as a boy. A second such man was Capt. Frank Wilson-Taylor. This jovial, red-faced mariner was English, and in the early 1920s he became a major carrier of finished lumber between Panama City and markets in Great Britain. His ship, the *Zinggara*, of Liverpool, was much larger and more powerful than the *Tarpon*, and its runs into our harbor were often on six-month intervals. This ship would tie up at the lumbermill dock, and usually the shippers would have made the arrangements for the loading of a full cargo. In those days this was a slow process, and to load perhaps five million board feet of lumber took several days. Capt. Wilson-Taylor was a precise man, and had his ship's maintenance lists prepared when he arrived. For such work he would contract with local boiler makers and engineers. He would spend his days on the ship supervising the several areas of work, but he would take advantage of his stay to book a room at the Panama, and he would be there for meals morning and night. The captain was a good customer of American goods sold in local shops; and he also made friends among the city's professional people. It was easy for Capt. Wilson-Taylor to make friends, for when he arrived he always carried a good supply of quality English spirits, wines and beer, and he would use these as gifts, or when he held parties on board his vessel. Captain Wilson-Taylor was always friendly to me too, inviting me, along with others from the hotel, aboard his ship to see his quarters and to watch the work in progress. He almost always had a little list of odd jobs that I could do for him, errands to the various stores in town. I looked forward to the arrival of the *Zinggara*. This handsome sea-going vessel—like the *Tarpon*—made an

Early in the century Minor C. Keith built the Bay Line Railroad between Panama City and Dothan. Keith had a record of successful railroad building in Costa Rica, where he had been in the banana business. Early in the century he hoped to develop banana imports in the United States, and Bay Line was to be his principal conveyance inland through the Port of Panama City. The cabbage stack wood burning engines looked like this, and engineers were friendly souls. If a man along the way needed a match or directions, he knew that he might signal the engineer and get the train to stop for his accommodation.

impression. Here again, the way people moved from place to place was important. By my twelfth birthday I had learned to catalogue such things, and to judge the place of a person in the world by the way he traveled.

It had been some years since the railroad had been engineered into Panama City. This was no intercontinental line with fancy passenger trains and porters in glistening white jackets. Instead, Bay Line ran about seventy miles from Dothan, Alabama to Panama City, and the route's principal products were related to the lumbering industry. The line was single track much of the way, and its equipment was probably second hand (or maybe more). I shouldn't say this, because my information was gotten by eavesdropping and not reliable sources, but I suspect that the line operated with a minimal investment in signal equipment.

I remember Bay Line for several reasons. As a boy I was like many another who liked to go down to the railroad's local yard and watch the trains, with their cabbage stack engines, come in, and to see workmen do the routine maintenance or the loading and unloading of cars. The train men were a legend to young boys. With their jaunty blue overalls and blue peaked caps, these men just seemed to exude excitement. The engineers were very special. Several of them wore red neckerchiefs, and once they got to recognize us boys they were not above giving their engine's whistle a friendly toot as they passed us walking towards the yard.

However, Bay Line had one story which was not good. I don't recall the date, but this event occurred at night. There is a point near Cottondale where the Bay Line's tracks intersect those of the L & N. At the time there were several accounts which tried to place blame for what occurred. In the dark of night trains from these two lines slammed together. Wreckage sent cars crumbling across the right-of-way, and there were several persons killed. As we sat around the hotel's dinner table for nights to come talk centered on this terrible accident. "There just wasn't proper signaling," one worldly wise drummer insisted. Another man was certain that one engineer had either gone to sleep or been doing something besides his job. We'll never know about that, for the poor man was killed.

However, that incident taught me another lesson which linked my transportation theme to life: no matter how good the equipment is, the success and safety of what occurs depends upon the person at the controls. Even the operator of a giant engine can be a victim when things go wrong.

I never forgot that.

In those days Panama City was like most deep South towns; people were strong in their support of their churches, and more than anything they enjoyed having opportunities to hear God's word preached in a powerful way. This was the era of the big tent revival, and the camp meeting. Just about everyone in town would attend these things, in part I suspect because their evenings were uncluttered by radio, television and the like.

It was in this period that a charismatic young man named Bob Jones came to town. Now I'll tell you that Bob Jones was something else. He stood tall, had the grace of a Roman senator and the voice of a Barrymore or Booth. When he expounded the scriptures people listened. Bob Jones's local ministry had not been planned as a long one, but people there loved him, and to keep him there they dug into their pockets and produced enough money to build Rev. Jones a sizeable tabernacle on the corner of Harrison Street and First Avenue. There Jones brought many a soul to the Lord, and of course he was fascinating to us boys. We would come, watch and listen, and by then we might just spend a little time watching those good looking girls in the audience. But . . . that was another story.

At length Jones decided that there was need in the Panama City community for a religious institute, and so he acquired use of land near Lynn Haven and began building his college. The buildings weren't large, and the faculty wasn't numerous, but for the next two or three years young people flocked to the Bob Jones College. It was something of which Panama City was very proud.

But then, as such things sometimes do, the bloom came off the rose, and enrollment at the college dropped. Meanwhile, rival backers appeared and began to woo the Rev. Mr. Jones away. Sure enough, the college in our midst faded and then closed, while Bob Jones University was being establishing in Greenville, South Carolina. I suspect that hardly anyone even remembers today that the college ever existed in Lynn Haven. The bigger university in Greenville has erased the Gulf Coast episode from most memories.

The story of Bob Jones and the building of his tabernacle helped to illustrate the generous spirit of the people of Panama City. They were, for the most part, poor and struggling, but they would open their hearts and purses to help others.

In those days everyone went to church. I won't say that everyone was truly religious, but church going was a way of life. It was a large part of family recreation. In summer months places like the sanctuary of the First Methodist Church were great Sunday or Wednesday evening gathering places, but they also could be hot as _____ . . . well . . . hot. There was no air conditioning, of course, and no overhead circulating fans. So each pew held several hand fans which the parishioners used, waving them lazily back and forth to create a modest breeze. Funeral homes furnished most of these fans, and that was true just about everywhere in the South. However, Dental Snuff got into the act at least one year.

Often during the summer months a congregation would call a revivalist, who might be in town for a week, giving hell-fire and brimstone sermons that always attracted a crowd. Sometimes these preachers were so popular that they commanded extra support. One case lives in memory, and this occurred in the Methodist Church building.

It was right in the middle of the morning service, with this preacher really wound up to a Class II frenzy when, suddenly, the back door opened and there—coming down the aisle in their white, hooded robes—were six members of the Ku Klux Klan. The preacher halted in mid-phrase, and the congregation seemed to be struck dumb. Down the aisle marched the visitors, and when they reached the front one stepped forward and gave the reverend a sealed envelope. "Here's a little something special to carry on your good work," said a very deep, hard to conceal voice. Then the sextet turned and started back down the aisle. As they did so a tiny girl, sitting with her mother, cried out: "Ooooh . . . look, Mommy, there's Daddy wearing his Sunday shoes!"

Immediately the cadence of the Klanners increased as they all but ran from the room.

In the early 1920s there were people in need who today we might classify as "the homeless." Two of these were an older couple, both of whom were blind. They had come to the area from who knows where . . . and had tried their best to keep body and soul together by selling notions, playing music and singing. People liked them, and pitied their situation, for often money was so scarce for this poor couple. Their plight was sad.

But then H. L. Sudduth raised the possibility of townspeople pooling extra dollars to build these poor people a little home. Believe me, this was no easier then than it would be today. Sudduth located a piece of inexpensive property, begged and borrowed building supplies and erected a nice little house for them. They were two grateful souls . . . and I will never forget the ways in which they expressed their appreciation. Yes sir . . . the people of Panama City were very special . . . and this incident proved it.

It was in the late 1920s that people from far away began to discover the Panama City area (again). As had been the case in Marianna, these folks began to arrive driving big, handsome cars (Dusenbergs, Cords, Reos, Packards, and I even saw a Stutz Bearcat once). We could spot these people half a block away as they walked down Harrison Avenue, which by then had been paved and even had lights too, for their clothes were of the latest style, and in the evening some of the ladies would strut about in their flapper gowns. Oh, they were something!

As had been the situation in Marianna, many of these folks had come to prospect for real estate. They liked the waterfront, and they saw other prospects around some of the beautiful bayous, such as Philips Inlet. Most of these folks stayed at the Pines Hotel, our really first class hostelry, though as they began to arrive still other fine inns were being constructed. One was called the Cove (and naturally it was located right on the water) . . . the other was the Dixie-Sherman.

Now I will tell you that prior to October 1929 land purchases around Panama City had gone into high gear, and many people who had never dreamed of selling property were out hawking "great buys." My mother was typical. Mother had many talents, and I suspect that she had long found time hanging on her hands as she lived life in one or two hotel rooms. Now selling became a possibility, and she quickly disclosed a new side to her character. Mother was a good salesperson. And, along the way I helped.

One of the business people I came to meet along the way was named B. G. Jones. He had a number of interests, and he was one of those friendly, outgoing southern gentlemen who would always be popular with youth. He was just a nice guy.

One afternoon, as we waited for the supper hour, Mother began telling me about a new piece of waterfront property that she now had available to sell. There were several acres, and it was going for one thousand dollars an acre. (That figure, incidentally, was an increase of probably one thousand percent over a very short period, for up until a year or so before land sales were at an absolute standstill in our area.) Owners who needed cash were willing then to unload at almost any price. Well . . . I made a mental note of mother's tale, not having any idea why. But the very next afternoon several of us boys were working for Mr. Jones in one of his enterprises picking up an odd nickel. Suddenly he began talking about how he would like to pick up a good bargain in waterfront land. I listened carefully, and then, when the others were out of earshot, I asked him:

"How would eight acres at one thousand dollars an acre sound? Is that what you're looking for . . . over on Red Fish Point?" Well, Mr. Jones' face lit up, and he said that sounded like his cup of tea. I told him I was in the business now, and next day I would help set up a viewing. And I did. I put Mr. Jones and mother together for a conference, and sure enough . . . he bought the property. After that mother was never shy about sharing her opportunities with me, but I'm afraid I wasn't too much help from that moment forward.

Among the visitors to Panama City were some who came as vacationers and stayed at the hotel. One of these was from the mid-west, and was named Carl D. Settlemeyer. Mr. Settlemeyer was a big, friendly man, who always wore fancy silk shirts and very fashionable clothes. One day after breakfast he asked me if I knew how he might do some deep sea fishing. I assured him that I knew just the right captain with a modest-sized boat to take him out. Whereupon Mr. S. said to me:

"Tell you what, you check this man out, and then if we can work something you come along, and bring one of your friends too."

That didn't take a whole lot of arranging, and next morning the four of us, the captain, Mr. Settlemeyer, my friend and I, left the docks, well-equipped for a day's fishing. We had hardly gotten out of sight of land when Mr. Settlemeyer dug into his belongings and brought forth a flask from which he took generous sips every few minutes. Before long he was stretched out in the shade of the small cabin, sound asleep, snoring deeply. He did not come to again until the day was all but over and we were approaching the dock on the return trip.

Meanwhile, my friend and I, with the captain's help, reached a good location and put bait and tackle to work. Sure enough, after a half hour or so we had a huge strike. The battle between fish and boys went on for well over an hour, and when it ended we had a 169-pound shark on board.

When we docked a big crowd gathered to see our catch, and there was even a *News* reporter (it may have been Mr. William Adkinson but I'm not sure of that). Photos were taken, and shortly a story appeared in the press noting Mr. Settlemeyer's great catch. We two boys were shown too, but the story credited the visitor with the victory. To read about it one would have thought that he alone had done battle with the fish, with my friend and me simply looking on.

Almost thirty years later the *Pensacola News-Journal* ran that photo again. But this time only my slim portrait appeared, sans fish and associates. The little story that accompanied the photo told of the fish, and then asked people to try and identify ME, as I stood there in the mid-1920s. What goes around comes around, or something like that.

To this point I've said little about my education. In fact, rattling along as I have, one might think I was a Huck Finn, never setting a bare foot inside the school house door. That wasn't so. Yes, Panama City did have a sound school system, and yes . . . I was a student. I'm afraid, however, that during the grammar school years my interest in readin', writin' and arithmetic was something short of sensational. So were my grades. I limped along, not exactly the bane of the teachers' existence, but then hardly the star pupil, either. That's the way it went through my days in the sixth grade, at age thirteen.

However, there was one subject I enjoyed a lot—art. Miss Bessie Norton was the teacher, and she made me feel that I was really an artist. I felt that I had talent, and along the way enjoyed the class exercises and doing other things too, out in the open, such as trees and flowers and the like. I never went very far artistically, but I did cover a good many sheets of drawing paper. I also had encouragement from F. M. Felix, the local sign painter. He was so good . . . and I spent hours watching and learning from him. Occasionally he would even let me help him. However, by age fifteen my artistic efforts seemed to have ended. Then, many, many years later, my hopes rose again.

It came about this way: I guess I had passed my seventieth birthday when one day an old acquaintance called me to say she had something she wanted to show me . . . something she thought I'd enjoy. We met, and there in a brown paper wrapper was a picture frame. “Braden,” she said, “I was browsing in an antique store the other day, looking for a particular kind of old fashioned frame, you know, something for use in our den? Well, there in this shop I spotted just what I wanted. There was even a picture in it . . . and when I looked at the bottom there was YOUR signature . . . Braden Ball, 1924. Well, naturally, I bought it, and here it is.”

With that she unveiled painting and frame, and sure enough, I could remember the work . . . done so many years before.

“That’s mighty handsome, isn’t it?” I began . . . admiring both art and frame.

“Oh, indeed!” she said. “Now, Braden, I’m going to use the frame, right where I said I would . . . and if you want you may have the picture.”

I was stunned. After all, she might have put out a considerable sum . . . I thought.

Then the lady continued: “Yes, I was very lucky. The man in the store was most accommodating, and even gave me his appraisal. Guess what I paid for this?”

Showing a great deal of modesty I declined to venture a guess.

“Fifty cents!” she cried, breaking into a laugh. “And you know, Braden, the store manager said that the price was the value of the frame.”

I still have the picture . . . and I’m proud to display it. And, in one sense, graphic arts would help to shape my career.

I was in the sixth grade when some events occurred which—unknown to me at the time—began to shape my career and my life. This began when Mr. William Adkinson became a “regular” at the Panama Hotel. Not that he was a resident there. He wasn’t. Mr. Adkinson was a likeable man, and I suspect that he had several strings to his bow, for he could hardly have made a decent living on the sole income from his work as “a stringer” for the *Pensacola News-Journal*. Pursuing this calling he visited the hotel regularly to pick up news tips. I liked Mr. Adkinson, for he was friendly and outgoing; and we enjoyed talking about the local stories he covered and telegraphed to Pensacola. As our friendship blossomed I had no idea that some of my own activities would soon link the two of us, or that I was taking the initial steps towards a career in journalism.

The first of these happenings occurred in mid-summer. I was out of school, and there was no time-demanding job at the moment. One morning I was available to accept an invitation from one of the "regular salesmen" who was staying overnight at the hotel. This man was a sales representative for the Lewis Bear Company, the large Pensacola-based firm which wholesaled a huge list of items for grocery stores and others too. As it turned out, this man and a second drummer who sold a similar line of goods were about to rent a motor launch and go across West Bay to the company store which served the large turpentine still there. This would be a day long jaunt, the weather seemed perfect, and since I had no conflicts I checked for my mother's okay and then we three took off.

Renting a launch was an accepted way to make sales calls in those days, for there was no road, bridge or telephone to the still site or other similar customers. Having two or more salesmen ride together to share costs was common practice. We set off and enjoyed a fine ride. We were getting close to the landing when—suddenly—our boat ran aground. We were on a sandbar, and since these men were not regular navigators to that region this was a not unusual happening. In any event, we were stuck . . . and we were out of sight or hearing of the shore. It was too far to swim to shore too . . . and so there we sat . . . hour . . . after hour.

Darkness fell, and by now people were beginning to miss us in Panama City. Mother was frantic, hotel guests scurried about seeking advice, and Mr. Adkinson, taking a few liberties with the known facts, pieced together an account of our absence which he hurried to his Pensacola editor. Next morning, when the *Journal* arrived, there was a prominent story which declared that two Pensacola-based salesmen and young Braden Ball, who had gone fishing in the gulf, were now missing and presumed lost.

Happily, the next morning's high tide floated our craft loose, the men made their calls, and we were back at the hotel by late afternoon. I'll tell you my mother gave me a piece of her mind. And at supper that night the folks around the table made us feel like celebrities. After all, we had been the focus of a search . . . and we had had our names in the newspaper. This was to be my first experience with journalism . . . and what I saw impressed me.

It wasn't long afterwards that Mr. Adkinson asked if I'd like to go with him across the bay to cover what might be a modest story, and though mother had reservations she said yes. We were getting close to our objective when, ahead and over a spit of land, we spotted the tall sticks of a four-masted vessel on the Gulf side . . . standing stark still. We beached our boat and ran forward over half a mile of sand, and there—sure enough—beached and immobile, was the *Cornelius H. Callahan* . . . . There were still a number of vessels of this type and size in the nearby Gulf, but this was the first time I had seen one up close . . . and the *Callahan* became even more of a curiosity when we discovered that she was skippered by a tall, gaunt red-headed woman. Immediately, Mr. Adkinson's nose for news rose . . . and he plunged into an interview. That evening, once we were back at a telegraph signal, he dispatched his story . . . and once again it was possible to see the end result in print.

It wasn't long afterward that I was browsing on the downtown docks when a strange sound was heard which caused us all to look up. There, circling just above the water, was a pontoon-type seaplane. The craft was in a steep bank, its engine sputtering, and one wing riding high. The plane was obviously in trouble and trying to land in the shelter of the harbor. Moments later she sat down . . . and as the pontoons planed the smooth surface the engine died. Now the plane settled down and began to drift toward the shore. Without power she was at the mercy of wind and wave action. Minutes later three naval aviators were visible, and as we watched they began several rather frantic motions, trying to alter the path their craft was following. Why? Because it was now obvious that one pontoon was headed straight for a partially submerged, cut-off piling. Their efforts failed; a few seconds later the lightweight cover on the pontoon was pierced with a sickening crunch, and the aircraft began to take on water. The fliers climbed onto the one still solid pontoon, threw a rope to the landing, and with the help of several bystanders drew the craft to the safety of the shore, where she was tied up.

This aircraft was novel to us onlookers for several reasons. Of course we had all seen airplanes before, but this model was different. She had been built by the Navy in Pensacola, and her frame was of locally milled hardwoods, probably mahogany. The design had apparently been done in the local shops, which may have explained the power malfunction. However, the trio of fliers had come to shore safely, and now were ready to remedy their problem.

The first thing that one man did as soon as the craft was fast was to reach deep into the rear seat. At first we thought he might be looking for a coat, or maybe even his lunch. But no. Slowly he withdrew one hand, and there carefully held was a pigeon. Now a second flier assisted, and he tore a small piece of paper from a pad in his breast pocket, and a message was slipped into a tiny tube already afixed to the bird's leg. Then, the pigeon was released, and up it went... circling first, then heading west. This was the first time any of us had witnessed use of a carrier pigeon for communication in the military . . . or anywhere else, for that matter.

The Navy men accompanied several of us to the Panama Hotel, where they booked rooms. Next they settled down at the hotel for supper. The next three days were like a side show, with the fliers as the actors. The three men were congenial fellows and obviously loved flying. As we boys gathered around they told us story after story of their harrowing lives, and with each episode we became more interested. Finally, a work crew arrived from Pensacola. In twenty-four hours the torn fabric had been repaired, and the engine's problems were corrected. Meanwhile, the faithful Mr. Adkinson was sending a daily account of this adventure to his papers. Each day another tale appeared. At length the plane taxied onto the open water and soon was gone. But the memory of their visit lived on. I was impressed by the news coverage they generated; and I was equally excited about flying. Here was still another way to travel... and being able to rise high into the sky and move with blinding speed... well... you can bet that I liked that.

Still another story, carefully prepared by the ever faithful reporter Adkinson, involved liquor . . . a yacht . . . and Prohibition. The national ban of liquor sales was, of course, an invitation to some to break the law for profit... and with Cuba and its supplies so close it was not unusual to have smugglers bringing cargoes of rum or whiskey slip into the bay by night. These rum-runners were wily creatures. Often they would slip close to shore, then send a man onto land to make contacts with the purchaser of their illegal cargo... and also arrange to refuel. On one occasion a handsome vessel arrived and anchored several hundred yards offshore. Word was quietly out to the receivers, while other crew members were detailed to "fill her up." Such vessels never came right to the docks, for this might have meant a quick identification and arrest. Instead, they remained several hundred yards out, and their fuel would be brought in large milk cans aboard a launch. And so things went this day. The gasoline arrived, and two men began pouring it into the vessel's tank. Things were going smoothly when one of the deckhands spotted a speeding launch heading south towards them. All on board were sure that the oncoming boat carried "Federal men." HURRY was the word, and that's what the fuelers tried to do . . . only as they worked, considerable gasoline was spilled. Finally, almost in desperation, the operator cranked the engine, which spit and fired. The combustion set off the spilled fuel, and in seconds a sheet of flame began to engulf the ship. All of the crew members dropped into the service launch and sped away. From shore several of us could see what had occurred, and we gave the alarm. Small boats hurried out to help, and soon had the blaze under control. When all was calm the high powered launch was towed to a repair shop, where under government orders she was stored. Then it was turned over to my friend B. J. Jones, who was instructed to use his waterfront boat yard to display and hopefully sell the vessel as a prize.

However, for reasons unknown, no one stepped forward. Mr. Jones placed the boat under careful guard at his own boat yard, expecting that the public would produce a buyer. That didn't happen . . . and so Mr. Jones, by default, became the vessel's owner. For years to come he had custody and use of this fast, larger craft. The missing bootleggers were gone, and apparently they had lost interest in their conveyance. As you might imagine, this too was one of Mr. Adkinson's stories well received in Pensacola. For B. J. Jones the *Glendover* was a prize with a history.

As you can see, events were beginning to shape my future.

It was at the end of the sixth grade that my parents decided to expand my educational horizons. I'm not sure why they did what they did . . . but perhaps they were afraid I would become the village dolt and be a charge upon them for life. But . . . whatever the reason, I was now enrolled in the Palmer College Academy, a combined high school academy and liberal arts school operated in the little town of DeFuniak Springs. Palmer College was a Presbyterian school, with a heavy church influence. It was also a place where the operators worked hard to provide quality schooling, and offered many opportunities for a person to work his way through.

The annual projected cost for me, room and board, and studies and books, was to be $365.

Some people might laugh at this today, but I know this meant a significant sacrifice for my parents, and at once I began looking around for a way to earn at least a little money to help offset those expenses.

DeFuniak Springs was the typical small Florida town of that day. There were no campus hangouts, and surely no fast food outlets. Students who had any hankering for extra food that they might enjoy were just out of luck. However, there was a small grocery in the town's center, near the railroad station. The combination gave me an idea. I visited with the store's owner, and discovered what he would charge me for several slices of bread (hand sliced on his new machine) and some sliced boiled ham, with perhaps a few leaves of lettuce. Then I sampled the market. Yes indeed . . . there was an almost daily want of ham sandwiches, and at ten cents apiece I could make several dollars a week. A new financial career had begun.

About this time I made the acquaintance of one of the young scholars who was part of Palmer College's athletic program. This young man was a fine athlete, excelling in several sports, and he had a full scholarship for which he had to clean one of the dormitories each day, using a so-much-per-day schedule. He also cared for the furnace. As we got to know one another better this young man confided that his schedule, for practices, homework et al, was making life difficult, and he wondered if I would take on certain aspects of the work, to be paid twenty-five cents per week. I jumped at the chance.

Then fate intervened.

I had done this cleaning work for just long enough to be known and appreciated by college officials for my efforts when my friend was hurt playing football . . . so badly that he could no longer be a sports participant. In a flash his schooling was over . . . and he was gone. Now school authorities turned to me, asking if I'd like to take on the housekeeping job *in toto* . . . with the full payment, not some paltry quarter a week. I jumped at the chance . . . and from that moment forward I lifted the financial burden of my education from my parents' shoulders.

Now . . . there are some good stories to tell about Palmer College and DeFuniak Springs in the 1920s . . . for both had a lot to do with my future.

I have a confession to make about my job maintaining college buildings. Even at a quarter per week this assignment had carried some wonderful perks. One was that, instead of taking my meals at the dining tables where one had to dress up, I got to eat with the cooks and student waiters in the kitchen. To a mature adult that might not have seemed a benefit, but to a growing boy with an insatiable appetite it was great to be in line for leftovers, which for most meals were ample. Take breakfast, for example. The fare seldom varied. It included cereal, eggs (fried or scrambled), grits, bacon and toast, and unless something unusual happened, there was always a heap of crisp bacon, and mounds of eggs and grits left. Of course, unexpected shortages could occur, and by chance they often involved milk. That might mean that we at the end of the food chain would have to pour water on our dry cereal instead of country whole milk. I don't recommend the substitution, but when you're young you can stand anything on occasion.

During summer vacations I went back to Panama City and stayed with my parents in the hotel, and each year I'd find a job to help meet my school expenses. The summer when I was fifteen things were a little slow, until a man showed up who worked for the Otis Elevator Company. The ten-story Dixie Sherman Hotel was being constructed, and at the time I mention, the elevators had been cased in, but had yet to be calibrated or lead treated. I talked to this gentleman about his work, and he finally took the hint and asked if I would like some part-time work. Of course I said yes.

For the next several days my task was to go up and down the hotel stairs, and at each level this man would move the car to me so that I could stand on its roof and lubricate the chains and guides with caster oil. It wasn't a difficult job, but it did require a lot of movement up and down those steps . . . and then I do not recommend the smell of caster oil. But . . . aside from that things went fine.

Finally, one day he changed our routine.

"Braden," he began, "now we're going to test the safety devices. I want you to get 2,200 pounds of sacked cement from the contractor, and put it in the left hand car."

I performed that little task with no strain. Then, we both rode the car to the top floor, and he gave me a second set of directions.

"Now," he said, "you know that as we've worked we've been bypassing the stops as we worked with this little chip..." And at this point he pointed at a chip with which I was already familiar. "Okay," he continued, "I'm going below, and when I shout I want you to pull out the chip and we'll see how the car performs."

With that he departed, and I entered the car to await his signal. Finally, it came, and I pulled out the chip. Immediately, the car started down . . . not slowly but with a jolt. I passed the ninth floor level, then the eighth and then the seventh. By now I was in what I can only describe as a free-fall. Down I went, one more floor, and then, with a great rattling of chains and screeching of brakes, the car (with me and the cement inside) came to a jarring halt.

At this my employer came bounding up with a big smile on his face. "Boy, that works just great. Wasn't that fun?"

Well, it sort of depends upon what one classifies as fun. You see, what he had done was put the cement in the car to approximate the posted safe weight limit the car might have in use. Then, with the safety stop pulled, he was making sure (or trying to) that the car did what it was supposed to do in an emergency. Fortunately for me it did.

"Okay," he then added. "Now you can shift the 2,200 pounds to the right-hand car, and we'll do that one the same way."

Well, we did, and that one worked fine too. But when we were through I had to question whether or not my mother had raised any stupid children. I wonder too what the today's OSHA might have thought of that stunt.

Plans to erect the ten-story Dixe Sherman was a topic of conversation for everyone in Panama City through 1927. After all, the city's prior hotels had been modest, and now the little city by the sea was to boast about its own skyscraper with a marvelous waterfront view.

The contractor worked hard through the summer and by fall the hotel was about finished, and the owners prepared for a gala opening. The community's "who's who" all received invitations to an evening on the hotel's roof garden for dancing and entertainment. Believe me, every household fortunate enough to have members invited could talk of little else.

Every household save one, that is. Dr. A. S. Hill, one of the city's patriarchs had been a highly successful country physician, former mayor and banker. He had a few years on him, and that made him what some folks call "set in his ways." He examined the invitation, then applied what he knew and understood of modern engineering and high-rise construction.

"No, we're not going," he told Mrs. Hill. "I'm not setting foot on the top of any skyscraper till I'm sure the building's quit settling into the mud. You never know what might happen. No sir . . . I'm not going."

And they didn't.

☞ ☞ ☞

At the academy (or college) my room was in the boys dormitory (there was a companion building for girls). Actually we lived very well. Palmer College had been founded and was operated under the direction of the Presbyterian Synod of Florida, and its format involved the standard years of high school plus two years of college, what today they might term a junior college. Right next to the Palmer campus was the Thomas Industrial Institute, which also was a combined high school and lower level college. These were successors to a state normal school which had been located there late in the 19th century. Our student body, which included day students, was about evenly divided between boys and girls, and the faculty was both able and strict. About sixty students lived in the dormitories. The college president, Dr. Herbert Love, was an able theologian, and our days began with a thirty-minute chapel service, and each day we had a sort of vespers too. These were conducted in the college lecture hall; on Sundays we walked the several blocks into town to attend services at the Presbyterian Church or the church of choice. The Thomas Institute, by the way had Methodist backing. It was no fly-by-night school, either. Among its graduates were future Governor Fuller Warren, future State Education Superintendent Thomas Bailey, and future Florida Supreme Court Justice B. K. Roberts.

At this time DeFuniak Springs was little more than a village. It had been founded in the 1880s when the Louisville and Nashville Railroad was built, and the town was located there because of the lovely little lake which stood not far from the railroad right of way. The town had a grocery, a tailor shop, a picture show and several boarding houses which were a legacy from the early days of Chatauqua . . . and this is a story that must be told.

Chatauqua had been conceived in Jamestown, New York, at a site on the western bank of Lake Chatauqua. Its origins related to an outburst of American desire for culture which followed the War Between The States. The New York Chatauqua grounds included a large number of frame boarding houses and several places where well known lecturers and artists might perform. As it grew, that version of the summer showcase lasted for several weeks.

When Col. William Chipley and Fred DeFuniak pushed the L&N through the piney woods of north Florida they were working in wilderness, and they knew that to make their new rail line prosper they must find means of attracting people from far away to see the land and want to buy it and live on it. Together, they conceived the idea of creating a Florida version of Chatauqua, and then to offer special excursion fares and bargain attendance costs. To house the enterprise they built a huge tabernacle on the lake shore . . . and for the next thirty years this summer series prospered. But with the coming of World War I and competing forms of entertainment, the plan faltered. By the time I arrived in DeFuniak Springs the original building stood idle, and the summer-long program of entertainment had been reduced to a single week in mid-summer. However, the Redpath Chatauqua was something no teenage boy would ever forget.

An advance party for the show would arrive several days in advance of the performers, and would erect a beautiful red-topped tent. Then they would do as many circus advance groups did . . . they would raise posters and signs, and begin ticket sales. By the opening night the tickets were usually all gone, for people from miles around had learned to appreciate the wonderful music, the plays, the serious lectures that made up the week's series. One might not have thought of little DeFuniak Springs as a cultural center, but for us it was . . . and I learned to appreciate things through that medium that would never have crossed my path otherwise.

Another similar summer event was the week's visit of the Coburn Minstrels. This was the fine old minstrel show, with humor, music, costuming and more. I can still close my eyes and see the banjo player as he strummed those great old tunes. It took a few coins to buy a Minstrels ticket . . . but students wouldn't have missed it.

And then there was football.

I was always a big kid, and even in the eighth grade I stood tall, carried a good deal of weight and could hold my own in physical contacts with boys who were much older. My first year at Palmer College I did not play ball. Between learning how to study, maintaining two dormitories and getting started with the college annual I had more than enough to do. But as the second season approached, the coach came to me and urged that I try out.

Now, trying out makes it sound as though there was a long line of prospective players and scholarship boys anxious to "do or die for Ol' Palmer." Not so. We had barely enough ball players to field a team, and Coach R. M. Brice, who had played for Davidson College, had to do some selling to put his team on the field. But he did.

I'll have to admit that those were good days. We practiced in the late afternoons on a field near the college, and then had a schedule that included games with Troy State Normal, Hartford College in Alabama, and schools in places like Blountstown, Tallahassee and a few others. Now remember—this was the mid-1920s, and there was just the beginnings of "big time college football." Yes, the Rose Bowl was played each year, and the Army-Navy game and the Harvard-Yale classic was reported in the papers. But the great stadia of 1995 were yet to be built. Places like Chicago, where the Soldier Field had been constructed to seat 120,000, were the exception.

Now, our games went something like this: we would drive to a game in a big old seven-passenger Packard touring sedan, with our equipment strapped on the top (or on the back behind the spare tire). I say seven-passenger, and that was the car's normal full load. Our team would stuff five or six more people into the available space, and that one vehicle was IT. We looked like a band of gypsies. There was no such thing as a "field trip." We drove to the game site early on a Saturday morning, would play the game and then drive back the same night. And yes—there was usually a pre-game meal, usually furnished by the host college.

When it came time to take the field we would come out dressed in uniforms that resembled the biblical Coat of Many Colors which Joseph wore. Ours, however, did not rely so much on different colors as it did on patchwork, for heaven knows how many seasons those poor jerseys had seen.

The game was played before an audience which might have reached 150 people, all of whom stood along the sidelines. There were no seats, except the low benches for the players. Usually there was a single paid official who had to have eyes in the back of his head to keep peace and order.

One of our rituals that always drew laughs came when a substitution was made. When a player came out of the game he had to quickly strip off his jersey and pass it to his replacement, for there was only one full set. And if we lost more than one boy to an injury we just played along as best we could. No one worried about having too few players on the field; too many, of course, was another matter.

Substitutions afforded an opportunity for trickery. Our coach had one play which he always kept in reserve for late in the game. In it a player coming out would pass his jersey to his replacement, who would come onto the field and then pretend that he had forgotten his helmet. Then he would start back to the sidelines. But instead of returning to the huddle he would lie down—inbounds . . . and hopefully out of sight of the opposition. Our quarterback would quickly call the play, we would line up, and the half-back would fade back and throw a pass to the boy who had been "hiding." It was all very legal, and the referee, if he saw what was happening at all, could hardly be sure of where that man had started the play. Many an opposing coach screamed "FOUL" after we had scored on that play, but somehow it usually worked, unless the pass itself went astray.

Most of the players on both sides were good old country boys, not too sophisticated in the football arts, but big and strong and anxious to go out and hit somebody. And they did. But after a game was over there would usually be a get-together to have fun. Often we would get to meet girls from the other school, and I'll confess that I liked that, especially when the older girls over-estimated my age. But once or twice I got left in the lurch very quickly when a sophisticated coed discovered that I was several years her junior. Oh . . . and when we would win, the coach would give us each a big five-cent cigar. Again recalling our opposition, I remember our Palmer College record as pretty even; we would win some and lose some, with no particular stars appearing against us . . . except one. In my final year we played Hartford and that school had a halfback that just ran rings around us. We couldn't stop him for sour apples, and after the game was over we all gathered around to congratulate him on his fine play. His name was Dixie Howell, and later he would go on to the University of Alabama and become an All American.

Meanwhile, there were numerous incidents and facts of life that made this era interesting.

It has been a fact of history that from time immemorial the mosquito has been a scourge for residents in this area. The swampy areas, the standing water, the heat and humidity encouraged breeding of the insects; and of course people everywhere sought protection or remedies. For peaceful slumber the mosquito net or bar was the usual thing, with the fine mesh protection strung across the bed and draped over the side. At other hours people used a vile smelling substance called citronella (a fluid which smelled for all the world like the oil furnished for lubricating sewing machines). A second option was called Sweet Dreams. It too was a liquid and came in a bottle which had a straw-like entry and then an arrangement on the top so that the user could literally blow a mist of the material towards any suspected insects. Sweet Dreams may have worked, I don't know . . . but it did have the virtue of smelling better than its competitor. However, there was also the possibility that a user might inhale instead of exhale. I'm not sure what kinds of dreams that produced.

In the late 1920s we were all becoming a little more worldly minded, for radio had opened the door to faster news coverage, and we were in tune to events taking place across the country . . . and indeed over the world. These were also times when a whole town would react when it was learned that a known personality might be coming through—or even over—the community. One of the first examples of this for me came late in 1927. That year young Charles Lindbergh had electrified the world with his solo flight across the Atlantic, and later in that year he began a sort of barnstorming tour across the country. The news would tell us where he was, and local newsmen then would forecast when he might fly over en route from, say, New Orleans to Jacksonville. I'll never forget the day Lindy was supposed to cross over the Panhandle. We all went about looking upward, and the slightest sound that might have been an aircraft overhead provoked excitement. To this day I don't know whether I ever saw Lindbergh's plane overhead . . . but I might have.

A little over a year later another similar event occurred, with a little more definition. Al Smith, former Governor of New York, had been the Democratic candidate for President in 1928, but Smith had lost to Herbert Hoover. Smith's friends realized how disappointed the man was over his defeat, and some determined to do some nice things for him. Early in 1929 Jacob Rascob, a major figure in banking and a big wheeler-dealer in the Democratic Party, chose to take Mr. Smith aboard Rascob's private car on a vacation to the hotel Mr. Edward Ball would later buy in southern Mississippi. Word got out that the train would pass through DeFuniak Springs, attached to one of the daily passenger runs. I'll tell you that it seemed like the whole town turned out at the station to see the car if not Mr. Smith. The train pulled in and stopped for its customary passenger exchange, and there was Al, graciously waving to us all. That was the first time I was to see an "almost American president," but not the last.

As it turned out, it was not my days in the classroom that fostered my future vocation but rather my opportunity to work on the Palmer College Annual. The annual was the school's yearbook, and even then producing such a volume was a year-long task, with a staff of volunteer young people laboring under the eye of a sponsor. As a freshman I became part of this staff. I guess my Panama City experiences with Mr. Adkinson and Mr. Felix had piqued my attention, and now the tough part of being a real news gathering and publishing organization seemed the right thing to do. That year the book had a business manager, but he held the role primarily because he felt the job carried with it a BIG MAN ON CAMPUS status. He really cared little for the work, and when I would volunteer for jobs he was only too glad to say YES.

One of the things which seemed obvious to me was that if the yearbook carried paid advertising there might be more dollars to work with, and subsequently we could produce a superior product. So, with the manager's permission, I began going about in DeFuniak Springs to sell ads. And I succeeded . . . getting commitments from the grocery store, the barber shop, the auto dealer, the Walton Hotel (which the Harbison family operated), the motion picture house and several others. Sure enough, those added dollars made a difference in the appearance of that year's book . . . and so when a new year came around I was named the annual's business manager.

With extra budget I could see us adding art work and a fine cover for our book, and so I began cultivating new people, like T. Hope Cawthon, West Florida's premier photographer. For a very modest sum he would come to the campus and use his glass-plate camera to make photos of class activities and more. Then, we found a way to get drawings made of some of the fine old buildings in the community, and they too were added tastefully to our book. Believe me, between class work, my housekeeping chores, the magazine and football . . . I was busy. But, I was young and had ambition . . . and when the next year's book was in the planning stage I decided that we had to expand our horizons. I had just about exhausted the ad sales possibilities in that little town, and so I decided to go into Pensacola, the area's BIG city and see if I might sell an ad or two there.

My first efforts were so-so. A few merchants could see the value of appearing in a college yearbook, for many of the Panhandle families came into Pensacola for much of their shopping. Then I had a great idea. I would visit the *Pensacola News-Journal* and sell space to Mr. John Perry's newspapers.

That meeting turned out to be a turning point in my life.

As I think of that first ride between DeFuniak Springs and Pensacola in a newspaper truck with W. O. Eiland, I never dreamed that I would one day own a portion of that very newspaper. But, that's what happened. And I suspect that it's honest to say that such a thing could happen only in these United States.

The papers' general manager then was Mr. John Payne, and from the first he seemed to have little interest in even talking with a young kid from the sticks. But, he heard me out, and then said, in more or less these words: "Young man, this newspaper and I could hardly be less interested in you, or your yearbook. I see no value in it for us, and you've shown me in even coming here that you know little about selling advertising."

At that point the aggressiveness I'd learned playing football, and the lessons I'd gotten from some "turn downs" in selling, came to the surface. I told Mr. Payne that he was making one giant mistake by not taking advantage of my offer . . . and that he was also wrong in his estimation of me. I ended by saying, "I'll tell you that I can sell better than anyone on your staff . . . I really know how to sell a product and I could do good things for you."

Don't ask why I said that. I wasn't looking for a job . . . I was happily at work as a student. But . . . out it came . . . and what I said seemed to impress this man. He stared at me for a minute, then said:

"You think so, eh? Well, now . . . suppose I offered you a chance to sell ads for us; what kind of salary would you expect?"

Talk about a change of subject. I was caught speechless . . . for a moment. But then, for some reason, I said: "I couldn't work for less than twelve dollars a week."

Mr. Payne paused, then said: "We'll make it fifteen. When can you start?"

I tell you that up to this moment I didn't have the slightest thought of coming to Pensacola for other than a day of selling. Now here I was . . . and fifteen dollars a week seemed like a fortune. I gulped twice, and then agreed to come to work.

Five minutes later we were in the office of a very soft spoken, pleasant man named John D. Thomas, who was the papers' advertising manager. Mr. Payne introduced us and told Mr. Thomas that the paper had just employed an advertising genius.

And so I approached the beginning of the end of my days at Palmer College. My arrangement with Mr. Payne and John Thomas was not for immediate employment. They understood that I still had some weeks to go to earn my high school diploma. I had other obligations too . . . to complete the publication of the annual, and to meet my role in maintaining the dormitories. And of course the newspaper had not exactly been waiting for me to arrive that morning. The whole arrangement was odd, but . . . that's the way it worked out . . . and so it was that I ended my high school days. They had been good times for me, and while I was not exactly the valedictorian I did complete my work there satisfactorily.

It was a rare coincidence that my half-sister, Sue Kelly, the wife of a naval officer, was at that moment living in Pensacola. Sue and I had always been close, despite the fact that in growing up we were years apart and she had been one of those children of my mother left behind in Virginia when our own family threesome moved to Florida. However there had been reunions, some of which brought my half-brothers and sisters for vacations on the Gulf, and once Sue's family was in Pensacola there were visits back and forth. Thus Sue and I were in good accord.

Now I approached her to see if I might find temporary lodging in her household. She agreed, and encouraged my mother to join us too.

You see, during my Palmer College days I had spent very little time back in Panama City. My mother had continued her real estate sales work, but as the decade of the twenties wore on, the outside public's interest in the area had waned. My dad had maintained a nine-month-per-year work schedule, doing little during the hot months when travel was so uncomfortable. Thus by the time I made my move they were in a position to relocate without great difficulty. So, as I joined the *News-Journal* they agreed to come to Pensacola too. The year was 1929, and a new chapter was beginning.

❧

CHAPTER THREE
I'm a Newspaperman (and a College Student)

My first year as a newspaperman came at an unusual time. We were still in that great era called the Roaring Twenties, with much of the country cashing in on the stock market binge, bootlegging, real estate speculation and similar actions which made for a free and easy lifestyle. Pensacola was not exactly in that cycle. There had been a bit of a land boom here just after the war, but the south Florida sell-off had had its ripple effect into the Panhandle, and so such sales were soft when I prepared to become a professional space salesman. On the positive side the town was still celebrating an announcement that the FRISCO RAILROAD would now terminate in the local port, and Armstrong Cork Company was to become a partner with Newport Industries in a new building board project. However, up and down Palafox Street business was anything but brisk. Because of this, selling space required finesse, and some carefully managed promotions.

My initial training was designed to teach me how to be a promotions specialist. As preparation I was placed in the charge of one of the paper's veterans, who took me with him from place to place. Promotions in that day usually centered around some gimmick the paper would develop, like flag pole sitting, dance marathons, parades for patriotic holidays and the like. The salesmen would design a big full-page ad with eye appeal, and then they would approach businesses that normally didn't advertise in the paper. Our job was to convince the barber or piano store owner that he could make a big impact by having his name, along with others, as a signature on this special page. Sometimes this worked well, especially if the promotion had wide-scale appeal, or if the businessman had some ties to the event, like the ad for Armistice Day. In any event, I went to call on a man who had more excuses NOT to buy than any human being alive. BUT my new partner was persistent. He talked, he argued, he pleaded, he praised . . . and finally, after several actual hours of dialogue, the man broke down and signed a purchase slip.

As the two of us were leaving the store and climbing into my partner's small car he looked at me and said: "You know, I thought that SOB would never make up his mind. Did you ever see such sales resistance?"

A little later we had reason to call back at the paper, and there, waiting for us, was a phone message from our recent conquest. He wanted to talk some more. My partner groaned, but picked up the phone and with the usual operator's assistance got through to our client. What happened next was a great lesson. The man didn't hesitate. "You know," he began, "When you two left my store you said to that young fellow that I was one tough SOB. You did say that, didn't you?"

My partner tried to hem and haw, but the man quickly continued: "You see, I'm pretty hard of hearing, and a year ago I had some training in lip reading. I could see every word you said, even though I was inside. So . . . Mr. Salesman, let me tell you that nobody calls me names like that. Cancel my ad."

My partner tried to get in another word . . . but the phone went dead.

Very swiftly I had learned that upon leaving a customer's premises it made sense to say only NICE things about him.

That incident was fairly typical of the experiences I would have through the next year. I learned, and I made friends among the potential customers on my list. I must admit that I didn't exactly burn up the world that first year, but then I didn't do badly, either. My bosses were pleased, and they liked to have a young man with ambition around the place.

Sometimes as one looks back at events long past it is difficult to structure a straight time line; things happen, and then as the memory process works they are sometimes out of order. Surely that's the case as one grows older, for as we try to call back memories we miss some only to find them surfacing later. That has been the case with me as I probed my history, thus I hope the reader will be understanding if, on occasion, I find myself jumping from one era to another. As I have done so I wanted to include small items which were interesting and helped provide an overview to those times.

All of this was difficult because for a time I bounced back and forth between Pensacola and Panama City like an India rubber ball (not a Braden Ball). For example, it was while I was in the second or third grade that my mother, father and I had a brief stay in a boarding house which then stood behind the Rhodes-Collins furniture store, on Chase Street. We were next to the Temple Beth-El Synagogue on the one side, and diagonally across Chase from the old County Court House, that giant red brick edifice which had been built there in the early 1880s.

This was a generally peaceful neighborhood, but one event was different. I'm not sure what sparked the incident, but in this period workers on the transit line went on strike. This was not a pleasant affair. After a time the company asked the governor for military aid, and the National Guard arrived and pitched tents up and down the Palafox Street median, and also between the Court House and the Presbyterian Church. That would not have affected me, except that one night there was suddenly an extensive burst of gunfire, and people were suddenly very aware that there was trouble, right here in Deep Water City. To this day I don't know what the shooting was about; no one was reported injured. After a time the strike was ended and the soldiers departed. But, for a time this made for excitement in the old boarding house.

I have to provide a little more background on the court house. It had been built with funds collected over the decade of the 1870s. The county's earlier facilities had been destroyed during the Civil War, and for a time the commissioners rented rooms along Government Street. But many citizens felt this was unnecessarily expensive. A tax was applied, and then beginning in 1882 the new building, a giant affair with an armory, was put in place. The court house was impressive looking, but by the time I was able to walk its halls the building was in a state of decay. It had always leaked badly, and by 1930 it was damp and smelled musty. Its rooms were small, and if one came in off the street to spend a few minutes watching proceedings at an exciting trial (which I did from time to time) he often had to stand. Those were good shows sometimes, for the city had several wonderful lawyers who were better than actors on a stage. The court house was a choice meeting place. I was in Panama City when the building's days came to an end, but I followed the story with interest. What happened was this: the Federal Customs House, which had been a combination customs headquarters, post office and court house, had been built at Palafox and Government in 1887. By 1939 it had been outgrown; the federal folks needed more space. In a trade, the county got the old federal building, remodeled it, and by 1941 was in its quarters which are still in use. The federals in turn tore down the red brick county facility and, with WPA funds, built what came to be called the Post Office, on the corner of Chase and Palafox. As I say, I watched that episode long distance, but I surely came to know both buildings once I returned in 1943.

In my early days with the newspaper I became fascinated with some of the unusual businesses up and down Palafox Street. The drug stores and clothing outlets were fine, but there were a few places that just had—well—atmosphere. Take Biazza's Barbershop, for example, on South Palafox. The owner, Antonio Biazza, was considered "the King of the Italian Community" here. Tony was a big man, and his shop was elite. The thing I remember about it was a huge, ornate brass fixture with lots of bright pipes which stood in the middle of the shop. Somehow the island had a feed of either very hot water or steam, probably from some hidden boiler, and from the portals of this device came very hot towels which the barbers used to soften the beards of those being shaved, or for a comfortable aftermath along the neckline following a haircut. The Italian-made machine hissed and there was always a sort of Vesuvius effect which fascinated the customers. I'm sure some patrons came just to look at this monster.

Another barber shop nearby was named Pon's. It was a big, eight-chair affair operated by a family of very efficient Creoles. Many people have heard of Pensacola's Creoles, whose background extended here from early in the nineteenth century. This was a very close-knit community that lived for the most part near St. Joseph's Catholic Church, and whose members tended to work in trades such as barbering. They were very skilled at their work, and they treated customers nicely. They also did women's hair.

Speaking of beauty shops, the city at that time had just two which catered solely to the ladies. One was in the Brent Building and named for its proprietor, a German named Klinger; the second, in the Theisen Building, was Irene's. It was at this time that a new piece of machinery called the Croquinole was developed for setting permanent waves. These were expensive devices, usually sold only one to the community. Mr. Klinger agreed to put one in his shop, and he did. But he did not advertise its presence or virtues, and this upset the sales representative, who told the owner repeatedly that promotion

Barber shops like Pons in Pensacola offered a great many "extras" in caring for tonsorial needs. Pons had seven chairs, and included fancy sinks like this one, where the barber would warm towels, or provide the basics for a shave. Such shops had begun to cater to the ladies by the late 1920s, giving what were called "bobs," a form of trim and permanent. When a man left such a shop he always had a wonderful smell, too, from Bay Rum or some similar tonic.

was part of the arrangement. Finally, the representative came to me and asked if I would go to Klinger, and tell him that if he didn't live up to his agreement that the company would take out the equipment and put it in Irene's shop. He figured that I would act for him since ad selling was my business.

I was young, and I also did not realize that Mr. Klinger had a terrible temper. I went to his shop, which was on the third floor and had a step down from the corridor into the shop area. In as few words as possible I gave him the message . . . and in a moment the man was in a fury. He grabbed a broom and made a terrible pass at my head. Ducking, I fell over the door step and landed flush on my behind (however, the broom did miss). I fled in retreat, not caring one whit whether any lady ever had the benefits of this seemingly valuable machine.

☞ ☞ ☞

As months passed, I got to know several of the local business people quite well, and a few of them began to work on me to continue my education. "You ought to go to college," one said. "There's really opportunity for the man with a college education. It isn't very expensive over there at Gainesville, and I suspect you've saved a dollar or two."

That was true. I had some money in the bank. I talked the situation over with my parents, and then with John Thomas and others at the newspaper. All agreed that I should try a year or so at the university. The paper's manager even said that he would hold my job open for me. Now that was something!

And so I chose to go.

I boarded a bus at the Pensacola terminal and made the long trip across the state to Gainesville. This journey across North Florida was another adventure in transportation for me. As we rode along, stopping in just about every hamlet en route, I saw folks of very modest means getting on and off, often seeming to carry their life's possessions with them. The trip was noisy, uncomfortable, actually unpleasant, for the bus itself had seen long service, and the seats and springs had seen better days. I resolved to avoid long-distance bus trips wherever possible.

As I arrived on campus (and of course that campus was a tiny portion of what it has since grown to be) my first need was for a place to sleep. As luck would have it a young man whom I had met in Pensacola was just exiting one of the nearby fraternity houses as I walked across the quad, and he waved a friendly greeting. When I explained my situation he immediately invited me to spend the night at the Kappa Alpha house, which I did. Thus came my first peek at fraternity life . . . and hi-jinks.

At that time fraternity pledges were somewhat hard to come by, and within a day or so I was being courted by several houses, including the Pi Kappa Alpha group which had as members several other Pensacolians, including E. Dixie Beggs. A fter some arm twisting I agreed to pledge there . . . and I did. However, I will say little about such experiences, except to confess that I felt very much out of place. I felt like an old man at a kindergarten picnic. I disliked the foolish paddlings, the Ffreshman beanie and much that went with so-called college humor. I had been a working man for so long, considering all of my part-time stints, that I felt such things were a waste of time. In the course of the next few months I tried out for the Glee Club (I didn't make the grade . . . though I can't imagine why, since I have always had a voice that might have done credit to the Metropolitan); then I became part of the fencing team. That I enjoyed. I gave just a moment's consideration to trying out for football, but when I saw the size of most team members I allowed that since my mother had not raised any stupid children I would not erase belief in that statement.

Did I study hard? Not really. I had money in my account, there was bootleg whiskey to be had, and there were many friendly and beautiful young girls about. I partied. I rented cars to take trips with a few choice friends. In short, I had a good time.

Not long after I arrived at Gainesville the national news suddenly focused on something which—for a decade—most people had considered impossible. The stock market, which had rocketed upward as millions played with borrowed money, suddenly went into reverse. Within sixty days people were using the harsh term "recession," and many a classmate was told by parents that he or she must leave the university since family funds had suddenly become "unavailable." Since I had my own limited dollars in a safe bank this had no personal impact; but then, day by day, I began to see or read about case after case where previously employed people were suddenly out of work . . . with no new prospects in sight. By March of 1930 money was becoming very tight, and everywhere one turned he saw worried looks on people's faces.

Two other bits of life remain in my memory.

The first involved trying to make a bit of money (as I had at Palmer College). By now I had a track record as a space salesman, and so I asked a worldly acquaintance about the status of newspapers in Gainesville.

"There's just the one," he replied, *The Sun*. It's run by a guy named Pepper. You might see him."

I marched to the *Sun* building at once. When I inquired for Mr. Pepper the little lady receptionist motioned me up the stairs, but made no effort to contact the boss. I romped up to the second floor, and there, sound asleep on a couch which had seen better days, lay Mr. Pepper. The man was in deep slumber, his nose rising and falling in a majestic manner. He lay on his side, his head supported by one arm. Viewing the publisher I attempted to awaken him by making a small sound. No luck. I coughed a few times. Nothing. Finally I stepped gingerly to his side and gently shook Mr. Pepper by the shoulder. With this he opened one eye and stared blankly at me.

"What you want?" he demanded.

I explained my background, that I was an experienced advertising salesman, and that I was seeking part-time employment.

Mr. Pepper grunted, then sort of shook his head to remove some of the sleep from his eyes. Rising, he shuffled to an old high top desk and rummaged among some papers until he found what proved to be a prospect list of potential clients, plus a rate card.

"Here," he said, "try this. Go to work."

And that was it.

For the next few months I tried my luck working for the *Sun*. I won't say I won any prizes, for I didn't know the territory, and the *Sun* was not eager to get into sales promotion. However, the experience was worthwhile, and I did meet several interesting people.

The second venture in Gainesville was my introduction to the gentleman's game of golf. This I tried at the suggestion of Prof. Walter Matherly, who proposed that I visit the local links and offer my services for odd jobs, trading out my earnings for instruction in the game. I took the professor's advice, and soon found myself with modest employment, where I helped to manicure greens and do odd jobs around the club house.

In the process, I did indeed get some basic instruction, and then the opportunity to meet and even play on occasions with the town's elite . . . the doctors, attorneys, bankers and the like. I liked golf. But . . . like many other forms of recreation, it took more time than I wanted to invest in such things. However, I did get the message that one can meet and move to a friendly basis by visiting with an ardent golfer.

By the end of the term I began to ask myself: "What am I really doing here?" That question was amplified when I had a letter from John Thomas, at the *News-Journal*. Mr. Thomas was inquiring about my progress, but he was also telling me that things on the paper were increasingly difficult, and that the paper could really use me, for a salesperson who produced was needed.

Thus I began that difficult self-analysis that one faces at such a time. What should I do? Would I be better off forgetting about this fancy education? After all, I knew that I had grown to really enjoy work on the paper. Then too, I had the offer of twenty-five dollars a week . . . when so many others were losing their jobs.

At length I made my choice. I would return to Pensacola. By mid-summer 1931 I was back in my little first floor cubicle in the *News-Journal*'s headquarters in the middle of where Jefferson Street should have been if the city had ever forced it through.

My return to the Pensacola of 1931 suggests a need to provide something of a community profile, since my whole business reason for being was to make contacts with potential advertisers, or to serve their needs once their companies had become committed to purchase of space in the *News-Journal*. At that time the paper employed somewhere between forty and fifty people, five or six of whom were the paper's sales staff. Each of us was given a prospect or client list, and our efforts were targeted at those specific organizations, unless some unique situations came to exist where we might swap a prospect for an identified reason.

It is also important to recognize certain fundamentals about marketing and advertising, since times and conditions have changed so markedly since 1931. For example, in 1931 Pensacola (and north Florida) had but one radio station, WCOA. As power was limited the station could be heard for only a short distance from the broadcast source. Even in 1931 radio was still a primitive tool locally for most. They had begun to manufacture receivers with large speakers by this time, but these were expensive items, and with a single signal source most local families chose to get along by using the old-fashioned ear phones. Of course this limited the number in any family who might listen at one time, but people were flexible, and they got along. Radio, for us, was not a major competitor. Of course, television for local citizens was still twenty-three years away.

There was a small county weekly paper. It did carry a few news items, but its principal purpose was to provide an inexpensive vehicle for required legal notices such as the courts and some attorneys would use. The *News-Journal* liked to get that lineage too, but even at that time our rates were considered too high for this very specialized presentation.

I had not been working for the paper long when Pensacola hosted a very unique deep-sea vessel. The 1930s were not a banner time for the port. The lumbering was all but gone, the docks were falling into disrepair and the two railroads had slacked off in their development. However, there was traffic, and one day there came to the Palafox Street dock a small vessel operated by the imaginative people at Woods Hole Oceanographic Center. They were here to load supplies and make a few minor repairs before they continued their regional project of "mapping" the floor of the Gulf. The officers and crew were a friendly bunch, and invited guests on board, and of course I went. These men were using a form of sonar which exercised a sort of doppler effect, which would send sound impulses downward, and these would then literally "bounce" off the Gulf's floor and indicate depth at that point. It was fascinating to look at the charting they had done, and to see their enthusiasm for their tasks. I will never forget the comment made to me by one of the officers. He said something like: "One of these days someone is going to turn this idea sideways so that a ship will be able to send impulses across the water. Then if there's an obstacle like another ship ahead of them they will be forewarned. I'm almost sure this will be developed." Of course it was, and fairly soon. It was called radar.

Another unforgettable event occurred shortly after the oceanographic vessel departed. At this time—the early 1930s—commercial aviation was still in its infancy, especially long distance flight over water. Our own Pan American Clippers were in the experimental stage, and other countries were working to this end too, including the French. At this time the French had developed a huge eight-engine plane which had enjoyed experimental success in

Europe. Now she was to be shown to portions of the United States. I'm not certain of this, but she may have been en route here to be demonstrated at the Chicago World's Fair. In any event, the plane, with her large crew of ten members in cabin service, her beautifully upholstered leather seats and all, came across the Atlantic via Martinique, and then on to Pensacola, where she landed on the bay and was berthed at a pier at the Naval Air Station, the only place where she could logically be tied. The plane was opened to inspection, and many townspeople went aboard and were duly impressed. I know that I was. Then, one evening, as crew members were being entertained ashore, a storm blew in, and the high wind gusts caught this aircraft and literally turned it over. Next morning there she lay, upside down, her underside displaying the design of her landing features. Sadly, the French had to send an oceangoing salvage craft for their airplane, and so take it back to Europe. Did it ever fly again? I don't know.

☞ ☞ ☞

Another point to remember is that in 1931 there wasn't a single local enterprise that employed a specialist who would design, write or lay out advertising. The proprietor or store manager would make up a list of the articles or services to be presented, then that person would meet with his newspaper sales liaison, who then would perform creative work, subject to the customer's approval. This was also a time when the methods of presentation were limited. In later years, when offset printing techniques would enable a paper to assemble all sorts of art materials, ad presentations could become far more creative, reaching their zenith when computer composition came into being. In 1931, illustration was almost always done through the use of stereotypes or, if one was very lucky, from original art work. Photographs required metal engravings, and at that time there was no such service in Pensacola. We just had to be able to use our wits and what was available through innovative type-setting, with one of the paper's linotypes, or hand composed headlines.

In pre-Depression days the percentage of local businesses that advertised was small. Now that hard times had come our job was to convince more business leaders of the value of promotion. Of course this meant making their advertising exciting, often linked to events that would capture the reader's attention.

Earlier I mentioned the use of specialties. In 1995 marketers still use such things, but today's big golf tournaments and Christmas generosity are far removed from what we came up with as I began my career. Take for example the dance marathon. These events were a national craze for a few years in the thirties, and they worked like this. A promoter would line up a number of cash-strapped couples as competitors. Then he would find a suitable arena or auditorium where these people would dance . . . usually to the music provided by an amplified phonograph. The arena had to have a fairly large seating capacity, for the promoter counted on ticket sales for part of his revenue. (As many as three hundred might show up to watch.) And he had to have revenues to award prizes, pay his expenses and earn a profit.

Our task at the paper would be to try to hype the event. We would go from client to client trying to get them to sponsor a dance couple. Once this was gained a special sign would be prepared for the dancers to wear on their backs. This provided a modest degree of exposure for the advertiser. Then we would prepare large display ads which we would sell to couple sponsors or others who wanted their firms to be linked to this form of local excitement. Then, day by day the paper would provide news coverage of what was taking place as these poor couples continued to drag one another around the floor, getting only a very small time break every few hours for nature's calls.

At first these marathons were conducted in the Venetian Ballroom, downtown; later, when some religious groups complained that this was cruel and inhuman treatment of the dancers, the city fathers passed an ordinance prohibiting the exhibitions, and the events were relocated outside city limits, usually to a pavilion in Kupfrian's Park.

Dance Marathons, like six-day bicycle races and flag pole sitting, went on for several years, in big cities and small. We tried our best to make them exciting, and to make them work for our customers and ourselves.

One other similar event was tree sitting. Don't ask how that got started, for I haven't the slightest idea. What occurred here was that young people, usually older teenagers, would build themselves a tree house, and then see how long they could stay up in it. Seville Square was usually the target zone, and these youngsters would be backed by their parents, who would bring food and clothing to the square, to be hauled skyward by rope. We covered tree sitting too, for often this would become a competitive event, and the townspeople would come out by the hundreds to watch and cheer.

Just think: there WAS entertainment before TV and the video store.

Boxing was another activity that had its place in the Pensacola of the 1930s . . . and my first recollection of it came in an unusual way.

For some time the American Legion Post had held wrestling matches in a small arena on their grounds near the Frank Marston Post on Barrancas Avenue. I liked going to the matches, though I'd never been a wrestler myself. The bouts were held on Mondays.

But then the *News-Journal* made a special arrangement for a substitute. One Monday, with the paper as sponsor, the matches switched from wrestling to boxing. The build-up by the paper was such that I figured I ought to go, and so I went—with a date. We arrived and I entered through the doorway that led into a sort of ground level auditorium that was at the level of the ring. However, the best view was always from a balcony that ringed the arena. One had to climb interior stairs to get to the balcony, and after showing my date the ground level we went up and found some good seats on the second level.

The bouts began, and before long the crowd got really into the action. Then, for some reason, the cheering began to go beyond shouting and clapping of hands. The patrons began to stamp their feet, and bounce up and down. Soon the none-too-sturdy structure began to vibrate. Frankly, I didn't like what I was seeing, so with my date's permission we departed, got into my car and began driving back towards town.

We hadn't gone four blocks when an ambulance came racing towards us, its siren screaming, and the car going very fast.

Sure enough, the action was at the wrestling arena. With all the hopping and stamping the fragile structure had collapsed, and altogether eight people were hurt, a couple seriously. Naturally I was interested in more ways than one, for this was a newspaper event. There were some damage claims, and for days this was front page news. Ultimately the old building was razed and wrestling came to an end. As one might imagine, I was mighty glad intuition had told me to clear out.

Many Pensacolians began to enjoy boxing about that same time in another setting. Once the bay bridge and the bridge across the sound had been completed in 1931 the YMCA began to stage summertime boxing matches on the beach. The one dollar bridge toll also covered a fan's cost to the fights, which were staged there every Wednesday evening during summer months. Dick Merritt was the boxing team's coach, and the fighters included such local zealots as Calvin Todd, Lefty Joe Lockwood and Joe Fields.

We would drive over early, and get ourselves a good seat (right on the sand). Then we would watch a long card of bouts, which were usually three rounds long. Ultimately one or two of those men went up the ladder in the Golden Gloves matches, but none ever became champion. However, in its time boxing was a lot of fun, and the matches were well attended.

To understand our market it will help you to have in mind a sketch of the downtown area, for virtually all of the community's major commerce was conducted in a relatively narrow business zone, for the most part up and down Palafox Street, though with a few exceptions on Garden and then on Wright Street. Merchants on Wright almost always had a tag line on their ads which noted that they were "Outside The High Rent District."

Some of these businesses were of interest to me as clients, while others were the places where I would support my personal needs. At age nineteen food was, of course, high on my list of priorities. The Dainty Del was one of my favorites. Chris Lochas' chicken and oyster gumbo was outstanding, and sold for twenty-five cents for the giant size bowl. Little Chris stood at the Del's oyster bar and shucked fresh bay oysters which were twenty-five cents per dozen, and thick ham sandwiches were fifteen cents. The Dainty Del was an unusual emporium. Out front, facing shoppers as they walked along Palafox Street, were large displays of fresh fruits and vegetables. One might easily have mistaken this for a vegetable market had he not known of the fine food served inside. Just down the street was Sol Cahn's Delicatessen. Sol specialized in all kinds of imported foods, many of which arrived on ships calling in the port. The tins of fancy sardines, olive oil, tinned fish, exotic vegetables and sauces made Sol's place very popular with the sophisticated trade whose large houses lined the streets of North Hill. Sol also had the services of Bill Tally, who assembled some of the finest sandwiches I have ever eaten.

Just down the street was the Electric Maid Bakery, whose saltrisen bread was a community favorite. Several blocks further south Bell's place not only had fine food but also specialized in live poultry, and live gopher. Here the customer might select her bird right on the spot, then have it killed, dressed and delivered in one of the firms fancy wagons. (At this point few businesses had gone to gasoline engine delivery vans.)

Drug stores were another great meeting place in the city, for each of them had a lunch counter where people liked to gather for morning coffee or a generous noon meal. Old Doc Harrell's drug store was not exactly typical, but it was most popular. The food at Doc's was prepared at home, by his wife, and her chicken salad and ham sandwiches were always a treat. At noon the place was always crowded with people who loved what they got, and where the management always made certain that they got enough to make them want to come back for more.

Then there was Walgreen's, and the Hamilton Russell Drug Store, which was one of the best merchandisers in town.

I'm not certain of the date, but it was in the 1930s; old Doc Harrell was very active in his drug store. As it turned out I was assigned to all three of the local firms, which made it rather ticklish when the proprietors chose to offer something competitive.

One day as I was calling on Doc Harrell, he sprang something on me that I didn't expect. Even though he was my friend he accused me of favoring Walgreens in some of our rate structuring. I protested, but Doc was not convinced. He said: "I won't believe that unless John Perry himself gives me the facts." Then I had a bright thought: I knew John Perry was soon due in town, and so I told the druggist that when my "big boss" showed up I would bring him to the store to explain the specifics of the paper's policy, and our ethics on this sort of thing. Doc grunted and allowed that this would be nice; he had always wanted to meet John Perry anyway.

Honestly, I had no real conviction that Mr. Perry would go anywhere with me, but with my business manager's help he was talked into the visit. The two of us called on Doc Harrell, and John Perry made a statement to him that could not have been more in keeping with what I had said. Doc was convinced. Mr. Perry seemed impressed too, that I would force an issue like this. That conversation was one of the first real talks I had ever had with the man who would become my employer and friend over many years.

There were a few other businesses that come to mind. One was the drug store operated by Dr. Herbert Bryans, on Wright Street. His father had built the building, and it even had (and still has) the family name in stone over the front window. Dr. Bryans was a physician here for over forty years, and was once president of the Florida Medical Association. He was also the president of the staff when Baptist Hospital opened in 1951.

Another of the general merchandise stores was operated by Mr. and Mrs. H. D. Rice, and then there was Philip Goldenberg's. (His son, Sam, would later run a wholesale dry goods business here.) Philip had come to town early in this century and had a small store in the south end. Now, let me be very candid here. Philip did NOT sell top-of-the-line merchandise. Instead, his was the shop where a man with a very limited budget could buy something to wear. He was a kindly man, with many talents, and his place was a favorite with many of the seamen coming off the ships which called here.

Palafox Street had its landmarks, of course . . . the San Carlos Hotel, the County Court House, the eleven-story American National Bank, the seven-story Blount Building, the Brent Building and the five-story Theisen Building. And there was the six-year-old Saenger Theater where Johnny Jones was the manager. (Tragically, the owner, Julien Saenger, who had built several motion picture palaces across the south, committed suicide in 1931 following a disaster in the stock market.) There was also the Isis Theater, and the Belmont.

The Blount and Brent buildings hosted the Kress and Woolworth stores, whose five- and ten-cent offerings became increasingly popular as hard times descended. Their lunch counters, with many five-cent selections, were patronized by many of the ladies of high fashion, who found these food services more attractive than those where the businessmen tended to congregate. Incidentally, those women, and that included many of the city's homemakers, were indeed fashionable. They always came to town shopping wearing lovely hats, fresh frocks and silk stockings . . . the ones with the seams down the back. The business community catered to their appearance too. Up and down Palafox Street, on both sides, tin roofs covered the sidewalks so that even during downpours such ladies might pass without being drenched. Incidentally, it was then that I first saw a woman in public with a cigarette.

There was, of course, an increasing number of stores selling ready to wear clothing. I use that term because it had not been too many years since much of the clothing worn locally had been custom made or prepared in the home since Mr. Singer's sewing machines were part of most households. The new "department stores" included Bon Marche, LaMode, Friedman's, T. L. Gant's, Silverman's, White and White's, Bland's Men's Furnishings and the Leader, where promotion-minded Harry Ordon was the owner. One word about Bon Marche. On the second floor Mrs. Philip Rosenbloum had a little cubicle where she produced ladies' millinery, and she was very talented. Mrs. R. was the wife of Phil Rosenbloum. Her son, Sam, later founded Sam's Style Shop, which ultimately was run by his brother, David.

Along downtown streets there were Reynalds Music House and Wing Hop's oriental specialties. The Gulf Power Company headquarters was on the lower and upper floors of the Theisen Building, and it was here that offerings of electrical appliances were shown. Fisher-Brown Insurance was on the second floor. The law firm of Yonge, Davis & Beggs, and virtually all of the city's physicians and dentists were in the Blount and Brent buildings. The Catholic High School was at Baylen and Garden, and of course the Manhattan Hotel was on West Garden Street, near Marston & Quina's furniture store. By 1931, WCOA had relocated to the seventh floor of the San Carlos Hotel.

Down near the waterfront the great fishing fleets of E. E. Saunders and A.F. Warren were going full blast. There was a huge demand for fish, locally and throughout our trade area, up into north Georgia, Tennessee and beyond. I really enjoyed watching this operation. When a fishing smack came in she would have been at work in the Gulf for up to four weeks, and her holds would be deeply laden with the new catch. Outgoing, the boats always were filled with ice, usually from the companies' own ice making plants. When fish were caught they were gutted and then iced down, where they would remain until the vessel returned. Now, with a smack at the dock, crewmen would load the ten-to-twelve-pound fish, mostly snapper, into barrels which had been made in Goulding by the Tart Cooperage. It was one of those "one layer of fish then one layer of ice" affairs until a barrel was full. Then it would be capped by a Croaker sack. When a shipment was ready the barrels would be loaded on a truck and carried to the L & N depot, where they would be transferred to a baggage car (not a freight car). One memory I have is that those barrels always dripped, for the ice would begin to melt almost immediately. The baggage cars obviously took on a fishy smell after a time, but that was okay with rail officials. They loved the extra business. Remember, at this time the city supported the two fishing fleets, so this was BIG business. This remained so until a decade after the war, when the smacks themselves began to fail, and the fishing grounds grew sparse in their production. One by one the vessels were taken out of service, and a colorful part of the local heritage died.

As I walked north I would pass the open doors of McKenzie-Oerting's chandlery shop, where the pungent odors of tar, canvas and rope made me realize that we still had a lot of sailing ships about.

Then I came into the downtown strip. One place I recall well was Marasa's Restaurant. This was what later would be termed a spaghetti joint, for the family served good, plentiful Italian food at tables upstairs. But what made Marasa's truly memorable was the display outside her storefront. There, every day, would be a display of mackerel. I guess they must have been salted, for they were not iced. I can still see those mackerel eyes staring at me as I walked by . . . and I would notice too that the tails all seemed to be in the same configuration, day after day. I doubt that Mrs. Marasa ever sold a single mackerel, but this was her image piece . . . and we all remembered.

Nearby was Mr. E. E. Walton's tailor shop. I guess Mr. Walton made clothing, or repaired it, but what made him a subject of memory was his pressing service. In those days it was the custom in many towns for shops such as Mr. Walton's to have what they called "pressing clubs." For $4 per month one would have the services of the shop whenever he needed them, and as things turned out that was a darned good idea. Pensacola has always been subject to many rain showers, and most business people then were very limited in their wardrobes. First, of course, there wasn't money to buy lots of suits in the Depression, so men (and women too) had to nurse what they had. If rain came and caught the businessman, he couldn't hurry home to change. So he hustled into Walton's for a pressing. There the customer would take off his clothes in a little waiting room, and Mr. Walton would sponge and press the rain-dampened garments, restoring creases and otherwise giving the suit back a good appearance. I can still see some men waiting their turn to step into the "waiting booth" so they might be served.

A few doors down was Peter Chackney's grocery store on Government Street. Mr. Chackney was an importer. Inside there was round after round of exotic cheeses, some foreign, some domestic, and exotic olives and pickles too. The odors were sometimes strong, and on warmer days these would blend and waft out the front door to assail the nostrils of the passersby. We all liked Mr. Chackney's place. Some of what he sold was wholesaled to the small groceries which dotted the neighborhoods. Here the city had a wonderful custom. For example, if I chose I could go into such a shop at noon and, for ten cents, purchase a generous slab of the cheese of my choice. Another nickel bought a handful of crackers, and all would be topped off with a nickel Coca-Cola. It was a meal fit for a king. Some of the cheese displays were out in the open, and in summer time, to be sure they were being sanitary, some proprietors would hang one of those fly catcher strips above the cheese plates. Then, I suspect, we were actually blending the smells of cheese and fly paper. But, who cared?

Another shop whose owners knew how to merchandise was the B & G Grocery. I don't remember who Mr. B. and Mr. G. were, but I do remember that they had a pipeline to a good supply of Florida gophers. They also knew that many Catholic families enjoyed gopher meat at the proper day or season, and so they would advertise that they had this special delicacy. People would line up to get a supply.

As I walked up Palafox Street I would often chance to meet Jim Dooley. Jim was an older man who had been blind from birth. But Jim was special. Each work day he would be dressed impeccably, and he would walk up, and then down Palafox. He had done this so many times that he knew how and where to cross the streets, and how to avoid pitfalls. Jim could recognize just about anyone by their voice. Their cheerful HELLO would be answered by "Why, hello Braden Ball . . . how in the world are you?"

Then there was Mr. A. C. Binkley, an attorney. I remember him because he always came to work, or went home, on the trolley, and later on the bus. Binkley lived on Mallory Street, and had a car stop in front of his house. He made his trip to the office, then home for lunch . . . with a repeat performance in the afternoon. Many people rode the cars, of course, but his routine was so precise that he stood out.

Palafox Street proper was still paved with creosoted wooden blocks, an innovation which dated from its initial paving in the mid-1890s. The blocks were fine, except when the heavy rains came. Then the flooding would literally pick up scores of them, washing them south from the high ground of Lee

Square clear down as far as Wright Street. However, the city was undaunted. There was a special crew trained to meet this challenge, and once the rain had stopped these men would go out, pick up the dislocated blocks, and then painstakingly put them back in place. A little later the community got smart and added a coating of tar and asphalt which helped staunch the flow.

Another part of the city which drew attention in those years dealt with illuminating gas. Before the turn of the century a plant had been built to produce such gas for use in the city's street lights. The small excess was sold to lucky home owners and the hotels. With the passage of time the plant's production was increased, but there was always a downside to this. The gas plant smelled. Walking or riding down Gadsden Street one would catch a whiff of the pungent aroma; there was never a doubt when the gas works were near. But then, largely because they needed gas for product drying at the Armstrong Cork Company plant, a pipeline was brought to Pensacola from Louisiana, and now the familiar yellow flame of manufactured gas was replaced by the brighter, cleaner flame of the natural fuel.

Up and down the main street the motion picture houses were doing a land office business, for many of the era's films were a measure of escape for many folks . . . and they were cheap. the Saenger, the Isis, the Belmont . . . all did a big trade.

There were businesses aplenty . . . Elebash Jewelry Company, Mayes Printing Company, the First Bank & Trust Company, the Citizens & Peoples National Bank, the T. M. Lloyd Funeral Home, Fisher-Pou . . . and of course fine churches housing the Presbyterian, Baptist, Catholic, Lutheran, Methodist, Episcopal and Jewish congregations. The automobile franchises were there too . . . Muldon Motor Company, Son Motor Company, Pensacola Buggy Works, Ed Lee Studebaker, Pepper-Taylor (Nash), Brockett Motors (for the Hudson and Essex) and others. On Wright Street freight and passenger trains rumbled day and night through the station which had been built there in 1905.

A dignified sign in a storefront window of the San Carlos Hotel read: Fenner & Beane, Members of the New York Stock Exchange.

The space occupied by the brokerage was narrow and long. Fixed along one wall was a large blackboard, which stood close to where the tickertape clattered its tick-tick-tick from morning until mid-afternoon. Opposite the board and backed against one wall was row of comfortable chairs. In those chairs, hour after hour, sat some of the city's well-to-do old men, the few who at that time of the Depression still had sufficient funds to be interested in the workings of the stock exchange.

Some naive people believed these men were true students of the market, and that their long hours there were spent in careful study of investment opportunities.

Those observers were at least ninety percent wrong.

You see, an additional fixure in the brokerage house was the presence of several very attractive young girls. Their job was to take down the fresh quotations coming in on the tape and to climb a four-foot ladder in front of the blackboard, where they would chalk the fresh data. Hour after hour this procession would continue, first one girl, then another, climbing those steps, making her marks, then retreating to obtain some more. It was, seemingly, a very efficient system.

And the men in the chairs?

Did they sit there with notepads and pencils or comprehensive data sheets? Well, one or two may have. But most just sit and watched. And not the information on the board.

I caught on to what was happening pretty quickly. But, since I didn't have two quarters to rub together, I wasn't considered "one of the group." Even so, I learned to drop by periodically . . . just to see what was happening.

☞ ☞ ☞

Palafox Street had several other bits of ambience which can hardly be omitted. At the Garden and Romana Street intersections there were traffic lights, and each time the light colors changed, and with them traffic direction, a loud bell would ring. Now, this may not seem like much, but if one's station placed him in close proximity the regular peal of those chimes could become very stressful. There were, to be sure, numerous complaints.

Then, there were the streetcars. In 1895 the car line had been double tracked as it moved north to south, to link with cross tracks at Garden and at Gadsden and more. The streetcars had bells too. These were operated in two ways. The conductor at the rear of the car would pull a cord, ringing a bell to alert the motorman that all passengers coming or going were now safely in place. That bell wasn't loud, but it could be heard, and there were many car startings and stoppings. The motorman too had a bell, operated with his foot. This he would ring in the same way the motorist might blow his horn, to urge progress by a slow-moving automobile, wagon or even pedestrians. There were several sets of downtown church bells too, and some of these rang out several times per day.

In mid-block on south Palafox stood Reynalds Music House, whose proprietor, George Emmanuel, had erected outside the store a large replica of the famous RCA Dog poised listening to his master's voice. Inside the dog Mr. Emmanuel had placed a speaker which would pick up on records being played inside the store. Sometimes the volume was moderate, sometimes the music was quite loud.

Now—imagine what the sound levels were like through that area as church bells chimed, the street signals sounded, streetcar bells clinked and clanked, auto horns blew and the dog at Reynalds' blared out John Philip Sousa at a high level of amplification.

Finally, people became exasperated and appealed to the City Council for relief. The city fathers obliged by passing an ordinance outlawing many of the sounds (including the traffic signal). A new atmosphere of near quiet descended, but this too was oppressive to some. Editorial writer for the paper, Leland Schwartz, could not resist presenting a sad lament which said that he longed for those good days when he could walk in step with the music.

By 1931 the automobile itself was becoming a noise factor. Parking was straight in, on Palafox, and there was a two-foot-high curb which was just high enough for many bumpers to scrape to a grinding halt. That meant another squeal, when the driver pulled out; and because his vision was limited by the parking method, the wary motorist would also blow his horn (as though this would make any difference to the party driving either north or south along the always crowded street).

Yes . . . downtown was a busy place.

Frankly, I loved it. And I loved the streetcars. For $1.25 per week I could purchase a pass which allowed me to ride anywhere, back and forth across the city. This meant that my business calls were handled conveniently, and, on my own time, I could hop on the cars and just ride. Lots of people did this, and many would ride out to Kupfrian's of a weekend, for there was always something going on there.

In the course of my story I've made several references to the electric streetcars. They were an innovation which came into existence in the 1880s in many American cities. Pensacola's first version had been cars drawn by horses or mules; this was upgraded to electric service in 1895. When I first came to Pensacola, and up to 1933, I enjoyed riding the cars. Many people did. But in the early 1930s, several motor car companies began producing buses which were suitable for in-city routes. Those car company people were good salesmen, and in countless cities they "proved" to political leaders and others that buses were superior to the streetcars, in part on a cost basis, and in part because the buses were more flexible. Streetcars ran on tracks; changing a route wasn't easy.

In any event, 1933 was the year in which the bus replaced the streetcar here. Gulf Power had acquired the electric routes in 1926, and I suspect that company's leaders didn't see transportation as their mission. In any event, they sold the franchise to Julius Wernicke and Jim Abbott, who promptly replaced the cars with 12-passenger Ford buses. There were reactions back and forth. Some people really liked the buses, for the drivers were accommodating, and on a rainy day, if one was a regular rider they would swing off the stated route and drive a block or two to drop the passenger dry shod at his front door.

But there were many who did not like the change. The buses operated with a single "driver," thus the old conductor, who was also a gossip and friend to many a lady carrying packages on and off the cars, was sorely missed. Those men missed having a job, since this change occurred in Depression times. When warm summer months arrived many travelers missed the open streetcars which had been nice and cool.

Where did the cars themselves go? I don't know. Many towns sold such equipment to cities in Latin America, and not too long ago people began talking about trying to bring them back, for today there is more and more concern in our country about pollution . . . and streetcars don't pollute.

All of these firms and services I've mentioned, of course, were considered as our targets for advertising sales, and all of the salesmen would gather periodically to try and develop ideas which might be used in promotions. One crazy one that—surprisingly—worked involved a man who called himself

PASHA. Pasha came to town shortly after the bay and sound bridges were opened. The 1930s had just blossomed, and everyone had hoped that these new bridges and the Island Casino would bring about a sort of boom . . . but they did not at first. We—and that included Pasha—elected to give the beach some help.

The idea was to bury Pasha in a coffin in the white beach sand. He would have an access only for food and drink, and the event was to have wide-scale promotion, to get the public interested in the man, what he was doing, how long he might stay buried, and so on and on. The sales staff composed special promotional pages to be sold to advertisers who might share some benefit from the gimmick. Many came on board. Coca-Cola, for example, became Pasha's official beverage. T. M. Lloyd's funeral parlor, which at that time provided the community's ambulance service, was standing by . . . just in case.

To help things along Pasha had an oriental background, and our creative skills tried to build up added mystique around that point.

The ideas worked. People by the legion paid the one dollar toll to drive over just to see what was going on. The Casino's lunch counter boomed, and there were souvenirs. Through one device or another Pasha stayed below ground for quite a while . . . and in the meantime the newspaper's sales department worked overtime.

Another of our successful promotions dealt with the annual World Series. Remember, this was the only major sports event of the year (unless one wanted to count the Rose Bowl). This was well before professional football became a widespread interest, or before there was such a thing as professional basketball. Of course this was before our local radio station could pick up the series from a national hookup.

What we did at the paper was to create a giant simulated playing field on the *News-Journal*'s east exterior wall. Then, using a series of strings and some white paper blocks, we would follow the game's actions as they were received via telegraph, play by play, in the paper's news department. As each ball, strike, hit, walk, run or other play developed, the news department would signal the "operator," who would move the markers to show what had happened.

Now, today that sounds so primitive. But, back then as many as 1,500 folks would assemble, some of them with little stools for comfort, and they would watch the game. Did that sell advertising? Yes it did . . . for we would develop a number of "special pages" for customers who wished to promote their businesses by encouraging folks to come out and watch. Some worked the crowd selling refreshments.

We were involved too, in helping promote the first PGA tournaments. I don't recall too much about those first years, but I do remember that the grand prize in the initial year was $3,500 . . . and that the paper's sports staff did a quality job encouraging public interest.

I mention the roles played by the city, for government here was important, and deserves a bit of background. A progressive stance by government had some roots that need description too. You see, up until 1931 the city had operated for eighteen years using a commission form of government. In the beginning folks had felt that having a three-person body of commissioners, who shared both policy and administrative duties, would reduce red tape and end the "cronyism" that had crept into the government. In 1931 the Perry papers cooperated with Prof. H. Clay Armstrong, who led the fight for a city manager-council form of government. The measure passed, and shortly George Roark became the city manager.

In today's world big time gambling has hit the South hard. The casinos along the Gulf attract thousands, and there are other ways that the addicted can bet on ball games, horse and dog racing and more. There was gambling in our city early on, especially during the 1930s . . . and beyond too . . . and it was spread all over Pensacola. The police obviously looked the other way, thus the little back room games and punch boards went on all the time. Those punch board games, plus the sporting houses, made this seem a wide-open town, and this did not give Pensacola a good name.

When George Roarke became city manager, he got down to business. He plunged in where angels feared to tread. It was he who hired Gene Forsythe, a former FBI man, to crack down on police corruption (no . . . I'd better not call it corruption . . . perhaps negligence is a better term). Most gambling houses disappeared, and more order was placed in handling other problems. By now motor vehicles had largely replaced mounted police, and there was even a motorized paddy wagon.

I wish I could report that Forsythe's presence led to a full-scale upgrading of our security force. He made an impact, but the overhauling was never completed. For example, the city never did impose real restrictions on the physical condition of its officers. It was common gossip that any man who wanted a job and had friends in high places could become a policeman. A few years later I had a wonderful example of this.

This occurred soon after my return to Pensacola from Gainesville. My family had moved into a house on the east side, which was quite far out in those days. One of the policemen at that time was a huge blimp of a man whose name I can't remember. But his girth was such that everyone called him Arbuckle, after the movie comedian, Fatty Arbuckle. Arbuckle was obviously not a prize physical specimen. He had difficulty walking a block at a good clip. Yet, he was friendly, well-liked and good at crowd control. Thus he kept his job.

One afternoon I was returning home and entered through the back door. My mother was at work in the kitchen, and after a greeting I walked to the front of the house. Just as I reached the living room I heard a fearful racket outside. A man was being pursued, and the pursuer was gasping commands to HALT and firing his pistol into the air. I stared out, and there, coming towards our house, was a man, obviously trying to escape from Officer Arbuckle, who was stumbling along in the rear. As a first reaction I slammed the front door shut, then hurried to the rear to do the same. Seconds later there was a fierce pounding at the front, and as I moved there I could see Arbuckle on the stoop. I opened the door. The poor man was gasping painfully, his air coming in deep gulps, his chest heaving as he fought for breath. As he saw me he handed me his pistol and whispered: "Here . . . here . . . you take this. YOU catch him. He went that way."

As I know you have already determined, my mother did not raise any stupid children. I did not move, except to invite the perspiring policeman inside for a chair and a glass of water.

The pursued man? Who knows what happened to him.

With my return to Pensacola in 1931 mother and I had enjoyed a brief time living with my sister and her husband, while my dad worked out of that apartment but also continued his nine-month-per-year sales routine on the road. However, after a time my fortunes began to climb, and the paper had raised my salary to thirty dollars per week, a veritable fortune for those times. With that increase our family did something it had never done before; we rented a nice little house at 16th and LaRua streets. This was a wonderful boon to my mother, who felt a great sense of relief in being able to do her own things. Mother relished the idea of being the cook. She enjoyed cooking and was good at it. Having to rely on the food at the Panama or the Chipola had not been bad for her, but she liked being her own master. Mother liked to sew too. Incidentally, the rent on our home was a princely twenty-five dollars per month.

By now—1932-33—the Depression had really begun to rock Pensacola. The first year or so following October 1929 had not had too bad an impact on the city, but by 1932 things were beginning to fare poorly. The manufacturing plants were operating on day-to-day schedules as orders arrived, the federal government was cutting savagely into its defense operations, and for two years not a single class of naval aviators was trained here. From Alabama and Mississippi hundreds of families fled from sharecropper roles because there was just no market for the products they had grown. Cotton was bringing ten cents a pound, and eggs ten cents a dozen. How could they survive on that? They came to Pensacola, hoping for work or relief. For the most part, there was little of either. The city appointed a commission to distribute what few funds became available from state, federal and local sources, but Carl Weis and Jack McCormack could make those dollars stretch just so far.

Some of these transients settled into what came to be called Hoovervilles . . . shanty towns built of old packing boxes, tin sheets from sign boards and the like. Some of these occupants were displaced farm workers, but others were what we called hobos or Knights of the Road, men who moved as best they could on the railroad, traveling from place to place, looking for a way to get a meal. One of those Hoovervilles was close to our new house, and I guess these men had a code of some sort to mark houses where they might be treated kindly. In any event, there was always a parade of them coming to the door, offering to work for a meal. We almost always tried to help, and those men did work; they weren't looking for something for nothing. They would cut wood, cut the grass or do other chores. It was sad to watch them, for in many cases one could see hope disappearing from their eyes as these hard times continued, month after month.

We also saw this in our own family.

I had an aunt (Nellie) who had lived in Coral Gables. Aunt Nellie was something of an artist, and she had lived an interesting if not affluent life there with her painting. But, as times became more and more difficult her ability to sell her wares faded. One day she called, and sadly told us that for days she had been reduced to eating nothing but potatoes and cabbage; could she come and stay with us?

We sent Aunt Nellie a bus ticket. She arrived and immediately tried to find a market for her artistry. With that I had an idea. The Hotel San Carlos had been built with a number of stores fronting Palafox and Garden streets, and now all of these stood empty, silent sentinels to our hard times. I went to hotel manager Conner Hagler and suggested that perhaps he might allow Aunt Nellie to display some of her art in the window of one store . . . to make the place seem occupied and perhaps to promote some business for her. He agreed, and shortly Nellie Ball's art was on display. I don't remember if she sold the first piece . . . but at least she tried.

Shortly thereafter we had another call, this one from Uncle Harry, also a south Floridian for whom times had grown tough. Could he come to stay with us for awhile, he begged. Again, I sent a bus ticket to my relative, and he responded, giving me his time of arrival.

In those days the bus terminal was at Garden Street, close to the newspaper, and so when the bus's arrival time approached I walked over to meet Uncle Harry. The buses of those days were not large, and when the vehicle pulled in the small number of passengers disembarked, one by one . . . but . . . there was no Uncle Harry. But then, at the very end, here came my relative. And what a sight he was. Harry was dressed in a pristine white suit, neatly pressed, and crowned by a Palm Beach hat. In one hand he carried his fishing gear. This was not the down-on-his-luck relative I had expected.

Uncle Harry joined our household and—to his credit—tried hard to find employment, but jobs proved elusive. But then Harry began to frequent the area pool halls where, to my surprise, he was very adept. Many a sucker was deceived into thinking Harry was an easy mark. Instead, my uncle began to enjoy a reasonable cash flow, if not a large income.

During these times our growing household lived well, by the standard of the day. Such a family could eat handsomely on ten dollars per week, with groceries always purchased at one of the neighborhood Mom 'n Pop stores which were found everywhere. They would even deliver the bags for that amount of traffic.

Late in the twentieth century those attending fancy golf tournaments are treated royally, with food and drink aplenty at convenient sites. That's now! But about 1930, a group of us took a converted baby carriage, equipped to carry soft drinks, ice, and a little more, to cool our days at the links in Panama City.

I have never been an avid golfer (though my wife, Theda, loves the game and was the driving force behind the par three course at Woodbine Springs). One of my few adventures with the game had come back in my Panama City days when I did play—poorly—with some good friends. Those were days long before golf courses would have strategically placed refreshments around the various fairways, and so our little group fashioned something that we should have patented. First we obtained a baby carriage which was past its prime. We stripped it down, then built compartments which would carry a variety of items—iced soft drinks, water, and a few others. We would take turns pushing our refreshment vehicle as we toured the links. As I say, it worked . . . and we should have written to Washington and prepared to make a fortune. But . . . in Depression times people didn't think in those terms.

In Pensacola, for one reason or another I have been a frequent spectator at golfing events, and beginning in the 1930s had the opportunity to witness what went on at Pensacola Country Club. Today, of course, this is a posh course, with a large and handsome club house. Back sixty years ago things were not quite that way. I recall one year when the PGA tournament here was still young, and Tony Penna, a local pro, was one of the darlings of the tour. All Pensacola wanted to follow Penna on the course, and they did. Also in the throng of viewers was an old man, wizened, thin, wearing a sweater from which both elbows protruded. The man was obviously very interested in the professionals' play, for he followed each move with a keen eye. But, along side the well-dressed country clubbers he seemed out of place, and one man muttered that the poor fellow would have been better off to use his one dol-

The Pensacola Country Club of the early 1930s had one of the more unusual lawn control systems in the country. Cattle browsed the links, neatly clipping slips of grass. Cattle bars made from railroad rails spaced in the ground kept the cows from interfering with auto traffic or the railroad which ran through the course. (The cattle were afraid to pass the bars for fear of catching their hooves.) Many a player missed a putt because Ol' Bossy had come up close to watch; other golfers, after "an accident," made sure that they stepped where cows had not ventured.

lar admission fee to buy himself a decent meal. Later we learned who this man was. He was Adm. A. C. Reed, one of the first Navy pilots to fly the Atlantic, the man for whom the Navy's golf course is named.

The PCC was very different physically. In those days entry was directly off Barrancas Avenue, and along the driveway the club had erected a cattle guard, for there were several cows roaming free on the course. The entire club grounds was fenced to control the animals, and golfers had to tread with care, for often there was strong evidence that one of the bovines had been there first.

The railroad ran through the course too. This was a trackage that once had served the old Dummy Line which carried passengers along the Bayshore to the Navy Yard. Normal freight from the FRISCO ran there too. Often during the course of a day trains would puff onto the course. If an engineer spotted a group of ladies playing he often would stop the train and make things as silent as possible while the female putters did their thing. However, if men were playing the engineer might take a different tack. Often he would have the engine glide forward, all but out of earshot. As the golfer prepared to drive or putt the engineer would release a giant blast on his steam whistle. I've watched that little move a number of times, and I tell you that the results have always been comic. Many golfers were not amused.

It was about this same time that W. J. "Pete" Noonan brought an innovation to Pensacola's golf. Pete was a road building contractor, and had been a star athlete at Notre Dame before going into business locally. He liked golf too. Now, in the early 1930s the game was still played here without benefit of wooden tees. When a player was about to drive he simply used his fingers to heap up a little mound of sand and placed his ball on that. It was Pete who discovered the wooden tee, but I don't know where. At any rate, he arrived here with half a dozen tees in his pocket and proceeded to demonstrate their use. As any golfer knows a tee can easily be lost on a drive, the club simply hurling it into the distance where it would be difficult to locate. Pete would have none of these losses. He developed a system to protect the tee which went like this: He would tie a string to the base of the tee, with the other end of the string attached to a red bandana handkerchief. The string would be—oh—three feet long. When Pete swung, both ball and tee were driven, but the handkerchief acted like a parachute. He seldom if ever lost a tee . . . but I will say that few of the club members copied his method.

In the downtown area at this point (1935) there were many people who sought board in one of several boarding houses. I remember three in particular. Mrs. Wilson's was on Cervantes Street, west of where a BP station operates today. Her's was a large, rambling two-story house (which still stands and is offices for attorneys). Mrs. Wilson managed "a respectable house" which was the dining table for young ladies who held clerical positions and who were away from home. She provided also a few nice, clean, decently furnished quarters, and good meals. However, her's was a table where "they passed the chicken once . . ."

Across the street, in a building which stood where the Town House Motel was later erected, was the boarding house operated by Mrs. Lyman Beggs (no relation to Dixie). Mrs. Beggs' clientele was a little better off than "the ribbon clerks" at Mrs. Wilson's; her rooms were larger and better furnished, and her table was more generous. As one resident put it: "Mrs. Beggs passed the chicken twice on Sundays."

At 900 North Baylen (where Hopkins Boarding House now stands) was Mrs. Irene McGaughay. People called her Miss Reen. She served meals restaurant style took in boarders, and also hosted parties. All three of these places were always well patronized.

In this era Pensacola often tried to add to its modest sophistication by staging events which seemed "big time." On one occasion one group (I can't remember just which one was involved) elected to stage a play, and imported a director who reportedly had great experience and skills. "Arty" arrived driving the biggest, best-looking foreign car I've ever seen. I believe it was a Dusenburg, you know . . . the kind with the long, long hood, with supercharger piping jutting from the sides. It was a convertible, and it was a car that demanded attention wherever it went.

Arty made quite a splash on Palafox Street . . . but then something happened. He was driving near the edge of town one night when he was robbed. Thieves cleaned him out . . . including the full content of his wallet. At that point, Arty was dead broke. He came to me with the story, and asked for help. I gave him some. It wasn't much, but it enabled the poor guy to live while he finished his stint as a director. Meanwhile, as compensation for my aid he let me drive the Dusenburg (or whatever). Now I was in hog heaven. If my life has been a saga based on modes of transport that car had to be a highlight. I was now a big man with the ladies, for every eligible maiden in Pensacola wanted to ride in that car. But, one day Arty scraped up enough money to go on his way and he did. However, I'll never forget him.

Arty's status at that time was in one sense unusual. I have no idea how he came into possession of that fine automobile, but like most other people he had little in the way of ready assets. No bank account, no stocks and bonds, no real property . . . he had nothing. Which made him like most everyone else. I've often heard veterans of that period say that they were poor but didn't realize it . . . because everyone else was in the same boat. People had enough to eat, though it was pretty plain fare. They had a roof over their heads, yet they seldom spent much on furnishings. Buying a small Philco table top radio was a big investment. For the ladies, a gift of a Lane cedar chest was outstanding. Oh, the family might spring for a mattress at Christmas time if their only one had collapsed, but my friends in the furniture stores had a slow time of it. We created our own forms of entertainment, and as I said, we were just about all in the same boat. Having a job and some kind of income made one feel prosperous.

Our Navy friends were in a similar shape, except that the young officers and flight candidates made sure they enjoyed a little fun. This was before many of the major improvements on the Navy base, and before the fine officers' club they now enjoy. In those days the officers and cadets pooled resources to maintain what they called THE BARN on North Baylen Street. The Barn was an old residence which had been transformed into a nice club, and on weekends the men would whoop it up there. They knew how to come by Sam's bootleg whiskey, and they had plenty of beer too. I can still hear the sounds that came roaring out of that building on a Saturday night. There weren't many neighbors nearby to complain, so things just rocked along. Nobody cared.

It was in this period that I had my first plane flight. I will tell you that I have never been an avid flier. There's something so solid about Mother Earth, and I have had enough little incidents in the air to make me appreciate my mortality. But, in 1929 I was introduced to flight by Horace Butterfield, who was by then an experienced naval aviator. Butterfield had suggested that it was about time that I had this experience, and he arranged everything, though to this day I'm not sure how civilian Ball got to go up in the old two-seater that was available that day. In any event, we strapped in, and he gave me my instructions, then began to taxi for takeoff, from the water's edge. (This was an amphibious aircraft.) About this same time a great wave struck us so that I was sure my days had ended. But . . . we went aloft, and I was at last part of the growing number of Pensacolians who had been in the sky. For the balance of my working career I remained a big booster of naval and civilian aviation . . . but I will never claim to have wished I had my own aircraft and been its pilot. No thanks.

I've already noted that the paper's staff was quite large, considering the times. A word is also appropriate to provide background on how and where we worked. The combined papers (*News* and *Journal*) had been gathered into a single company in 1922 when John H. Perry Sr. acquired them from separate owners. He then assembled the operation in a three-story brick building which stood in the intersection of today's Romana and Jefferson street corner. The first floor held the old press which served until Mr. Perry acquired a more modern unit from England. The advertising staff also had offices on that floor. The second floor was used for storing the large rolls of newsprint, and held the offices of the news department. The third floor was for composing . . . that is, the five linotype operators who composed the news columns and the compositors who used hot lead to create the stereotypes from mats.

The *Journal* was the morning paper, the *News* the afternoon edition, and in those days our circulation carried papers all the way to River Junction on the Apalachicola River. As each edition rolled off the press company trucks would load its copies and take off, making contact in town after town with the circulation person for that area, who employed young boys to carry the papers door to door. A great many successful business men of a later day, such as Fisher-Brown's Dave Johnson, liked to brag about how they began their business careers selling the papers on street corners across town, or delivering house to house on their bicycles. I suspect that there were more claimants than delivery people, but I like to think that men looked upon delivering papers as an honorable profession.

I've already mentioned John Thomas's name, yet I must record one other bit about him, even though our working relationship with him was brief and early. John was a wonderful person, and would leave the *News-Journal* to become first an Episcopal clergyman and then pastor of the First Presbyterian Church. Many referred to John D. as "a saint," with good reason. But John had one ongoing problem: he was always in financial difficulties. From payday to payday he was fending off creditors, and when I arrived there he had a routine which deserves recalling. On pay day John would take his money (we were paid in cash at that time) and then begin putting one dollar in each pocket . . . one in each shirt pocket, one in each jacket pocket, one in each pants pocket and so on. At this time the paper had windows which opened on an angle into the street, thus bill collectors could slip up, look in through the window and determine if their prospect was in sight. John's desk was near the window . . . and so when one of his creditors would stick his head through the opening John would straighten up, pick out one dollar, and say: "You see, George, I promised you I'd have a dollar for you on payday." And so he did. This routine would be repeated several times in the course of the day, for John owed a sum to a lot of people. They tell me that even when he was a very successful minister this problem continued, though perhaps in not exactly the same form.

In this period . . . especially through the Depression years . . . the paper always had a procession of printers and so-called newspaper people who would arrive in the city, trying to make a few dollars to take them on to the next point of opportunity. These men would come in, boasting of great things past . . . and the paper would almost always give them a typewriter and the chance to write a column about something in which they were expert. Then we would pay them enough to get to—say—Tallahassee. Some of their columns were pretty good too.

It is difficult to tell some stories about the 1930s, for those times were so atypical, so unusual that young people today tend not to believe what were true facts. The telephone and its uses are a good example. In those days the telephone exchange was on Romana Street, where a city parking garage was erected later. In those days phone subscribers were few in number, so few in fact that most homes and businesses had just three digits to their numbers . . . like . . . 123. Calls were made through an operator. The caller would lift the receiver of his instrument and the operator would respond. She would then "plug in" the call to the proper number. In that way just about everyone got to know the operators, who were real community personalities. (Incidentally, when the telephone service was inaugurated locally back in the 1880s the manager of the system had initially hired young boys as his operators. That was a short-lived experiment, for the boys enjoyed playing pranks on their customers . . . and that just wouldn't do. Thus young ladies stepped in and took command of this profession.)

Some companies used the phones a lot in the early 1930s. For example, The Lewis Bear Company's big wholesale company office on south Palafox was in constant touch with its customers or with its sales people on the road. The Lewis Bear Company had just three instruments, all on the ground floor in an office which was part open bull pen, part official cubicles. Watching their use of telephones was fun, for as a call came in there was no orderly transfer. The recipient would learn who was wanted and would then shout the person's name, with the message: "Call on line three." That was a busy office, and their phone handling made it a madhouse. The Peninsular Lurton firm and West Florida Grocery Company were not quite as large, and while their methods were similar they were somehow a bit calmer in atmosphere. I made calls at most of these, but the latter two were infrequent advertisers.

I particularly enjoyed visiting the West Florida Grocery operation, for in addition to their staple lines they were an outlet for wagons and buggies. Now, you may think that's funny, with the automobile age then almost thirty years old. But Pensacola still had its share of horse- or mule-drawn vehicles, and this one company continued on as a headquarters. In the same way the Lewis Bear firm was still active in distributing feed for horses and mules, and for the chicken farmers in the area too.

In 1933, with the inauguration of President Roosevelt's era, the Congress repealed the Volstead Act and, one after another, beer, wine and then hard spirits were once again legal. That meant that bars, saloons and the like opened once more, and some of them became advertising customers. So did the distributors, who touted the merits of Budweiser, Schlitz, Pabst and then Spearman beers. The return of alcohol also boosted the fortunes of pool halls such as one that operated right across the street from the newspaper. That particular operation also had a gambling set up for shooting craps and the like, all carefully concealed in a back room. The police often turned a blind eye to most such things.

It was 1935 that the *News-Journal* assigned me to a project that had some wonderful opportunities. There had never been an auto show in Pensacola; in fact, the idea had been used only once or twice across the country, and during the Depression years there had been few showings. Now, however, the manufacturers were pushing such events, and so the paper agreed to become a local sponsor, in concert with the San Carlos Hotel. We went from dealership to dealership, and each was anxious to show his wares. The plan was to have the various makes and models enter the hotel through the south side entrance, along Garden Street. To do this we had to build a short ramp to ease the way up the steps, and this we did. The sign-ups included Chevrolet, Ford, Pontiac, Buick, Oldsmobile, Nash, Studebaker, Chrysler, Packard, and the new English-made Austin.

The evening before the show the cars were brought in. They were placed in the lobby and down the concourse, called Peacock Lane, towards the main dining room on the first floor. The plan went well until about the time for the move in, and then it began to rain heavily. We didn't want to stain the floors, so I sent for some smaller rolls of newsprint paper, and these were laid as a sort of runway. This went fine for the first models in . . . and then came the Austin.

Austin was something of an innovation as far as Americans were concerned. Our own domestic cars were small by some of today's standards, but the Austin was a true midget . . . tiny in size, light in weight. At any rate the driver brought the car to the doorway and then gunned the engine to move up the temporary ramp. Down the hall he went, past the barbershop and registration desk, and was about to turn right to his allotted place. However, as the driver turned he also applied the brakes, and this action, combined with a damp floor and the unsecured paper took the car into an abrupt slide. The car only went three or four feet, but it ended with its front end wrapped around part of one of the support columns. It was a mess. I think we can say in retrospect that this Austin was the only vehicle ever to have a major crash in the hotel's public areas. The car had to be removed . . . and Austin was among the missing on show day.

On another occasion in the same period I ran into another new car story. This was in 1934, a time before all cars except convertibles were to be made with what the manufacturers called "the all-steel turret top." Earlier models had a roof area which had a perimeter of steel, then was closed by a wood frame over which a padded fabric topping was installed. Needless to say this was not the safest material should an overturn occur.

In that day all new cars arrived in Pensacola in railroad boxcars. On one occasion in mid-1934 one dealer's shipment had a misadventure. The rail car was thrown from its rails and turned over. The cargo was bumped about, but because the autos had been well secured there was little metal damage. But one car did have a tear in the roof.

The dealer accepted the car, then had tapestry specialists repair the damage, placing new fabric on the top. The car was then placed on the showroom floor, ready for sale as brand new.

A Navy man arrived, admired the car. He bought it and began commuting to the base, but as he did so he was disturbed by a constant rattle in the car's top. The buyer returned the car to the dealer, demanding that the problem be checked out . . . while he was present to see what was wrong. The dealer brought in a craftsman, who began by removing several finishing tacks and then a portion of the topping. That's when the fat hit the fan. There, just under the outer roofing layer, was a copy of the *News-Journal*, into which were laid a score or more of unused tacks. In his haste to finish his work the original worker had overlooked these items and had just sealed them in. I don't know what arrangement the buyer and seller came to, but I'm sure there was one red face.

In the final year of Prohibition (1932-33) Pensacola was still in the throes of living without readily available alcohol. You'll notice I said "readily available," for the products were available if one would only look. Take home brew, for example "Pop's Place" on the Gulf Beach Highway was a standout. Pop had this nice little establishment, with an outdoor garden and tables, under some moss-hanging trees. Pop produced an excellent home brew. If one wanted to down a few cold ones he had only to make that short drive and there was as good a beer as he could want.

Bootleg whiskey was available too. Now, I'm sure that many local folks of that era tried the illegal brew, and that many would say that it tasted just awful. But Sam's was different. I'm not sure what his formula was, but Sam (I'll just keep wraps on the last name) knew how to make a smooth, taste-tempting, palate-pleasing drink. People would literally come from far and near to get a supply, and our Navy trainees would conceal bottles in barrels of pecans bound for the west coast. Yes . . . between Pop and Sam, one could get his little drink if he was so inclined.

Food in this era was specialized too. Now, this is long before Pizza Hut, Colonel Sanders or McDonalds . . . but that doesn't mean that we were deprived. No indeed. If one wanted barbecue he drove out to Joe Johnson's, which stood near where the Martine's Restaurant would be located later. Joe had a genuine pit barbecue, and the aroma alone almost forced a car's wheels to turn in. Joe served large portions, and his cheery manner made his place popular with the Navy boys. That of course attracted local girls. Joe's disappeared from the scene after he went to prison for shooting a man, but to this day, the word barbecue conjures up memories of that fine little restaurant for me.

Another popular spot, though small in size and somewhat remote, was Henry Bartell's restaurant and winery in nearby Alabama. Henry had quite a large farm, where he raised scuppernong grapes and chickens, and then parlayed the two into some fine eating. His family developed a special style for preparing chicken, and their manner of serving was family style, with platters piled so high that the normal diner could never finish what was served. The scuppernong wine, too, was superb . . . and once again people would try to come from miles around. However, as I said, the restaurant proper was in his home and was small, and on key days one had to have a reservation or risk being left out in the cold. As a precaution I would send a message to Henry via one of our delivery trucks, asking that he set aside four or five places for us on a given evening, and he would. The Navy fliers used a different tactic. They would write a note and wrap it around a rock, then drop the packet with a little parachute made of a handkerchief or rag. The note would be the request for reservations . . . and they tell me this worked just fine. Later Bartell's moved their restaurant into Pensacola, where it passed to different ownership when the family died out. Only in 1995 did that memorable place close.

The Wisteria was the youth hangout. It was located across the street from the San Carlos on Palafox Street, and had a drive-in as well as inside service. This was where the younger set could come for a Coke or a shake, and they did. It was a most popular place for many years. (This should NOT be mixed up with the place of the same name on Twelfth Avenue. That came much later.)

The Volstead Act, or 19th Amendment to the Constitution, put a partial lid on the manufacture and sale of alcoholic beverages in the United States. But that law couldn't stop a good Southerner from having his little nip. Many a family made its own beer and wine, and the "Moonshiner" became a part of regional lore. Signs such as this, boosting Near (non-alcoholic) Beer were seen in many places, north and south.

Most people don't realize that the Morrison cafeterias had their origin in Pensacola. I'm not sure of the year, but Morrison opened his little place and served very good food, but for some reason the place failed, and he went bankrupt, I believe. Then he moved on to Mobile where he opened once more, and this time he succeeded. Of course, the resulting company is a national provider today. I should mention the Warfields too. They had been in the grocery business, and when the original Morrison's shop closed Warfield reopened it, again as a cafeteria. I'm not much of a cafeteria fan, and so I didn't keep track of when that closed. For a time in the 1930s it was very successful. Another who succeeded in his time was Laritz. He opened a conventional restaurant across from the Knights of Columbus Hall on North Palafox, and was quite successful. But then he had the idea of trying to provide similar food downtown, and so opened what became the Laritz Cafeteria, across from the *News-Journal* on Jefferson. That was a great success, and was ultimately taken over by Morrison's in the 1950s.

It was in 1933 (I believe) that Guy Spearman began his production of 3.2 beer . . . and then of course Guy shifted gears to more potent brews when the law allowed. The Spearman Brewery (its motto was THE PURE WATER DOES IT) shipped products over a considerable area, including the towns to the east on the coast. I was back in Panama City at the time of the *Tarpon*'s sinking, and I will always connect Spearman with Capt. Barrow's last run, for this reason: the *Tarpon* was loaded to the gunnels with cases of beer, in odd-shaped cans which had sort of a spouted top. At any event, the beer went down with the ship, and by that summer the wreckage had been located and it thus became a target for divers. Several of us from the paper (Bill Cummins as well as myself) rented regular diving suits from Greek sponge divers who happened to be in port. With that equipment we would go down and play in the wreckage. As we did so we would send up the beer . . . only to see the cans literally explode from the pressure change when they hit the surface. Thus we had fun, but we drank no beer. I'll never forget the experience, for being down in a diving helmet, and with someone pumping air to you, is rather weird. You see, the diver has to equalize pressure by regularly hitting a valve inside his helmet with the side of his head. Otherwise the full suit would fill with air and the man inside would float to the top, helpless as a wounded fish. Cummins did just that, and we kidded him unmercifully for days over his imperfect skills. (Incidentally, I'm glad I had that experience one time . . . but once was enough.)

As the Depression continued, the San Carlos Hotel suffered along with other businesses. Travelers were not traveling, and the San Carlos was primarily a hotel for the traveling public. Social functions sometimes graced its dining rooms, but they were not the heart of the hotel's business. For a number of years new management had been talking about changing decor, to try and give the hotel an interior appearance in keeping with the city's heritage. Thus when artist Joy Postle came along she found an interested client in the hotel management. Joy was given room and board (and perhaps a little more) to paint beautiful murals which graced many of the lobby and dining area walls. One ran elegantly down the main staircase. Others were in the main dining room. Bits and pieces appeared above doorways. Joy's colors were vivid yet appropriate, and her figures out of the past gave meaning to the hotel's name. It was this same time that my Aunt Nellie came to Pensacola and opened her art shop in the hotel. She and Mrs. Postle got along well.

It was at this time that I purchased my first automobile. That first car was a slightly used Model A Ford, in my opinion one of the greatest automobiles ever produced on this continent. The price was $125, and while I didn't pay cash I did pay off the loan balance swiftly, and with gasoline at about twelve cents a gallon I felt very mobile indeed. A year later I moved up . . . purchasing a used Chevrolet from Filo Turner Sr., at the Pensacola Buggy Works. Then, in 1936, as my fortunes seemed to be really climbing, I went back to Filo and traded for a new Chevy business coupe. The only sticker on this deal was that the car he had available wasn't the color I wanted. "No problem," he said. "What color do you want?" "Bright yellow," I replied. And so it came to pass that I became the owner of a newly repainted, new Chevrolet . . . with an appearance that stood out from a mile away. I was twenty-four years old, single, a man of the world . . . and despite the Depression my family and I were doing all right.

In those days—pre-war and wartime—the celebration of holidays in Pensacola took on a sort of tradition. Christmas Eve there would always be big parties, sometimes at the office, many times in private homes. Thus by late evening many of the celebrants were more than a little tight. But then many would march off to church for the midnight mass or service. There would be fine music and the usual ceremonies, but then many who had just been barely awake in the pews would return to their parties . . . determined to be insensible when morning came.

New Year's Eve was a little different. Hundreds would go to the Saenger late in the evening where, in addition to a special motion picture, they would have a stage show, a sing-along, favors and general fellowship. People liked that, and the theater would usually be jammed. For some there would be house parties too. But by then a new year had officially begun.

In 1935 John Perry had purchased a weekly paper in Panama City, from the White family. Immediately his staff had elected to convert the *Herald* to a daily, and their efforts produced a flood of red ink. Ad sales were poor, and there just didn't seem to be any answer. Perry contacted his management in Pensacola and asked for suggestions.

"Why not give Braden Ball a chance?" the Pensacola manager George Willings suggested. "He sure can sell . . . and remember, he lived in Panama City for some years. He knows the territory."

John Perry agreed, and I was confronted with a new opportunity . . . the chance to become business manager of the struggling daily. Oh . . . and I was to get a princely salary increase, to thirty-five dollars per week. On April Fool's Day 1936 the arrangement was confirmed. I headed for Panama City and a new step in my life. As I went I was in my handsome new car . . . and once again the role of transportation in a man's life appeared to me. I had driven to Pensacola from DeFuniak Springs on a *News-Journal* truck, a ride hitched from the driver. Now I was departing for my new station driving a fine new car.

Becoming a newspaper business manager at my tender age sounds very special, and I guess we might say that it was, except that the organization which I had been named to was hardly the *New York Times* or *Chicago Tribune*. The *Panama City Herald* had become a daily paper very recently, and it had some fierce competition, offered by another converted weekly, the *St. Andrew News*, owned by Mrs. L. C. West. The *News* was managed by her very capable associate Cecil Kelley. At the time of my arrival Panama City had 5700 residents, and there were untabulated hundreds in several outlying suburbs. However, this was no booming metropolis, and at the time there was little to suggest that the area was on the verge of a population explosion. The city faced the Gulf. There were miles of pure white sand beaches and a number of handsome bays and inlets, but we were still decades from those times when waterfront property commanded one thousand dollars a front foot.

Panama City's commercial district was small by comparison with Pensacola's. In fact, much of it was squeezed into a zone about two blocks long. The main street was paved, as were several cross streets. And Highway 98 was partially completed in its path along the coast.

What were the local businesses? I can remember some: there were, surprisingly, several drug stores, run by Travis Chiles, Jimmy Daffin, Crawford Adams, and the Brewers. There were clothing shops, operated by the Powells and the Cogburns. There were two motion picture houses, the Panama and the Ritz, and two banks, the Bay National and the Commercial. There were several automobile agencies, a funeral parlor, Bill Cook's Ford dealership, Nelson Chevrolet, and others. The Cove, the Dixie-Sherman, and the Marie were the principal hotels, and Christo's Five & Ten was among the more popular stores, for in those Depression days people were always looking for bargains. Also in the downtown area was the Bungalow Restaurant and Bar. On the waterfront was the city dock and the wharf where the *Tarpon* would continue to berth until she was lost in a storm.

As an aside, things were so depressed in Panama City that several blocks which had been lighted by street lamps now remained dark at night; the city just couldn't afford the cost of the electricity.

When I walked into the newspaper that first morning I was moving into a significantly different atmosphere from that I'd enjoyed in Pensacola. The *Herald* was housed in what had been the Panama City National Bank Building, a typical 1920s-type banking structure which at this point was owned by Edward Ball and Alfred duPont and leased to the paper's owner, John Perry. The staff was made up of about a dozen people, including the sales personnel, editorialists, printers, circulation folks and all. I walked into an office which I had seen once or twice during my earlier years in the city . . . the handsome office which had been the domain of the defunct bank's president. Now this was to be MINE. I had arrived.

The *Herald* had two linotype machines, a warehouse out back, and an ancient flat bed manually fed press which literally had to be stoked one sheet at a time. (And it would be some time before economics and demand allowed Mr. Perry to modernize this production.) As I examined the paper's reports I discovered that we were producing eight hundred copies per day, and that our actual subscriber list was about half that large . . . the balance of each run being sold through street sales. The staff pay scale was hardly handsome. Printers were paid twenty-five cents per hour; the editor and circulation manager each received twenty-five dollars per week, while Toni Veverka, who was our Girl Friday, handling calls, editing, proofing, doing news bits and more, got a princely ten dollars each week. Since our subscription rate was ten cents per week the paper was hardly awash with money. In fact, the balance sheet showed that we were losing about two hundred dollars per week, and Mr. Perry's first communication to me was "THESE LOSSES HAVE GOT TO STOP." Obviously some new and drastic actions were required, but to meet our current cash crunch I was able to borrow about one thousand dollars per month from the Pensacola operations.

At this point we obviously had a marginal product, and what made matters worse was that our competitor, *The News*, had converted to a daily at almost the same time as the *Herald*. Both papers had been weeklies and now were struggling for readers, for circulation was the lubrication for advertising sales. As the business listing showed, the roster of potential advertisers was small, to say the least.

Our first goal, then, was to boost circulation.

My initial move was to make an effort to fill our paper with names. I felt that name recognition, and coverage of local events, would interest residential readers. Toni Veverka and one other staffer were on the phone constantly, asking folks if they might have hosted a party, had visitors from out of town, enjoyed an anniversary or even a significant birthday. Day by day our editions began to present those things which made for local news.

Then we began to move beyond the city proper and into the suburbs, trying hard to convince people to become subscribers. There we used recent editions to illustrate that reading the *Herald* was the way to keep up with community happenings.

Next we began to focus on things that might interest business operators. "Is your store about to celebrate an anniversary, say a fifth birthday here in Panama City? Let us help you celebrate by preparing a nice ad." Or, "Has your business just developed ties with some big new distributor or supplier? Wouldn't it be effective to let people know about that through a nice series of ads?"

I will tell you that our efforts bore fruit, slowly it's true . . . but we did make progress. Week by week we were matched, stroke for stroke, by Cecil Kelley and the *News*. Each of us would make broad claims about our circulation, and of course we exaggerated some. Then Kelley challenged our numbers by telling advertising prospects that our statistic or numbers of papers printed was false. I confronted Kelley about this, demanding: "How do you know that? How can you make a statement about how many papers roll off my press?"

Kelley smiled. "Mr. Ball," he replied, "that old flat bed press of yours makes a sound like a man slamming a door every time you pull the handle. All I had to do was stand across the street and count the strokes. You can't fool me. I KNOW how many copies you print."

What could I say? He was right. He was also one darn good operator, and I told Mr. Perry that I felt that both papers were doomed to disappointment and failure so long as there were two dailies competing for a small market. He agreed, and so we made an offer to Mrs. West, who was struggling just as hard as we were. Our offer was $18,000, and we agreed to put Mr. Kelley on our payroll. Mrs. West didn't like it, but she was a good businesswoman. She shook hands on the deal. Promptly we converted the pair of papers into a single company, and called the unified paper the *News-Herald*. Now we could sell one edition and concentrate on both circulation and ad sales. As our circulation people went into the street they could tell potential customers that they would receive five papers . . . all for ten cents per week.

Immediately business improved.

Please don't get the impression that our growth was being developed strictly through the addition of trivia. No indeed. Instead, we began to take on the role of solid investigative reporting, and we also added solid efforts to become the promoter of events which would improve the entire city. When violence occurred (as it did from time to time) the *News-Herald* was on top of things. One great example was the famous murder of Roy Van Kleeck.

Roy Van Kleeck was a kindly man who lived to the north of the city and ran two little businesses, one a hardware store downtown. He had just a handful of employees, and everyone seemed to like him.

Well, one summer Saturday night Mr. Van Kleech put the store's proceeds in a canvas sack, turned out the lights, closed and locked his front door, and climbed into his car parked in a dark area. What he didn't know was that a disgruntled employee named Brown was hiding in the car's rear seat, holding a pistol. Van Kleek sat down, and immediately felt the gun to his head. The man grabbed the sack, and, at that moment, the gun went off. Van Kleek slumped down, dead.

The employee, Brown, slipped into the driver's seat, drove to the west side and came to a small bridge over a big lagoon. He got out and dragged Van Kleek's body to the bridge rail, and then dumped it in.

He then drove back to town, washed his hands, and headed for the bus station.

It was morning before Mr. Van Kleek's remains were found. They were discovered by a passerby, who rushed into town to tell the sheriff. Then, for a reason I've never been sure of, the sheriff hurried to our office to bring us the news.

Now he, my associate Toni Veverka, and others began trying to assemble the facts. I suggested that a quick check be made of Van Kleek's employees, to see if they might have information. When Brown came up missing he immediately became the suspect.

"What would you do if you were him?" the sheriff queried.

"Well," I said, "since he's left the car here my guess is that he took the first bus north, out of town."

Now I must add here that the operator for the primitive telephone service in town was named Audrey York, and she soon became a vital part of what happened next. We placed a call to the local bus terminal, and yes . . . someone there remembered a man bearing Brown's description buying a ticket. Since the next transfer point would have been Marianna we called there, and—yes—they remembered Brown too. He had purchased a ticket for Jacksonville.

I was familiar with Jacksonville, so I suggested to the sheriff that the hotel closest to the bus station was the Seminole. Also I happened to know that the desk clerk there was a Panama City man named Campbell Bannerman. Another call went out . . . and sure enough, with Audrey's help we were on the line to Bannerman, who said that Brown had just checked in.

Well, it didn't take long for the sheriff to get hold of the Jacksonville police, who arrested Brown. He was brought back for trial. Trial day was very hot. The courtroom was filled with men in overalls, with just a few ladies to the rear. Everyone had a fan, and some of the men passed the time shelling and eating boiled peanuts.

That trial wasn't like the ones today. It was over in a day, and Brown was found guilty. He was then taken to the sheriff's jailhouse.

That night, as the jailer became drowsy, men slipped in, knocked him out took his keys, and made off with the prisoner. By morning this was the story of the century in Panama City.

Now, everyone began looking for Brown. We all expected that he had been lynched, and in a small town there weren't too many places his body could be hidden. At this point we had our new press which could turn out eight pages at a crack, and what I proposed to do was prepare an extra, using a new front page with all of the trial's details and—hopefully—the finding of the body. Deadline for an extra—the first ever anticipated in Panama City—was 11 A.M. I sent out just about everyone we could spare, including the assistant circulation manager, a young, very high-strung fellow named Percy Oliver. Hour by hour these people combed the town and outskirts . . . and then, about ten o'clock Oliver found the remains . . . dragged off a dirt road and into some tall grass. The former prisoner was very dead, but it looked like we would get our extra. But then the impossible happened. Oliver FORGOT to call the office with the details. Our own employee had found the corpse . . . but he failed to give the word that would have set the press moving. Our one great opportunity for an exciting EXTRA ended in failure.

Of course, violence wasn't our only editorial tool. We were also blessed by happenings that swept the public's interest. One of these was the arrival in our city of Clarence Chamberlin. These were still pioneering days in aviation, and Chamberlin had been one of the first to solo fly the Atlantic (I believe he made his flight just after Charles Lindbergh's), but like others, Chamberlin's success drew only small mention in the press. Now, some years later, he was owner of a vintage Fokker tri-motor aircraft and was trying to make a living barnstorming and giving rides. Chamberlin arrived in Panama City just about dead broke. He was down on his luck, and after he had landed on a grassy strip outside town he made his way into the city and one of his first stops was at the newspaper. He introduced himself, honestly explained his plight, and asked for help. I asked him to give me twenty-four hours to think about it, and he did. My suggestions to him came in two parts. First, we would become his promoter, using the paper to boost his reputation and then to offer low-cost sightseeing flights aboard his plane. We even paid for the first tanks full of gasoline. With our buildup, people flocked to the landing strip, and within a day or so Chamberlin had about as many passengers as he could handle.

Then we tried a second stunt. I hired a local photographer to go up with Chamberlin. First we took the door off the plane to give the cameraman good vision; then we tied that man securely into place . . . and I even went along to hold onto his legs . . . just in case. We flew around the city, taking pictures of landmarks AND local businesses. We printed a few of those photos, but then began selling the idea of giving the businessmen enlarged copies of the pictures of their buildings. We even suggested that photo-ads would be effective. Boy . . . did that ever work.

I don't recall how long Chamberlin stayed around, but it was for several weeks. When he left we were good friends, and both he and the *News-Herald* had profited. This was one of our best early promotions.

When his tour with us ended, Chamberlin flew to a new opportunity in Lakehurst, New Jersey, and, by chance, arrived at that airport on the day of the fateful crash of the dirigible *Hindenburg*.

Our second promotional effort involved a crazy character named Happy Jack Miller, who billed himself as "an auto daredevil" . . . and he was. Jack had a powerful car in which he did what he termed "auto jumps." That meant that he would set up a sort of lift onto which he would drive at high speed, and the lift would propel his car into the air . . . and over other cars which had been placed strategically in his path. Jack was a man of great good humor, and had several parts in his act, which he put on before an audience which had to be promoted. I saw this as an opportunity to involve the paper in something which would liven peoples' lives, and so we agreed to be his sponsor. One problem: No one was willing to volunteer his car as the object over which Jack would jump. And so it was Braden Ball to the rescue. I was still driving my canary yellow Chevrolet coupe, a car which I treasured, but Jack assured me that his efforts never failed. After considerable lineage designed to draw a crowd, the great day came and Jack Miller performed . . . and did very well. My vehicle ended the day unscathed, and the crowd went away happy. We had charged admission to the event, and then offset Miller's advertising costs and gave him a modest return.

On the side, Jack admitted that men in his profession did run risks, and that it was not unusual for their cars to tip over and roll after such stunts. But, he said, there were seldom any serious injuries because the men had learned to drive using a special harness. This was my first introduction to what came to be known as the seat belt, and we wrote considerable copy about that too. The *News-Herald* was thus considerably ahead of its time on some things.

It was about this time that work began on the building of the St. Joe Paper Company in the nearby town of Port St. Joe. Naturally I saw possibilities for some special advertising in this, since the entire area would want to have details of this mammoth mill which would be linked to almost one million acres of timber land in the region. The key appeared to be getting a hearing (and support) from the mill's key financial figure, Edward Ball, and so I held a sales meeting to see if any member of our staff had any connection with the financier, who was one of the executors of the huge estate of Alfred duPont. One of our men, surprisingly, volunteered that, yes, he had seen and met Mr.

Ball while visiting the lodge at Wakulla Springs. With this man's aid we obtained an appointment to visit with Mr. Ball in Jacksonville.

The meeting day came, and Mr. Ball received us courteously. Just as we began to talk business he asked my salesman if he had been a recent visitor to the springs, since his name sounded familiar. "Oh, yes!" the salesman responded. Mr. Edward Ball then produced a clerical item which he passed across the desk. The slip noted that my employee had indeed been present . . . and had left leaving a worthless check for five dollars. Embarrassment? You'd better believe it. My man was red as a beet, and our meeting might have ended right there had Mr. Ball been a lesser man. But, after receiving assurance that the debt would be paid promptly, he settled down with us and helped plan what was to be a giant section of the newspaper, to include aerial photos of the mill site, sketches of the planned construction, and text of the mill's plan of action. I'm happy to report that a host of advertisers, including many firms involved in the mill's construction, came on board as advertisers, and that a beautiful rotogravure section was printed for us by the *Atlanta Constitution* (our plant was of course not equipped for that sort of work). Thus began my relationship with Edward Ball. He would be my friend and associate in many business ventures until the day of his death in 1981, at age ninety-three.

☞ ☞ ☞

As I worked out of Panama City my calls occasionally took me to Chipley, where Major Olin Shivers ran the Chipley Hotel. I always made a call there when I was in town, to have a cup of coffee with the major, and to chat about conditions. I'll never forget one visit, which came when the economy was at rock bottom. I asked Shivers how things were going, and he replied: "Terrible. Just terrible. And the few people who do come in . . . well . . . we're just swapping water with 'em . . ." I'd never heard that saying before.

Earlier I had mentioned the name of Cecil Kelley, who had been a part of the *News* acquisition. Cecil was a very able newspaperman, and also a great inventor. (He would later assist John Perry Jr. in major changes in paper production.) Cecil became a strong right arm after the *News* and *Herald* were united, and became a great help as we began efforts to broaden circulation into the five suburban communities. As we did this Cecil and I discovered that one major problem in paper delivery stemmed from the duplication of street names. As one suburb after another came into existence the founders chose the same persons or events as the source of street titles, thus we had a very mixed up system community-wide, despite the relatively modest population. Also, it was not easy for anyone to be able to analyze deliveries or even find people. We determined to pursue a project which had never been attempted in that area; we would prepare a community directory, with names, addresses, telephone numbers of all who lived there.

This was NOT an easy task, especially since we were also trying to end the duplications. Developing a directory design required special skills, for we were going to print the material in the paper . . . and then encourage recipients to cut out and assemble pages from a unique format. Well . . . we plunged ahead, and in the process just took it upon ourselves to change names, often by adding a form of suffix. (For example, Bay Street might become Bayview Street, or Panama Street might become Panama Drive.) It took weeks of work to gather all of the names, numbers and political boundaries, and then to formalize the design . . . but at length it was done. In the process we took advantage of an opportunity and sold one inch advertisements to businesses which might profit from having a mention in a booklet that was likely to be retained. That sales effort did well too.

Rose Printing Company in Tallahassee did the actual directory printing for us, for which we promoted distribution day heavily in the paper. When the directory came out it was a huge success, taking on the role of the Polk directories which had been done for half a century in larger communities. Of some interest, I kept several copies long after practical use had ended, and only recently I made a present of one to the University of West Florida Library. The directory was one good promotional effort with staying power.

With the growing popularity of our paper we decided to try to further extend our overall area of circulation, and once again this required a little ingenuity and money. The goal was to sell subscriptions in places like Blountstown, Bristol, Marianna, Bonifay, and other towns. Our kickoff was brilliant.

For it we printed fliers which said that as of a given day newspapers were going to literally "come out of the sky" to the specific community. Each circular was localized.

On this great day we rented a small airplane piloted by Gene Schwab and one by one flew to these towns. The right hand door of the plane had been removed, and one of our staff was with me to do the drops. As we swept over each town we would throw out the circulars, which drifted down like falling snow. The drop was made over the business district, and of course the combination of the noise of a low flying aircraft AND the unusual paper falling from the air attracted a crowd in each town. (For the drop my assistant would lie flat on the plane's floor and I would hold tight to his legs so that we didn't also start dropping people.) Once the leaflet drop had been completed we would regain altitude, circle the area for a few minutes, then soar back once more, dropping small bundles of newspapers which were carefully tied to prevent them flying apart. From above we could watch the townspeople swarming over the bundles, snipping the strings and then begin to read. Of course there was a special front page story which detailed how one might arrange a subscription.

I forget just how many towns we visited that day, but it was quite a number, and I will say with some pride that the tactic worked. NOW the *News-Herald* was extending its sway.

Our work to improve circulation wasn't limited to the incorporated towns and cities. To reach large numbers we also tried to sell papers to men and women who worked for the large mills, most of which operated in the woods, or near them. Many employees lived in company-owned villages. One of these was the Kenny Saw Mill, where the whole operation was built around a company town. Remember, this was Depression time, and this wily company (like many others in the area) paid employees in company script, not in cash. This meant that family purchases had to be at the company store, where they sold food, clothing, shoes and incidentals. However, when we tried to collect the ten cents per week for our subscriptions we ran into trouble. These poor people had no money, only paper script, and I couldn't see myself buying my shoes at their store. This whole matter took a lot of negotiating . . . but we finally found a solution.

As the paper gained stature we found it possible to go into league with others to promote events and causes. One of the first of these was a regional beauty contest. This was done in connection with the Martin Theater group which owned the local motion pictures houses. The idea was to generate some fun, and to draw people onto the area's beaches at a time when those pure white sands were hardly appreciated. There were prizes offered, and with circulation now in effect over an area of more than fifty miles we drew contestants from most of the area's communities. The young ladies came, posed, looked attractive and were ogled by quite an audience. We repeated that exercise for a number of years.

Next came promotion of what we called the Gulf Coast Fishing Carnival. By now there was a growing number of fishing boats in the port towns along the coast, and Panama City had its share. There also was such activity in Mobile, Pensacola, Fort Walton, Apalachicola, and Destin; our goal was to try to promote such sport to areas well beyond the Gulf itself. Small ads were run in distant papers, and through the efforts of fishermen and boat owners we rounded up a goodly list of prizes. The carnival, first held in 1937, came to be a highly successful annual event, drawing substantial numbers to the city. It was a bonanza for advertising sales too. We had a paper which ran between thirty to forty pages in the key issue. In a similar manner we began gathering interested local folks to try and bring substantial numbers to the community as tourists. Our problems in this were huge. The beaches had no facilities to speak of, and many of the little roadways that led to the white sands were lined with pathetic tar paper shacks which did anything but encourage visitor traffic. Our first big promotion of this kind was targeted for July 4, 1937, and for this everyone involved pulled out all the stops. We advertised fireworks, patriotism, beautiful water, and plenty of family fun. From the first this idea paid dividends, and before long an estimated 50,000 people were swarming to the waterfront for the holiday. When one considers the level of local population, and the limited facilities for tourists, that was quite an accomplishment.

On a parallel track, the paper began promoting the building of better streets and roads, and changing the form of Panama City's government, which was still an old-fashioned and ineffective council system.

Recently, Edward Ball and Alfred duPont had done yeoman service in promoting the building of major highways east to west, and by now Highway 98 had been completed from Pensacola to Carabelle. But Panama City lacked connectors north and south, and from the city onto the beaches. In this work J. R. Asbell, a former member of the State Road Department who knew how to approach such needs, became my advisor. Now, let me be very clear on this: the work of road building was no overnight affair. We worked at it and promoted it heavily for many years. But . . . step by step, the work got done, and this opened up Panama City to many forms of improvement. In later years some people asked why Highway 98 didn't follow the shoreline, to gain the waterfront view. The answer was that much of the land near the water was very swampy and unsuited to highway construction.

Establishing a timeline for those busy years is not easy, for many of the things that came to pass fed upon one another. The success of the papers began to be felt by 1938, for by then circulation had multiplied, and now the space needed for operations exceeded what was available in the bank building. A deal was struck for purchase of a corner lot at Harrison and Fifth Avenue, and plans were made for a single story wooden building which would house the *News-Herald* and afford a space for a lease property which we offered to the A&P. A&P already had one small local store, and they were very unpopular with other merchants, for this was a day when many small business owners felt the threat of "the chain stores" and were vocal in their opposition.

However, A&P was present, and they were of a size to afford the paper an opportunity. We were still in the period when retail space advertising was largely restricted to very small ads . . . four column inches . . . six at the most, and the A&P was about our only sizable advertiser. However, like the others that did buy space, their insertions were very small. Other retail firms used what they called fliers. These were small printed pieces, often on multi-colored paper, which they had delivered to homes, other businesses or even stuck on the windshields of automobiles. My goal was to get A&P's management to increase the size of their ads and thus set a trend. I could not do this through the store's local manager, for he had no such authority. Instead, I worked through the regional headquarters in Jacksonville. I finally talked the regional manager into considering using larger ads. When they became serious about opening a second store, I offered them space in the building we had planned. The monthly lease payment was to be very low . . . $125 . . . but was predicated on their taking at least one weekly ad of considerable size . . . 2 columns by 12 inches . . . a monstrous affair by the standard of the times. The general manager finally accepted what I saw as obvious economics, and the deal was struck.

The paper's portion of the new building had multiple street-front entrances, and had a fine space for press work at the rear. This brought into play our second move . . . which involved acquiring a used rotary press from Horace Hall and his paper in Dothan. Horace was well known to me, and his operation, the *Dothan Eagle*, had grown to a point where he needed a larger press, thus we worked out a deal. We paid four thousand dollars for the unit, and had it moved. In the process I wooed away James Peavy, the Dothan pressman, without whom I probably never would have gotten the new machine into production. James was a craftsman, and soon we were running smooth as a kitten purring. The combined development illustrated how far and how fast we all had moved in a few years. Mrs. West, from whom Mr. Perry had purchased the *News*, continued to snipe at us a bit, calling our young team "Perry's Kindergarten," and I must say that she got on my nerves from time to time. Mrs. West was a much older woman, but a very capable one, and I know how she must have felt about seeing her paper in someone else's hands. Another lady whom we continued to have much contact with was Mrs. Beulah Penny White, from whom Mr. Perry had purchased the *Herald*. She remained on our payroll and was a very capable part of the staff. She was my right hand.

Efforts to build circulation and a new plant, and to promote community growth were one thing. Advocating change in form of government was something else. As one might expect, any such suggestion treaded on sensitive, entrenched political toes, and there were some who would have liked to have run the aggressive publisher of the paper right out of town. The City Manager form of government had been installed in Pensacola in 1931, and it was working very well . . . helping undo the core politics which often accompanies the form then in use in our town. To push the project we helped establish a Good Government League, with W. C. Sherman, the civic leader who had recently built the Dixie Sherman Hotel, as the league's president. That image strategy didn't hurt one bit. Finally, after many months of wrangling and debate (and numerous skillfully written editorials) the change was made. Gov. Cone signed the amended charter . . . the change was made. A few weeks later I received something of a shock. Much of the legal work done in this campaign had been performed by a man named Tom Sales. All of our committee members had performed their functions as a public service, and I had assumed that Tom had too. No indeed. We got a handsome statement from him . . . and getting that resolved took some big league diplomacy.

The late 1930s saw Panama City beginning to open up more as a town, and some of what I saw I didn't like. Not that this all occurred overnight; it didn't. But step by step the community began to host all sorts of gambling, houses of entertainment, and a few other things that attracted a poorer sort. At the paper we tried to stand up for what was good in the community, and, as we were able, we put such places and stories about them in as poor a light as possible. As things turned out one of the county's more aggressive figures became involved with one establishment, and after his name appeared in print in such a way he paid me a visit. This man was big, far bigger than I was at twenty-four, and he was not smiling. He came right to the point: "Sonny," he began, "you 'uns printed my name in that story about the card games, and I'll tell you right now I didn't like it. Now, you'd better quit . . . and right now."

My knees sounded like castanets, but I looked him straight back, and said in as strong a voice as I could muster: "Yes sir, we did print that . . . and I'll tell you this. So long as you are properly identified with things like that we're going to continue to put your name there . . . right out on page one."

He looked me in the eye once more, then sort of grinned. "I guess you mean it," he said.

And you know, from that day forward we became friends, and his name did stop appearing, not because we had backed down, but because he had.

In the 1930s there were many institutions which came and went in this region, some of them of lasting duration, some which were modified as years passed and are still with us in some form. One of those which I remember with humor was the juke joint. This name was usually applied to the tavern or roadhouse (or whatever it might be called in Prohibition days) where there would be refreshments, a record-playing machine which came to be called a juke box, sometimes slot machines, and if the proprietor wanted to live dangerously a punch board, which was technically a gambling device.

The juke joint was a hang out, or better still, West Florida's version of a pub. It was a place where people sought companionship, where news and views were exchanged, where "singles" sought contacts of the opposite sex, and where the music encouraged dancing and the like. For many years these places were the epitome of our Southern culture, for the music was often the wailing, tearful, tragic stories which told of lost loves or worse. People of many stamps visited juke joints, and usually they would have a good time.

But on too many occasions someone would consume too many beers and would become aggressive or even violent. I can remember once when I visited such a place as a young man. I had a date with me, and when a record began to play I suggested that we dance. She agreed, and we glided back and forth to a record that may have been cut by Roy Acuff or Skyline Scottie. It was a soft, slow, doleful melody, and we enjoyed it. There was only one other couple dancing. Then we sat down. I had hardly warmed the chair when a tall, heavy, red-faced man grabbed my shoulder. He was part of the other dancing pair, and was a solidly built character, obviously with too much to drink. He also must have been affected by some personality-changing event. As he grabbed me he shouted: "Buddy, you ain't dancin' on my nickel no more!" Who was I to argue with a man of such stature? My date and I fled into the darkness.

On one other occasion, however, I made out better. I was en route to Tallahassee to visit several young ladies in one of the university's sorority houses. I was short of cash, but when I entered a juke along the way I was struck by inspiration. There on the counter was a punch board, with only eight chances left. And . . . there were eight prizes waiting to be won . . . each a pound box of quality chocolates. For my last three dollars I could buy all available chances. I jumped. And, of course, I won the candy. When I arrived at the sorority house and the girls discovered how well I was endowed with gifts, I became the man of the hour. (I don't recall what tune was playing when I won.)

Prior to the late 1930s our Panama City post office had been a very modest structure. These were still WPA times, and it was possible with a little good politicking to get Uncle Sam to come forth with monies to build such a structure. Our plan was approved and the post office was built. Then, through the efforts of John Perry, the city got Postmaster General James A. Farley, one of FDR's true lieutenants, to come to the city for the dedication. Our paper covered this from stem to stern, but I also wanted the message of Farley's presence to blanket an even wider area, so we made arrangements to have Pensacola's radio station WCOA broadcast the event. We agreed to pay what I considered an outlandish fee for a fifteen-minute broadcast, but it was worth it. On that day Panama City seemed to have its spot on the map . . . recognized nationwide.

By now we were midway in the second term of Franklin D. Roosevelt. The war had not yet begun, but the world was very tense. The President was in the process of winding up a visit to Central and South America to try to implement what he and Cordell Hull called "The Good Neighbor Policy." Now, Mr. Roosevelt was returning to this country aboard a Navy cruiser which was to dock at NAS. Then, the President was to motor through the city and then board his private car, *The Magellan*. The eighteen-car train was backed into what was then the L & N freight station which ended with a terminal along Garden Street, just west of Alcaniz.

You can imagine that this was a BIG day for Pensacola. There must have been two thousand people packed around the freight station, and on schedule the President arrived, riding in the rear seat of a four-door convertible sedan. They had placed a sort of ramp arrangement at the point where he left the sedan, and there, to assist him, were several aides. It was then that I, now a veteran newspaper man with over a decade of experience, received a shock. Mr. Roosevelt alighted and made the transfer, but only with much assistance. The wheel chair was positioned for him, but obviously his legs were all but useless. The President was a helpless cripple, and this was obvious to see. Yet ... to that moment, I had never become aware of his handicap. He had passed through two presidential elections and been much photographed in many places—yet the news networks had glossed over his condition and had NEVER, to my knowledge, photographed him being cared for as he had been that day. From that point forward I held the views and news presentations of the wire services with great suspicion.

By now the war clouds were growing darker, and as a result the activities of our military forces were expanding. At Valpariaso the commander of Maxwell Field in Montgomery had established a little runway where fliers might land and take a break during exercises from that base. Recently, National Airlines had begun service across the panhandle, flying twelve-passenger Lockheed Lodestars from Jacksonville into such towns as Pensacola, Tallahassee, and Mobile. Now I had a great idea. Why couldn't we get the Army Air Force to blacktop a runway in Panama City that would enable the town to get commercial air service as well as a tie to the military? I posed the concept to several business leaders, and they agreed that this might be a great step for us. And so, working through our United States Senator, Claude Pepper, we got an appointment in Washington with General Hap Arnold, who then commanded the USAAF. All of us flew at our own expense to the nation's capital on a commercial DC-Three.

Arnold was a tough customer. He was congenial, but he made it plain that he could see little value to the Army Air Force in spending money for something it didn't need. But then he posed a question: was there per chance a major acreage near Panama City which might be obtained for a new military air field? We assured him that there was . . . and so conversations began. I won't detail all of the negotiations, but in the long run large acreages were obtained from St. Joe Paper Company and others, and the result was the 1939 establishment of Tyndall Field, which to this day continues as a major base. The only sad note in this was that it seemed like forever before all the property owners were compensated, and Edward Ball was forever unhappy about his treatment on this project. The commercial airfield and National Airlines? They had to wait until much later. Then the city put up the money to acquire property and build the facilities.

When 1939 dawned I was still living in the Cove Hotel, and my parents were in the small rented house in Pensacola. I frankly had given little thought to any change in these arrangements, when an opportunity knocked that I could not refuse. Along a stretch of beautiful St. Andrew bay front was a lovely vacation home which had been built by Asa Candler Jr., son of one of the early developers of Coca-Cola. The main house had three bedrooms and baths, a huge living room, a magnificent dining room and splendid kitchen. There was a caretaker's house, and a guest house with four bedrooms, all on three hundred feet of beach front. Mr. Candler and his brother had built the property as a summer vacation home, and then the brother had been killed in an auto accident. That took the bloom off the property for Candler, and so he placed it on the market for $7,500. I was interested. I made a call on the seller, and finally offered him a $125 payment of "earnest money." Quite frankly, I didn't have funds in the bank to even cover the check, but I went immediately to make that bid good. I had no sooner put the process in motion than others responded to Mr. Candler's ad, and I was put in the interesting position of becoming a broker, for I now was technically the one who had control of whether to sell or not sell. Several of those seekers went away disappointed, for I saw little value in even talking with them, but then came an automobile dealer from Georgia who offered me one thousand dollars spot cash for my option. That was a lot of money, and so I said yes. He gave me his check, which I promptly cashed. It looked as though Asa Candler's house and I would quickly part company. But things didn't turn out that way. The auto magnate went back home and found that his banker would not finance the house purchase. His cash flow just didn't justify it. And so he called back and told me to just keep his money . . . the deal was off.

I moved in . . . and shortly my parents joined me. Now we were really living. The house payments were steep, $51.57 per month, but I could make them, and we took great pride in this truly luxurious surrounding. (So that I do not overlook the end of that story, the Balls lived in the Candler house until 1943, when I was promoted to the publishership of the Pensacola papers. By then it was wartime, and selling a house was like stealing. I ended up with a $12,500 profit on the deal, overall. This beautiful home came fully furnished—but it had one drawback: as a summer home it had only fireplaces for heating. We thus struggled through one winter, but then a suitable system was installed.)

The Candler house had a long pier built for the first owner's yacht jutting into the bay, and fishing off the pier was good. As a result, my employees had an open invitation to come and enjoy themselves. One Saturday afternoon I looked out of the window and spotted Bill Cummins, our circulation director, escorting a striking looking young lady. They carried fishing gear and were about to test the waters. I could see Bill any time, but this girl was fascinating, so I walked down to say Hello. Bill introduced me to Theda Sims, who was a Panama City native but was then working in Birmingham for a real estate firm. Theda and I struck sparks right off. I liked her, she liked me . . . and before long we were courting, partly by long distance telephone, often through my visits to Alabama. I won't say that we became engaged exactly, but we more or less developed an understanding. I was with several friends in New Orleans on September 1, 1939, when a German submarine sank the British vessel Athena. Now war was for real, and I realized that it might soon come to our country, with who could tell what consequences for personal relationships. Later that week, I called Theda, and that weekend I drove to Birmingham and proposed . . . formally.

We were married in the Catholic Church in Birmingham on April 10, 1940.

Fred Philips, our advertising manager, was my best man, and Roy Hickman, then in the engraving business, was in the wedding party. (Later Roy would go on to be the president of Rotary International.) I had known Hickman since my days in Palmer College. His engraving company had been involved with preparation of that school's annual, thus he had been my advisor as I worked at getting an improved book out for them. We had stayed in touch from then on, in one way or another. It was a beautiful ceremony, after which we departed for New Orleans for our honeymoon. I will tell you that even with my exalted salary at the paper money was short. Monthly house payments of $51.77 took a big bite out of earnings, and so I had to borrow seventy-five dollars on my life insurance for that trip. We had a wonderful time, but I will always remember the cold treatment we received from a waiter at Antoinne's, who seemed to sense that we were traveling on a budget. I never forgot that moment. I still hope that one day I can go back there and get revenge on some waiter in that restaurant as a symbol of what we went through.

At that point we returned to Panama City, and took up housekeeping in the Candler House with my folks. War had yet to come to the United States, but by now the work done over several years at the paper had shown results. I do believe that Mr. Perry, the owner, was pleased with what we had done.

Life for the expanded family living in Candler House had some unique twists. Because there were additional facilities outside the dwelling itself it was possible to entertain in a broad sense, and we did. My parents developed strong friendships with several couples their own age, and enjoyed having them in for poker parties. Some, like eighty-three-year-old Sam French, came for overnight visits from Pensacola. This was possible because of the extra bedroom in the main house. One event in Mr. French's story bears retelling.

French was a retired Florida state engineer, a man of many talents. One of these was the enjoyment of his little toddy of an evening, and sometimes, if sleep came with difficulty, later in the night. For this he kept his bottle of bourbon handy in the kitchen. To reach the kitchen without turning on lights which might disturb others French had a "seeing eye route" which carried him into the living room, where he would put one hand on the edge of a large marble-topped table which ran almost the length of that room. This routing carried him straight into the kitchen. This was his nocturnal route, and his technique was faultless, despite the total darkness of the downstairs room.

Shortly after our marriage Theda decided to rearrange some of the furniture, including that large table. When repositioned it now ran at right angles to its former place. It was just weeks later that Mr. French arrived for an overnight visit, and sure enough, about three in the morning he began his move to get a little "putter to sleeper." All went fine at first, but then the unexpected happened. Now, with the table going in a new direction, he was lost. He went round and round, always keeping his fingers on the marbled surface, but the kitchen never appeared. At length his cries for help were heard . . . and all of us came rushing to see what was wrong. The chagrinned Mr. French was forced to admit that he had become totally disoriented in a forest of tabletop . . . from which only our arrival released him. We never forgot that night, or ceased to laugh about it.

Others came to visit too. Eugene and Anne Elebash were guests who stayed in the other house. Ditto for Lansing T. Smith and his wife, Julius and Mrs. Wernicke, and George Archer and his wife. There were many others too, for when our Pensacola friends learned that there was a waterfront vacation spa available they didn't need much urging to come and spend a night with us.

☞ ☞ ☞

It was 1939 when Mr. Perry, examining the improving results at his radio stations in Pensacola and Jacksonville, decided that he would like to have a station in Panama City too. The ball was passed to me. However, we faced one problem up front. At that time the Federal Communications Commission would not allow a newspaper to also own a radio outlet in its market. This was deemed a hazard to competition, or something like that, and so we had to find a way around this roadblock.

Our remedy was simple. I enrolled three leading businessmen, Bill Cook, the Ford dealer, Phil Roll and Ed DeWitt, and furnished them with the $25,000 necessary to plough through the permits and paperwork, and to acquire the equipment necessary to put WDLP (the call letters were for the initials of Mrs. John Perry, Dorothy Lilly) on the air. The agreement was that at some future appropriate time the paper would take the obligation off their hands. Not a word of this transaction between the four of us was put on paper.

Cook, Roll and DeWitt proceeded, neat as clockwork, and on schedule the station was ready to go on the air. We wanted to do this up RIGHT, for it was important to get WDLP off well in the eyes of possible advertisers and influential folks. For a master of ceremonies we obtained a regional figure named Charles Francis (Socker) Coe, who did fight broadcasts play-by-play and was well known. We knew he would draw an audience. Then, we paid the high phone fees ($12.50 each) to get direct remote line coverage from the Methodist Church and the local armory. The Bay High School band was to play at the church, where a crowd was to gather to hear speaker presentations from the station. Other town figures were to assemble at the armory. The two remote locations were established because the station's studios were too small to accommodate a crowd.

You must remember that this was 1939 and that Panama City was considered a prime part of the Bible Belt. At the precise moment, the microphones were opened and Mr. Coe took to the air. For the first moment he did beautifully, setting the scene, giving credit to the three apparent founders of the station, and noting what a community benefit this station was sure to be. Then, he said, using true radio technique: "Now . . . to begin our entertainment for the day, we transfer you by the miracle of radio to the First Methodist Church, where the Bay High School Band will begin its concert by playing *The Beer Barrel Polka*. No one thought he was serious, but he was correct. The band, with no one having checked their selections, WAS playing the Andrews Sisters' favorite. The Methodists were horrified. So were other conservative churchgoers. Negative phone calls poured in.

Coe was light on his feet. He made a frantic signal to the engineer to get back the mike, then announced: "Now . . . we take you to the Bay County Armory, where Tom Yancy, head of the local Chamber of Commerce, will greet you . . ."

Yancy was right on his toes, ready to do some *vox populi* interviews . . . and the first man he talked with was asked: "Sir . . . in your opinion, what do the letters WDLP stand for?"

I have no idea who the clown was who answered, but his reply brought another cry of anguish from the radio folks. The man said: "I think it stands for WE DRINK LIQUOR PUBLICLY."

Once again the phones rang, bringing calls from angry church people.

Again the mike changed hands . . . and so the day went. Mr. Perry was present for the event; so was his private secretary, Earl Kettel. We were off, I would have said, to a rocky start . . . but somehow we got through the day. The Methodists weren't going to advertise much so we could more or less write off their reactions. Other townspeople felt that the program was "very entertaining . . . and different."

All went fairly well for WDLP for several months, and then, just before the Christmas holidays, an inspector for the FCC arrived, asking to see any records we might have related to the radio station. I smiled . . . and was as cordial as any man could be. The inspector then began his search. I believe he went through every sheet of paper in my office and in the newspaper's files. He checked things at Bill Cook's, and at Roll's and DeWitt's too. He found nothing illegal. Finally, on Christmas Eve, he came in to shake hands and say he was leaving. I invited him to sit down and have a little toddy. He did. As he was about to leave he said:

"Mr. Ball, I don't know how you did it. But I know you did it. You folks are mighty sly."

I replied: "Sir, some day I'll send you my whole file on this, the special secret agenda . . . and then you'll know how we did it."

I waited about a month, and then I kept my word. I mailed him a large manila envelope . . . which contained one sheet of completely blank paper.

And, as planned, when the time was right the Perry organization became the official owner of the radio station.

It was in 1940 that our next blockbuster occurred. By now Hitler's panzer divisions were running wild in Europe, and the United States was finally trying to get its military act together. In June (I believe it was) it was announced that General George Patton would lead a column of armored equipment, with ten thousand troops, from Columbus, Georgia, to Panama City, where they would participate in some special maneuvers. Now, I will tell you that this was a new exercise, for the troops, for the area, for the area's road system, for our city, and for the armor, much of which dated from World War I and was in terrible shape. The general began the movement, and as might have been expected, they had problems every mile of the way. George Patton arrived in the vanguard, his flashy revolvers at his waist, his uniform spotless and sharply pressed. But his column was strung out for almost the full hundred miles. As a chamber official and newspaper manager I was among the welcoming committee. When he learned of my newspaper connection, the general took me aside:

"Ball," he began, "I know what you're seeing, but I want you to print a story that says that every vehicle in my command arrived in Panama City, on time, in good condition, and with the morale of the men at the highest. Do I make myself clear?"

He didn't have to say it twice.

Accompanying the general was a young man who held the title of communications officer with the division of public relations, who he was expected to prepare a story about the march and get it on the wire — pronto. Well, this poor guy had no experience along these lines. He looked at me mournfully, afraid that the general would eat him alive if something went wrong. I beckoned for the man to follow me, and within minutes I had him in the company of our best reporter, who helped prepare a story AND get it on the Associated Press wire. In Panama City and across the country it sounded as though Patton's march had proven that the U.S. Army was in perfect condition, and was the equal of fighting forces worldwide. I tell you that the young PR guy was grateful. Later, when he was fighting in Europe, he wrote back with a very special Thank You to us all.

The general's arrival caught Panama City flat-footed where services for off duty military might be involved. There were no services—period. My good wife and some other ladies who made up the Pilot Club saw this void. These included Beulah White, Eunice Robinson and many more. Each took time from her war work to join several business leaders in putting together what became the first stage of the city's USO. It was primitive, but it worked. The boys in uniform soon had a place to relax, to write letters, take a shower, *et al.*

When General Patton's force left our area I believe they felt that the community had adopted them . . . and done all that it could to make their visit pleasant.

One other major event occurred during this period.

There was a time while I was a business manager at Panama City when I was called to serve on the federal jury, with the court meeting in Marianna. It's not a long ride between those two cities, but in the summer months, before auto air conditioning, it could be a hot trip, and for the first four days of that week I would go, sit and be questioned, and then released. For some reasons the attorneys on both sides just didn't want me to serve. Finally, on Friday afternoon, I was selected, and the case began.

This was a moonshine case. The revenuers had caught two young men coming out of a nearby swamp where the federals had already staked out a still. One of the men had a sugar sack over his shoulder, and when the pair was arrested this was the primary piece of evidence. The trial didn't take long, for which the jurors were thankful. It was hot in that courthouse, and the jury room was small and stuffy.

Well, we began our deliberations, and to me this was a farce. Here we were, men who had wasted a week going back and forth, and now we were on a case where the evidence was of the flimsiest, and the result not too important anyway. So I said something like this to the other jurors: "Men, isn't this foolish? Those fellows had a sugar sack, but what else did the federal boys prove? Nothing. I suggest we take a vote right away, and as for me I say we ought to turn 'em loose."

The others agreed, and moments later the judge received our verdict, nodded and acquitted the two young men.

That was the last case of the day, and so we prepared to leave. As I approached the courthouse door an older man approached me. He looked as though he hadn't shaved in a week, and his overalls had seen better days. He said "Hello" . . . and then added:

"You were on that there jury, weren't you?" I said I had been.

"Well," he continued, "I sure do thank you for turning my boys loose. They're good boys . . . but I told 'em I knowed the law would get 'em, I told 'em not to come out of the swamp that day. So . . . I sure do thank you."

☞ ☞ ☞

Shortly after our marriage Theda felt that she could not remain idle. After all, she had been enjoying a fine career in real estate, and now she wanted to be productive, and so I arranged for her to become the manager of radio station WDLP. She loved it. The station was small, as was its staff, thus the manager had the opportunity to do many things . . . including being one of the station's liaisons to the community. For a time, this was a perfect role for her.

My own position in the community was enlarging, and people were paying more attention to the importance of the newspaper.

Since my work was thought of as different, the Kiwanis club program chairman invited me to present a program on a given date, and I said that would be fine . . . only I promptly forgot about the obligation. On the very day of the meeting I was entering a drug store when, by chance, the program chairman reminded me that I was "on the dais" that noon. To this point I hadn't given the prospect a minute's thought.

As I walked into the store there, seated at a small round top table, was a dark-skinned man who was studying some papers. By his elbow stood a small sign which announced that here sat Prof. Melton, an expert at handwriting analysis. A light went on in my head, and so I approached this stranger and began a conversation about his profession. He spoke well, and finally I asked if he had ever spoken in public about his work. He replied that he had not . . . but that he could. Quickly I did a little selling. I suggested that he would make a fine speaker for that day's Kiwanis Club, that there would be a free lunch, and that he might even get a little business. Prof. Melton was delighted. Then I added that I felt he should change his title from professor to Doctor; it just sounded more . . . more up town. He agreed. Soon we were off to the club site.

I will tell you that Dr. Melton was a smash hit. The members loved his talk, and many did ask for analysis. Now I had another idea: I felt that if Dr. Melton made his pitch on radio he might draw a lot of traffic, and so I drove him to Pensacola and arranged for him to appear on WCOA, which by now was owned by Mr. Perry. The doctor obliged, and his broadcasts always concluded with an offer to analyze handwriting for just ten cents, if the listener would send his dime and a stamped, addressed envelope. Well! Talk about a smash hit. Pretty soon George Bowes, then part of the station's sales staff, had upped the ante to one dollar per request, and still the mail poured in. Later I helped Dr. Melton begin a tour of stations to the west along the Gulf, and he was a smash hit wherever he went. They tell me that ultimately his tour ended when a certain federal official stopped him, though to this day I can't imagine why. Certainly he was doing nothing wrong. But . . . whatever . . . his radio days were over, but my understanding is that he continued as a handwriting analyst all through the area for the rest of his days.

About this same time another event occurred that helped to make me realize that, no matter how hard one may plan, sometimes things just get out of control.

I was president of the Chamber of Commerce for this year, and in keeping with local plans to try and get people excited about our community we ought to stage a major meeting with a well known celebrity as speaker. The man we selected was boxer and former heavyweight champion Gene Tunney. Tunney was to address a very large throng in the Cove Hotel, and ticket sales were excellent. It was winter, and as is often the case air traffic was snarled by fog. We had no local commercial field, thus the speaker had to arrive in Tallahassee and then be driven to our city. Our committee was there to meet the plane, but of course it was many, many minutes late. But . . . finally it arrived, and they raced to Panama City. When they walked in I tell you that the women of our city simply swept the former boxer off his feet. He was handsome, charming, articulate, and the ladies loved it. The planned initial welcoming speech went by the board, and when dinner time finally came both Theda and I lost our head table seats; others had simply taken over. I guess the event was a success but it surely did not go off as planned.

☞ ☞ ☞

My father and I had decided to go fishing on December 7, 1941, and were driving along listening to one of those clear channel stations on the radio when we heard the first flashes about the bombing of Pearl Harbor. We were near Philip's Inlet, and the first place we passed that had a phone was in a bar whose owner was known to be a sympathizer of Mr. Hitler's Germany. I rushed in and called Theda, who was at work at the radio station. Yes, she said, they had been getting a steady stream of bulletins off the teletype; the word was on the air. As I walked back into the bar room I announced to the men drinking beer that Japan had struck at our naval base. From the rear came the muttered words:

"Hurray for the Japs!" I was tempted to throttle the man, but instead I left before I could do something that would end up by getting me charged with assault.

World War II changed Panama City, as it did everywhere else in this country. One of the first major happenings was the building and opening of what was called the Wainwright Shipyard, named for the general who had been captured at Corregidor. The yard was owned by a major steel company, and they immediately began siphoning off just about anyone who could wield a wrench or hammer . . . and of course men in the specialized construction trades. Several employees of the newspaper and radio station left to accept the higher paying jobs (who could blame them?). Ultimately Theda too left, to become an assistant in the engineering department of the shipyard. Incidentally, by war's end that yard had produced 102 ships for the Navy and Merchant Marine.

As thousands of service men and others descended on the area for one form or another of the defense effort, housing fell into very critical supply. Military commanders begged householders to make housing available to those who were eligible. And as a result I rented our caretaker cottage to one family, utilities included, for twenty-five dollars per month. The guest house was remodeled into two apartments which were used by fine service families.

Soon there were well known celebrities among the service personnel. One was Clark Gable, who was assigned to Tyndall Field. Col. Bill Maxwell, who was my neighbor, gave me a no-nonsense statement that he did not want the movie star's presence widely promoted, for that might cause all manner of problems. I could not entirely overlook the news opportunity, however, so I placed a small one inch squib in the personals column which stated that a Capt. Clark Gable was currently staying at the Dixie Sherman Hotel. The colonel was not pleased, but I think he understood.

On another occasion, before Theda left the radio station for shipyard duty she took a call from a musician who asked for help in promoting his band's appearance for the military that week. He was a relative unknown, named Louis Armstrong. Theda wasn't sure what should be done and so sent Mr. Armstrong to me. I gave my okay. Later, of course we both chuckled about our first contact with the trumpet virtuoso who would become world famous.

When war came it affected us in many ways. By then I had joined the newly formed Rotary Club, and it was here that I became involved (along with the paper) in promoting the various scrap and war bond drives which the war effort required. It's hard to believe these things were true, but they surely were. The government urged families to collect scrap fats to be used in the making of explosives. And there soon were scrap drives . . . for rubber, steel items, aluminum foil, other metals and more. Many of these campaigns were conducted with civilian leadership through groups such as Rotary, and I had the privilege of leading several such movements. I remember one in particular. We were trying to get more metal for a campaign, and I asked the club members to respond by each bringing in some metal article which they truly cherished . . . I felt that this would have a psychological effect, for in really giving of self the drive would bring the men closer to the war. The club responded beautifully . . . to the man. My own contribution was something that I called my Special Dollar, for it had been given to me by my brother-in-law. This piece of metal was really a medallion made from materials taken in a military raid. He had received it, and cherished it, but then had given it to me. I shared his feelings, thus giving it to the drive was not easy. But, it was typical of what Americans were willing to do to "do their part."

Another great contribution came from a very old (one hundred years) black man named Hawk Massalina. He and his wife lived on the edge of town, and despite his age old Hawk got about a good bit and was well respected. When the new drive started he came into the newspaper office bringing is wife's flat iron, a true antique from the era when irons had to be heated in a stove before use. I don't know how old that flat iron was, but it was something this little family cherished, and their contribution was considered really something. I had their picture taken and a big story done for the paper, illustrating how some people were digging deep for the war effort.

I had another type of early contact with the war effort which came to the paper's profit. I reasoned that the several unions that were present in the shipyard might want to sound the klaxon of their patriotism by placing large ads, announcing their work on behalf of Uncle Sam. There was a separate union for every trade, and of course all of their meetings were at night. My practice became standard. I would lay out a handsome full page, ask for an appointment, then visit the union hall to make my pitch. Many of these men were tough, hard traveled fellows, not usually the kind to buy ads . . . but one after another I made the rounds, and in every case the men voted to put up the $150 cost. Then I came to the really tough group . . . the Mechanic's Union. Here I could see in the faces of those assembled that they weren't too interested in my prospect. They as much as said so. So, before unveiling my layout I talked about their patriotism, and how much the war effort would profit by this show of worker solidarity. Then I unrolled my ad rough. To my dismay, I had brought one made out for the Carpenter's Union . . . and when the men saw this they broke down laughing. To my surprise that did the trick. They allowed that if the carpenters were in, they would be too. I left the hall with their commitment.. and their laughter still ringing in my ears.

By now I approached my thirtieth birthday, and the waves of patriotism that were swelling over us affected me too. I talked about this at length with Theda and my parents, for we were a close family. My father was now retired and it was sad to watch him age almost by the day. Theda had resigned from the radio station and taken her position with the shipyard, where she felt she was performing essential work. With their blessing I went to New Orleans to apply for a commission in the Navy. I applied, we talked, but the Navy's officials looked at the roster of adult dependents I had and turned me down. "We don't see any possibility that we can take you this year, Mr. Ball," they said. Thus I went back to the paper and rolled up my sleeves.

Late in 1942 my counterpart at Pensacola, George Archer, who was business manager of the *News-Journal*, had similar military urges . . . and he was accepted for service. This opened a void at that larger paper, and Mr. Perry turned to me, asking if I would accept a transfer back to Pensacola. This was a wonderful opportunity, but it was also fraught with problems. My parents loved our Panama City home, and this job would be a large responsibility. By now we had made any friends in the business community and elsewhere, and leaving all of that was difficult. But, the family agreed. The *Pensacola News-Journal* was an opportunity that could not be passed by. By now Theda was pregnant with Suzanne, it was wintertime, and late 1942 was hardly an optimistic day in the war. There were still scares about Nazi submarines in the Gulf, and we were all dealing with the wartime restrictions that rationing brought on. But . . . we made the decision. In mid-December I boarded one of the newspaper's trucks which made regular runs between the two communities, and so began my next great career move. By then my beautiful Lincoln Zephyr had suffered from age, and a twisted crank shaft, and I had traded it for a used Ford V-8. However, we were a one-car family, and so that vehicle was left with Theda and my parents. I rode on the truck. Somehow, that seemed out of synch with my theme of transportation as a beacon in my career. But it was wartime, after all, and we all had to make sacrifices.

My first stop in Pensacola was at the front desk of the San Carlos Hotel, for I had to have a temporary place to live. I negotiated with Conner Hagler, the manager, and walked to the elevator pleased at a "deal" which would provide me with a room for twenty-five dollars per month. That sounded fine. However, it wasn't long before I discovered why the price was right. My room was on the north side of the hotel, facing St. Michael's Catholic Church. That part was fine . . . but what I hadn't realized was that St. Michael's church bell struck—loudly—three times each day, signaling a special mass or other service. One of these ringings was very early in the morning. That first night I was very tired and as dawn broke I was still deep in the arms of Morpheus, dead to the world. Then the bell rang. Now . . . this wasn't a single peal. The bell rang and rang, for the sexton wanted to be sure all who were to be alerted to the service heard the call. I felt as though I were sleeping inside the bell tower. And you know, if I concentrate I can still hear that darn bell ringing.

When I stepped into my new position I quickly discovered some major problems. George Archer had run a tight ship, for he was a fine newspaper man, but wartime problems were present everywhere. We were critically short of newsprint, with only a working inventory of a month. Men were being called into service and some women were volunteering. Or, in some cases, people were leaving for war work which paid more than the newspaper could afford. George had done his best to plan for and overcome these problems, but there were scores of loose ends awaiting me . . . and on top of that I came down with some undiagnosed malady. Within just a few days I felt terrible . . . and with no one to care for me I did what seemed the wise thing . . . I hopped a *News-Journal* company truck and returned to Panama City and the bosom of my family.

It would be nice to report that with their ministrations I was a well man in jig time. Not so. I got worse. Dr. Horton Lisenby was summoned and seemed baffled. What I had was no mere cold . . . and so he summoned a specialist from Tyndall Field, who added his knowledge, pills and potions. Gradually I regained my health, but all told I was out of action for almost four weeks.

The return to Pensacola saw me back in harness in mid-January, and I was no sooner there when Theda called: the baby was coming. "I need you here," she declared with some emphasis. I responded as a good husband should, telling her to go ahead and have the baby and that I'd be along as fast as possible. Once again I claimed a seat on a *News-Journal* company truck and so reached Theda's bedside shortly after Suzanne's arrival. All was well with mother and child, and for this happy event we paid Dr. Lisenby the princely sum of twenty-five dollars. After a brief stay I was once again at my desk. Now some serious problems had to be addressed.

The major one was newsprint. There was a critical shortage nationwide, and the price had been skyrocketing. It was no secret that there was a black market for this item, and I spent considerable time trying to come up with some tactic which would allow me to crack the system.

You'll remember that my friendship with Edward Ball had begun in 1938, and during the ensuing few years our contacts had continued. Now I turned to him for advice, or perhaps it's better to say that I was going to try and get his specific assistance. The plan we worked out was this: Mr. Ball made it possible for the *News-Journal* to acquire from St. Joe Paper Company five thousand tons of brown, kraft paper. Now, kraft is a versatile item, and can be used for many things, including carton making, bag making, wrapping paper and more. We reasoned that having this paper would give me a trading item, and with that I might barter for newsprint.

There was a paper products convention scheduled for Chicago that coming month, and so my advertising manager Bob Rainey and I did two things: we had some little fliers printed up which said in essence that we had five thousand tons of kraft available which we were willing to trade, two tons for one, for newsprint. Then we bought two railroad tickets and off we went.

We had left for Chicago knowing that we were heading into a big convention, but Bob and I fully expected to get a room at the Palmer House, or nearby. No such luck. Everything was packed to the walls, but the convention bureau was helpful and said they would find us a place. They did. However, it was not on the Miracle Mile or in the loop. No, we were in Chinatown, which is about Twenty-Second Street South, a good long ride by streetcar from the convention headquarters. This hotel was a very simple affair, with virtually only Chinese as patrons. The guest rooms began on the second floor, and were directly over a large Chinese restaurant. When we checked in we quickly found that the aroma of egg foo yung and chop suey were a permanent part of the ambience. But . . . it was better than sleeping in Grant Park.

As soon as we had gotten settled Bob and I headed for the Palmer House with our fliers, and went door to door, floor to floor, sticking them under doors. On the flier was a note asking interested parties to page us in the hotel's lobby. With our communications out we bought some newspapers to read and sat down to wait.

Quickly we began to receive calls. Some of the callers had little to offer, but ultimately two men in the trade did indeed meet our terms, and we came away with a plan for receiving 2,500 tons of the needed newsprint. As things turned out, our paper even made five thousand dollars extra dollars in the exchange on freight rates to move the two inventories back and forth. Our neck was out of at least one noose.

Pensacola, 1943, was in the midst of a major upheaval. The sleepy little port town was being overrun by naval aviation candidates, people using the seaport for specialty cargoes, and then through growth of activity at Newport Industries, Armstrong Cork Company, and the Florida Pulp and Paper Company. The mahogany works was doing well too, and on Bayou Chico crews were at work putting together what would be called the Pensacola Shipbuilding Company. Housing was in short supply, as were many food items. Supplies of household goods such as appliances were non-existent. However, everyone was feeling a patriotic surge, and every merchant was doing his or her best to keep things rolling "for the war effort."

What did the community look like?

Well, I had been away for more than six years and had to get my orientation back in place. I spent a good bit of time, at first, browsing up and down Palafox and the principal cross streets, to survey the prospects for advertising sales, and other things which might benefit the paper. I quickly transferred to the local Rotary Club, and really beat the bushes for talent so that the papers would not miss a beat in production, sales or circulation.

Walking towards the docks I could see a host of ships being loaded with cargo, and bunkered with coal. Out in the bay there would be a dozen or more freighters sitting at anchor, loaded (or waiting for their turn), and also waiting for the moment when they would join an outbound convoy, to be guarded by Navy warships. It was in that year too that Calvin Todd and some others worked through the Civic Club Roundtable to encourage Sen. Phillip Beale to enter legislation to create a local port authority. Beale did so, but it would be many years before the new authority owned a single foot of waterfront.

When I had returned from Panama City and took over the papers' reins one of the first professional groups I tried to study in community affairs was the attorneys. Part of this was because the courts generated news, and often there were legal notices which provided ad revenues. The men themselves were fascinating. Whom do I remember most? Phillip Beale Sr., Judge Dixie Beggs, Forsythe Caro, William Fisher Sr., Will Watson, J. E. D. Yonge, McHenry Jones, John M. Coe . . . and more. There was another reason to study these men: newspapers have always worked hard to avoid being parties to law suits. Juries are notoriously anti-newspaper, thus if a suit ever pended I tried my best to make a settlement outside the courtroom. I recall one situation where a client of Montrose Edrehi had us over a barrel . . . dead to rights. But for one thousand dollars and a box of good cigars we got off the hook. When our pages said some things that were indefensible about Rep. Bob Sikes I apologized publicly. That's what we did on another occasion when one of our reporters who had a wonderful and witty style went a little too far when describing the products of the newly opened Spearman Brewery. He called the business the Bearman Sprewery . . . and suggested that a chemist who had analyzed the company's product had declared that the horse involved would be dead in ten days. Mr. Spearman took exception . . . I apologized.

By now I was taking steps to get the family, new baby and all, relocated, and that meant selling the house in Panama City. No one wanted to do that. My parents, especially my father, loved that house and its on-site fishing. But . . . it was fairly obvious that I would never return there. The house was put up for sale, and after a few of the customary selling adventures we made the transaction with a $12,500 price tag. Thus as we finalized this latest move in our family life and career we were doing so with a sizeable bank account . . . something that surely had never been the case before. The 1938 Ford was not exactly a limousine, but it ran well, and at this point in the war having a car with four wheels and decent tires that could run a long way on B or C gasoline ration coupons was, well, a great benefit indeed.

Pensacola in wartime was not unlike Panama City, though we did not face quite the blackout restrictions. Everything was bursting at the seams, and I was fortunate to find a house for sale . . . and so the family was able to move into new quarters in East Hill. I will confess that my father really hated to leave his fishing grounds, and as the group arrived I was more than ever aware that age was creeping up on him. He had worked very hard in his lifetime, with a routine that was far from easy. It was not pleasant to see him uprooted once again, especially as the family faced numerous war induced restrictions.

Those restrictions related to just about everything we did. Food was the number one problem, for all persons, adults and children, had to get along by trading ration stamps for what they ate. Meat and canned milk were the biggest problems, but anything related to fats and cooking oils was very tight also. Poor Theda. She had to stand in line at the various shops, sometimes acting on rumors that such-and-such a store should have a supply of a much sought-after item on a given day. I can remember that as Suzanne grew a little older she liked lamb chops, and so the ration stamps were used for chops. The little girl ate the meat and the grownups sucked the bones, so they wouldn't forget what meat tasted like. However, vegetables were usually plentiful in season, and fish and bread were never rationed. So . . . we got along.

The same shortage was felt in shoes. Any article made of leather had a ration point value, and one had to make choices. There were shortages of clothing items too. With the military taking almost everything the factories produced there was often little to buy. Men's suits, for example, were very scarce. Of course, there was a trade-off. Almost from the outbreak of war there had been price controls, so that scarce items could not be legally boosted in price by manufacturer or retailer. There were black markets, of course, but I don't recall that Pensacola was deeply involved that way. We did have to struggle along on bald or recapped tires, and if a car's battery went dead the owner had a real problem.

By mid-1943 producing a newspaper had become something quite different. The newsprint shortage remained. My one great windfall in Chicago could not carry us forever, and by mid-year it was necessary to literally apply rationing to our product too. We did this in several ways. First, the size of each edition was scaled back to either four or six pages. The advertisers were rationed too, with a plan in place which doled out precious inches as fairly as we could. Of course, this was not as bad a situation as one might think, for since the retailers had very few things to sell they also had little to promote. Most of the ads dealt with matter that was ongoing and not war-related. Of course, a smaller paper meant less to do for the staff. We were losing some people through attrition or military call-ups, but I was determined to sustain the core membership, for one could not produce a quality product without people. Since there were major lulls in each eight-hour day I gave the okay for those who wished to do so to retreat to the third floor to play poker . . . or read. Some did, and thus we had a rather unusual work schedule. There was even one brief time late in that year when the paper supply literally did run out. We were at our wits end, but Jim Allen, who then headed the Florida Pulp & Paper Company, came to our rescue. Jim sold us a quantity of brown wrapping paper being run at the Cantonment mill. This was hard to turn through our press, and surely did not give the reader an easy page to enjoy, but it was better than nothing, and I can say with pride even now that we never missed an edition.

In 1944 our family grew once more when Kirk was born. Now Theda really had her hands full, trying to run a household with two aging parents and two small children, along with the many shortages. But, she did magnificently. The older generation tried to help, of course, for everyone was being patriotic. My father had one chore that I'll never forget. Dad loved coffee, and coffee was very hard to get in the stores (though it was available in restaurants, and occasionally I was able to get an extra pound from "a friend"). But for the most part we had to really stretch the supply. At one point my dad would literally run the water through the grounds three times to brew a pot . . . and even then the result was mighty weak.

It was about three months after Kirk's birth that my father died. This was not the result of some lingering terminal illness; he just sort of "wore out," spent just one night in a hospital, then passed away peacefully. That was a very difficult time for me, for my father and I had been very close, despite his odd working and travel schedules. He was a product of an earlier time, and in his last years I had the feeling that he sort of felt "left out" as the world changed. I truly missed him.

Then, within months my mother suffered a paralytic stroke. Here was another severe blow. Poor mother lived on for another eighteen years . . . but in all those many months she never uttered another word. She was lucid, and ambulatory to a degree. My poor wife was a saint through all of these difficult times.

It was about this time that I was introduced to the Carmelite Sisters, who then operated a small home for the aged near Lillian, Alabama, about fifteen miles from Pensacola. These sisters were the heart of compassion, and their work, making senior people comfortable and happy, was exceptional. Soon after our meeting they invited me to visit their home where I could witness first hand what wonderful things they did. They also had some problems. Their building was old, and very hot in summer and cold in winter. There was no air conditioning. As an observer I could see that these ladies wore their heavy wool habits summer and winter . . . and in the hot months they literally suffered from the heat.

I took action on their behalf. Chester Rabb, the manager of Bon Marche, was both my advertising client and my friend. I felt at ease putting a request in front of him. I asked for enough light weight brown material to make summer habits for these gifted women. They did the sewing themselves, and now they had a new look on life in the summer. Next, I was able to arrange some basic air conditioning for their home, and with some friends was able to add some other amenities such as a music system. By now those ladies began to call me Father Ball. Along the way, during one of his visits to Pensacola, I introduced the sisters to Edward Ball, who was equally impressed with their ministrations.

By now the condition of my mother had worsened, and so Theda and I, with many misgivings, elected to make a trial of having mother as a guest at the Haven. What a great decision that was. I know that mother enjoyed her final years as a resident there. On each of our frequent visits joy could be read in her face.

It was not long before the sisters found their home at its absolute maximum in guests, and I began to prod them to consider moving into Pensacola, to a new site. The five local ladies thought the idea had merit, but, they declared, such a move must be approved by the Mother Superior, who was resident in Holland. Getting that lady to Pensacola for talks was not easy.

Invitations were extended, and many letters written to encourage one of the Mother Superior's regular visits. Finally the good woman agreed to come. When she arrived we were very impressed, for one could not miss her. I say this because of her pleasant appearance, and also because of her girth. She made two of me. The morning drive to the Haven was pleasant, and the day could not have been more perfect. The sky was azure, the temperature was temperate, and yet at first these things began to work against us. "Why," she asked, "with pleasant days like this would you want to move away from this lovely spot on the water?" That day air conditioning would not have been needed at any time. The good lady stared out of the window and suggested that she might like to continue our talks down the path towards the beach . . . and so we did, taking along a stool for her to sit on. Sit she did. But then, as we talked, the Mother Superior appeared to shrink before our eyes. What was happening was that she was slowly but steadily slipping off the stool, her bottom sinking towards the white sand. What to do? After a time our Dutch lady was all but prone, the fancy lacework of her underdrawers in sight of any who might dare to look. Oh my! Several of us attacked the problem, and with the greatest difficulty raised our guest to her feet. I'm afraid we all laughed, and for a moment I was certain that all was lost . . . but no. Once we had talked more about the prospect of bringing many more senior people under the care of the local sisters our visitor was convinced. "Yah," she said finally, "I can see what you are saying. If you wish to move, I give my approval."

Thus the story of the Haven of Our Lady of Peace took its new turn. With the aid of Dr. W. C. Payne and others we raised the funds for construction of the new home site just north of the recently constructed Sacred Heart Hospital. Edward Ball, already enamored of the work of this order, personally financed the dining suite for the home. Almost every time he came to Pensacola Mr. Ball would want to visit that home. Often, if he had visitors of his own, he would take them along. At the conclusion of their tour he would turn to the chief sister and say something like: "Sister, I know you can always use extra dollars, and I'm so happy to give you my little check for one thousand dollars . . . and . . . I know that Mr. MacGregor Smith and Ambassador William Pauley here would like to make a similar contribution." The two men (or others in time) would have been caught completely off guard . . . but I believe that there was never a time when such a guest failed to contribute on the spot. And me? I was Father Ball.

By 1944 the war had turned around and the news became brighter, even if living conditions had not. I remember well that ladies were by now very vocal in their feelings about some items. One was underwear. Rayon-based undies were in very short supply, and I can recall hearing several say, "I sure hope I won't be in an accident and have to go to a hospital. My underwear's in shreds."

It was at this same time that nylon stockings came into being. Now, as a man I really can't understand to this day why women became so excited about them, but they did. Nylons became a black market item bringing great returns to a seller or trader. The same was true with our military personnel overseas. I understand that a pair of nylons could be traded for . . . well . . . a lot of things.

At the paper I used some of the "free time" that smaller editions permitted to make some physical changes. Previously a lot of the so-called "heavy work items" had been housed on the upper two floors. That really didn't make sense, either from a logistical or a safety point of view, so I used some of the modest financial surplus the paper had accumulated to buy a piece of property behind our building. This land already contained a fair-sized shed which could be used for newsprint storage. There was also a large house on the property, and I'll come back to that shortly.

Now I moved our newsprint (what little there was of it) from the second floor to the shed, and then moved the huge volume of newspaper files from the third floor, also into the shed. That created a modest problem, for the files had not been stored in an orderly manner. Finding containers of a proper size was not easy, especially in this time of shortages. Then one day I was walking down the street and noticed a shipment of coffins being carried into the local funeral parlor. Those wooden crates seemed just about the right size for my filing needs. I asked if I might measure one, and sure enough . . . the size was perfect. At very modest cost I obtained a number of those crates and had them moved to the shed . . . and so another problem was solved.

Then I had another great idea. We were currently negotiating (again) with the three unions which had contracts with the paper. I say again because it seemed that negotiating never ended. These were the ITU, and unions for the pressmen and the stereotypers. These folks were never easy to deal with, even in wartime, so now I had a plan that I felt sure would help me psychologically. I scheduled our union meetings in the shed, where the men had to sit on the crates which once held caskets. The building itself was rather dark and gloomy, and there in one corner was our meager supply of newsprint. It was the perfect atmosphere for an employer to conduct such discussions. It worked. But, finally, one of the stewards begged me to change the location. "Can't you rent a room in the hotel?" he pleaded, "this is . . . well . . . so depressing." I took pity . . . and we moved. But the casket boxes had surely paid dividends.

Another word now about that second building on the new property. It had been under lease when we bought it, and the lessee was a madam who ran a high visibility, high quality whorehouse. Zaragossa Street, for example was lined with such establishments, most of which catered to Navy personnel or seamen. Of an afternoon one could ride or walk by those houses and see the girls, all decked out in garish fashions, many with flapping feathers, seated on the porch. When a man walked or drove by they would all wave and call out . . . in a most friendly way. Those houses had been part of the local scene then for half a century, and they were not suppressed until the Navy finally put its leadership foot down. Then the local police closed the houses.

I've mentioned the wartime popularity of motion pictures, but the story deserves still other comment. At this time the Saenger had a very talented organist named Anne Gayley, who was a music teacher. Miss Gayley would play for all kinds of events, and had a daily hookup over WCOA too. Often she would do mini-concerts, sometimes in company with Pat McIntyre, a local photographer who had a fine voice. I remember one summer morning walking down the street past the theater when their combined music came wafting out of the front door. It was many hours before showtime, and of course the manager held off turning on the air conditioning as long as he could. It was quite a sound, listening to that duet on Palafox Street. How many cities had anything like that?

Our employees stayed close to the war news, of course, and with just a little arm twisting each of them became a regular subscriber to war bonds. We all did that. Even the troops overseas, whose income was pathetically small, had a small amount deducted from their pay each month for bond or stamp purchases. During that same period I helped our local Rotary Club lead several war bond sales campaigns. Everyone got into the act.

It was in 1944 that I made my first survey of what was then called Fort Walton (earlier it had been known as Camp Walton, apparently named for the early 19th century Secretary of the Territory of Florida). What I found was fascinating. Fort Walton had about 450 residents, and stood in a marvelous position for the attraction and entertainment of visitors. The beaches were beautiful, the water looked superb, and nearby the 450,000 acre Eglin

Field was already being turned into what would become the nation's largest Air Force base.

Actually, I began this work without so much as a word to Mr. Perry. What I did called for establishment of a weekly paper which would be run on our presses in Pensacola. The news could be largely a remake of the past week's regional items, with whatever local input we could get. Since there were several other small towns nearby (Niceville, Destin, Valparaiso) and they had already dubbed themselves The Playground, I even had a title for my prospective paper . . . *The Playground News*.

When I advised him of my idea Mr. Perry told me to proceed, providing it appeared that there would be at least minimal advertising support. (Incidentally, the *Playground News* was the only paper his company ever started from scratch.) And so I called a meeting of the business people of the village. There was no suitable conference area, so we met in the old Magnolia Bar, and there I told these men that we would begin a paper if each of them would commit to fifty dollars per month in ads. They hemmed and hawed a bit, but in the end they said yes. We were ready.

Now Mr. Perry and Edward Ball both got into the act. Our second need was for space . . . not a printing plant but suitable offices for advertising sales, news collection and circulation management. The town was, as I said, very small, and I located a place where a new, short street could be placed, one which would intersect the main drag, Highway 98. Mr. Ball agreed to take half of the frontage property to begin a bank. Mr. Perry opted for the remaining land. And so we got busy. The land purchase was made for $18,000 shared equally by Mr. Perry and Mr. Ball. On our property we erected not just the newspaper offices but what would be called the little city's first shopping center, a strip which would be occupied by eight stores. Dewitt Lamb was named as our first editor.

Meanwhile I went to bat for Edward Ball to pave the way for his bank. A charter had to be okayed by both the state comptroller, Jim Lee, and the governor, and at that point Mr. Ball was not on the best of terms with either one. That meant a lot of politicking, and I became Edward Ball's point man. In the end I was successful, and the charter became available. In the meantime, Mr. Ball had also been seeking a charter in the Central Florida town of Bushnell, and now he had to make a choice. He could have one . . . but not two. Thus despite my efforts Fort Walton did not get its bank (at that time). Instead Mr. Ball opted for Bushnell. In later years I wonder how many times he examined the later growth of the two communities and wondered at his poor judgement on that occasion.

The *Playground News* got off to a fast start. In fact, not long after the initial publication a Texas visitor came through town and after looking at Fort Walton itself AND its newspaper, commented: "I've never seen a town so damn small with a newspaper so damn large."

The presence of the paper enabled the playground area to begin a more formalized promotion of itself. I began to place ads in Birmingham newspapers promoting visitor traffic and subscriptions to our paper . . . thus it wasn't long before tiny Fort Walton began to grow. As visitors arrived it became clear that it was the beaches that were our big attraction, and what brought them back time after time. At about the same time I happened to be in a newspaper conference with a publisher from Daytona Beach. His advice proved invaluable. "Braden," he said, "our town was originally known as Daytona, but then I got them to add the word beach. You'll not believe what a difference that made in terms of outside acceptance." I believed him, all right, and so suggested to the town's leaders that Fort Walton ought to do the same. With their concurrence I put the matter before the state legislature, which had to approve any name change. Shortly thereafter we became Fort Walton Beach, and I doubt that there was ever an objection to this brilliant move.

The paper had gotten off to a fine start under Dewitt Lamb's direction. However, he moved on and his successor was killed in an automobile accident, thus a new leader had to be chosen. To my misfortune one of my great ideas here did not work. This began with my discovery of Art and Heddy Cobb, a husband and wife team of able journalists whom I chose to put in joint charge. I reasoned that she would handle the society and name recognition duties, while he would be the editorialist and administrator. Wrong! Mrs. Cobb wanted equal billing, and the idea of having a two-headed editor was no good.

Once the paper had a head of steam it was obvious too, that I was getting more personal work out of the operation than I wanted, and we were stretching the Pensacola press capacity. I turned to my friend Cecil Kelley, who had become the manager in Panama City, and told him that I felt it appropriate to put that whole Fort Walton Beach operation under his direction, printing, circulation and all. Cecil's papers needed extra activity and cash flow and could profit with the link with the *Playground News*. Cecil was not exactly delighted by this move, but he accepted it graciously . . . and did an excellent job. In fact, a few years later, after John Perry Sr.'s death and his son's takeover, Cecil became one of young Perry's disciples in moving from the traditional hot type to the more flexible cold type operation. Cecil also became one of the first newspapermen in this country to appreciate what the computer might do to makeup and overall production.

As those years passed there were other forms of new activity for me. First, Governor Millard Caldwell named me one of the early members of the state's Advertising Commission, where we made decisions on how to promote the welfare of the state's visitor and manufacturing opportunities. Then, a few years later, another governor named me to the Florida Turnpike Commission. Both were no-pay but honorary positions, and I enjoyed my work on each one. However, like all such work, these required travel and time away from my office and responsibilities.

A third fascinating public service assignment came when I was appointed as a member of the state's judicial council. This was a body of legal specialists who were to work with members of the business community to overhaul some Florida laws which had been outgrown, and which were restricting commerce. Here I worked closely with the council's chairman, Justice B. K. Roberts, who would be my friend for life . . . and who provided exceptional leadership in this task.

One of my more successful endeavors in the 1940s dealt with insurance. There are many fine insurance carriers serving Florida, and fine agents in virtually every city. Over the years our paper had worked with several, but when I returned from Panama City in 1943 I chose to place our business through Fisher-Brown. Johnny Hoefflin was already becoming a strong participant in community affairs, and I liked his style. (Johnny had previously been manager of the Greyhound Bus Terminal here and had been tapped for FBI by Hunter Brown, the Fisher-Brown president.) Johnny was good, and after a time his service and skill proved very valuable to us. At this same time—the mid-1940s and just beyond—Mr. Perry and his son, John Jr., were in the process of buying up a number of small papers throughout Florida. Each of them required insurance, and Mr. Perry, who always admired success, turned to me for advice on where that coverage should be obtained, at the local level for each publication, or on a concentrated basis. I recommended that the bulk of the business be placed with Fisher-Brown. And that's the way it went, for papers all across Florida. We were never sorry. Later, when my son, Kirk, began his career with that firm I knew that he had made a good choice.

Along the way I have noted our relationship with Dave Johnson, who also was a career man with Fisher-Brown (and who had actually begun his economic life by selling the *News-Journal* on street corners). However, it was not Dave's influence that brought me to work with that company; nor was it Hunter Brown's. It was just good service. Mr. Brown was a compelling figure, always immaculate in well-pressed suits and linen. His little eye glasses gave a certain impression too, and because by then he headed a fairly large business he was held in awe by many.

When I returned to Pensacola I immediately transferred my membership in Rotary to this city, continuing my unbroken record of service. As had been the case with the Panama City club, local Rotarians were then active in so many areas of the war work. People like Tom Kennedy and Wright Reese headed boards and campaigns, and club members did much to sell bonds, support the military through such things as the USO, and entertain men and women in uniform. The Rotarians met then at the San Carlos Hotel, offering an active program at weekly meetings. It was in that period that we devised what I called the Good Samaritan Plan in which the club gave each Rotarian a set amount of money and four weeks to make it multiply . . . by any means. It was amazing how imaginative those men were as they raised funds for fifty care packages for needy townspeople in Wales, the home area of member T. M. Lloyd. We had fun too. Harry Ferriss and Tom Kennedy became joint chairmen of the Sunshine Committee, starting a precedent which still lives. And new members were always assigned immediately to the Indian Affairs Committee, so that they would have time to meet people and do absolutely nothing.

That club had been solidly behind creation of the Pensacola Sports Association, and even farther back had helped to bring the New York Giants to

Pensacola for spring training. That year—1938—manager Bill Terry spoke to the club, as did Branch Rickey, future general manager of the Brooklyn Dodgers, who told the club about his plans to bring a rookie named Jackie Robinson into the National League.

In the mid-1940s there was another Rotary event which also involved John Perry. It was during that period that he had somehow come into contact with a gorgeous woman named Garnet Gardner, who until recently had been with her husband in foreign affairs in such places as Shanghai and Hong Kong. Mrs. Gardner was now divorced, and she was not just a handsome woman, she was smart and intriguing. In any event, she arrived in North Florida and spoke at a club in Panama City. I picked her up there and drove her to Pensacola, where she addressed the Rotarians. She was a smashing success, telling some of her wartime adventures in the Far East. That visit coincided with our son Roger's birth in Pensacola Hospital, and with some rare bit of inspiration I asked Mrs. Gardner to accompany me on a visit there to see Theda. I cannot claim that as one of my more successful maneuvers. Later Theda would say: "Don't you EVER do something like that again!" I didn't.

In short order Mrs. Gardner performed a number of services for the Perry chain out of Jacksonville, then moved on to Washington, where she became something of a lobbyist and then married Baron Stackleburg. For a time she was a toast of the town, and also wrote a specialty column for the Perry papers. However, time takes its toll. It wasn't too long before the baroness began to age, and as she did so she more or less slid off stage.

I have mentioned my automobile problems of the early 1940s . . . and how I had been forced to trade my handsome Lincoln Zephyr for a used Ford V-8 during wartime. Well, Theda and I were still chauffeuring the Ford about when the war ended, and the great rush began to try and get a new car. I had saved some money during the war years, and I was ready . . . but to the dealers I was just one of hundreds hoping to get new wheels. Then I got a break. Over the years I had become friends with Dominic Rand, a risk-taking entrepreneur who, among other things, operated a taxi service from a base near the newspapers. One day Dominic and I happened to be talking about the need to replace vehicles, and he announced that he was soon to take possession of a new fleet for his cabs. These were to be especially made Packards, built in Detroit. The cars had a number of features that made them especially appropriate for taxis, and this model would be used in big cities by both Yellow and Checker fleets. I was interested. Dominic pulled some strings to add one more unit to his order; then he sent half a dozen of his drivers to Michigan to get the cars and drive them back. You may think that I looked a little odd driving that unusually designed Packard, but remember: the Big Three and their competitors had made only modest cosmetic changes to the pre-war models in 1946, and anything unusual had the look of being "new." I kept the Packard for about five years . . . and I'll say now that it was a fine automobile. That company's slogan for years past had been "Ask the Man Who Owns One." Many people did ask me, and I had only positive responses.

I have one more memory involving Packards. This too was in the early post-war years, when former representative Millard Caldwell had become the state's governor. Caldwell was a North Florida man, from Milton, and for years he had some of his auto service on his Packards done at a filling station there. Once in his new office, the governor decided to do something that I doubt a politician would do today: he opted to buy a foreign car. And not just any car: a new Rolls-Royce. Millard went off to New Orleans to pick up the car (there were no Rolls dealers in all of North Florida) and came back across on Highway 98, stopping in Pensacola to show friends his fine machine. We all admired it, and then he was on his way to the east.

The story goes that Mr. Caldwell wanted to show off his car in Milton too, so he drove there, making his first stop at the gas station. There the old, faithful attendant who had served him for years came out, greeted the governor, and then said something like:

"Law ze, Mr. Caldwell, don't that old Packard look fine. She is one sweet car, and you take such fine care of her that she'll run on for years. I'm sure proud to see that car again."

Needless to say the governor HAD driven Packards for years, and this incident left him speechless.

Again looking back into the 1940s I like to remember an event which got a good deal of news coverage. Spessard Holland, who would later go on to be our United States Senator and was my close friend, was governor from 1941-1945. Like many of us, Mr. Holland was always a critic of high tolls on bridges. He agreed that people who use a facility ought to help pay for it, but he also felt that once the out-of-pocket cost had been recovered the road or bridge toll ought to be removed.

Well, when our Pensacola Bay Three Mile Bridge opened in 1931 it carried a one-dollar toll, and there was a toll booth at the logical place where collectors were stationed. Once he was in office Gov. Holland discovered that the bridge had in fact been paid for, and so he was instrumental in having the toll removed. To make his point and to show his political concern for the people, Mr. Holland came to Pensacola for the ceremony ending collections. There, on the bridge, with the aid of the tollkeeper and others, the governor picked up the toll booth and threw it into the bay. Front page stuff.

☞ ☞ ☞

It was early in 1946 that word came via special invitation that leaders in the press were invited to Eglin Field to see and meet our new president, Harry Truman. Needless to say, I went. This was to be a morning meeting, and surprisingly the response to the invitation was small. We gathered outside a small building near the runway, and shortly Mr. Truman walked out the door. He was alone, not flanked by secret service men or aides. He just walked forward several steps and then paused. Our group hung back, seemingly paralyzed and tongue-tied. It was downright embarrassing, especially since this was supposed to be the hard-boiled media. Finally I couldn't resist; I broke the spell and walked forward a few steps and said, "Good morning, Mr. President, and welcome to the Gulf Coast. By the way, have you read Drew Pearson's column in the morning paper? He had some things to say about you."

Pearson's column had run in the morning *Journal*, and I must confess that what he had said was not complimentary to the president. Mr. Truman didn't hesitate:

"No, I haven't," he began, and then he continued. "What did that SOB say this time?"

That broke the ice, and for the next several minutes we enjoyed a wonderful, man-to-man exchange with a President who was Mr. Informality himself. I came away much more impressed with him than I had been before.

A decade or so later I had a similar invitation to go to Eglin to meet and greet another new President, John F. Kennedy. I went. This time the throng was much larger, and we waited as a group for his plane to taxi up to us. In came Air Force One, moving with engines howling to within a few yards of us. Then it stopped. An aide got out and moved forward and then the President followed. He walked straight to where a marker had been placed on the tarmac, and there he stood, waiting for the press to take pictures. He posed left, he posed right . . . and he didn't say a thing. There wasn't a whole lot more to the "interview," and I couldn't help compare the visits of these two presidents. Mr. Kennedy did not come off too well in my eyes.

☞ ☞ ☞

As my new role as publisher of the *News-Journal* broadened, my re sponsibilities and my travel schedule increased. In part this was met through travel by train, for in the mid-1940s our airline services here were still primitive. Eastern Airlines was still a year away from operating in Pensacola.

Going to the east, which I usually did, my train would arrive here about 9 P.M., have a fifteen-minute stop for passenger and mail exchanges, and for taking on water. I would board at that time. As the train stopped it blocked the traffic lanes on Alcaniz Street, which at that time was the principal artery for motor cars. While all of this was going on, I discovered by observation that the train's fireman had a special duty. He would slip out of the cab and trot across the way to the Deluxe Package Store . . . and there he would pick up "a package." That package in hand, he would re-board, the engineer would blow the whistle and ring the bell, and we would be off.

Now, that may not seem very important in a man's life story . . . but think of it this way: how would you have felt, riding as a passenger, thinking that the man at the throttle of your train, charging through the black of night at seventy miles an hour, was taking heaven knows how many swigs out of his bottle of bourbon? Even today I get a little nervous thinking about it.

☞ ☞ ☞

In the late 1940s I had gotten hold of some of my first property and was getting ready to clean it up a little. There was plenty of overgrowth, and among the brush was some sumac. I didn't know this at the time, but sumac, when burned, gives off a very toxic substance which can create a severe allergic reaction in some people. I had been working in shorts, with a shirt cut off at the sleeves, so this substance got all over me, and within a few hours I was in misery. It was so bad that I could hardly move . . . from head to toe. Theda used some home remedies, and then I turned to professional help. Marion Gaines' father was the area's only dermatologist, practicing in Mobile, and with the greatest difficulty they got me into a car and we went to get medication from him.

As we approached Dr. Gaines's offices Theda suggested that I get out in front of the Merchants Bank building and wait while she parked the car. I agreed, for walking was terribly painful. I dismounted. There I stood, on the sidewalk of this busy thoroughfare, with many days growth of beard on my face, slippers on my feet, wearing clothes of a loose and hardly fashionable nature. As I stood there blood began to course down my arms and my hands tingled, so I raised them, holding them out in a sort of cup-like motion. At that moment a kindly looking man came by, stopped, looked at me, and quietly took a dime from his pocket and deposited it in my outstretched hand. I stared at him, not knowing what to say. Then he realized that I was not really begging (except for a cure). At the same time we both began to laugh, and he walked on.

Nothing Dr. Gaines suggested helped much. Meanwhile, I was in pain, and I could hardly move. Finally we decided to go to Ochsner's in New Orleans, where the good doctor was just beginning to build a reputation. They put me in this big place which had been something like a military barracks, and here they tried all kinds of treatments. Nothing worked. Finally, one afternoon, a well-dressed, formally acting woman who was trying to be helpful and cheerful came in and said: "Now, Mr. Ball, I know things are going to get better . . . especially after you have a good, big dinner. Now . . . here's what we've got for tonight. You choose."

I listened, and with every item this woman listed I felt worse. I finally said, "I don't care what you've got, 'cause I'm not going to be here tonight."

She left . . . perhaps fearful that I intended some drastic action, possibly suicide. Moments later I managed to get myself together and just walked out. I didn't check out . . . I just left.

It took additional weeks to fully recover . . . but I finally did . . . and I'll tell you that I never burned sumac again.

Years later, during my close workings with Edward Ball, he discovered that he had a small cancer on his nose . . . and in looking at me he diagnosed that I had one too. Mr. Ball suggested that we both go to New Orleans to see Dr. Ochsner, who by then was one of the nation's foremost surgical specialists on cancer. Mr. Ball made the appointment, and we went. The fine doctor saw us as outpatients. As we sat there he surgically removed our tiny tumors, with local anesthesia . . . and he charged us each twenty-five dollars for his service. When I think on what surgical charges are in 1996 . . . and how things went then, it is hard to believe. Oh . . . one other thing: Dr. Ochsner's work was perfect. Our problems never returned.

CHAPTER FOUR
The Post-War Pensacola

When I returned to Pensacola in 1943 there had been gambling in what I would call "the friendly games," and I was soon privileged to be invited into the oldest ongoing group of this kind, one that met every Saturday night. Who were the players? They were much older than I was, and most were high on the hog of the city's power structure. There was Filo Turner Sr. of the Buggy Works, City Manager Adrian Langford, jeweler Eugene Elebash Sr., banker C. W. Parker, insurance agent Knowles Hyer, Frisco Railroad manager Tom Humphrey, motor magnate Guy Yaste . . . and later Tom Brent too, of the Brent estate. We did not play for high stakes, and our poker was definitely a friendly game. Those were days too, when local Saturday night entertainment was limited, thus the wives seemed not to care too much that their husbands were out regularly.

Actually, such gatherings were beneficial in many ways. Pensacola was a small city, and its power base was tiny. Men who made decisions knew one another well, because they had fun in business and elsewhere (such as poker). Golf had come into the picture, of course, but it was not the all-absorbing game it would become later. Such gatherings as ours continued well into the 1970s . . . and I can still remember one power group that met every Friday at the Driftwood Restaurant, with a standing reservation for the big table near the window. That group included John and Dick Pace, Francis Taylor, Henry Hilton-Green, McHenry Jones, and sometimes one of the Johnsons. Others in the restaurant would watch them, and many would wonder what was cooking!

As the war finally ended, so did the problems we had faced putting out two newspapers six days per week, plus a Sunday edition. As peace came all of us were focused once more on selling . . . and on the role which the papers might play in developing the community. Businesses we had cultivated in the difficult days slowly began to advertise more with us . . . places like Pensacola House Furnishings on Wright Street, for example. I can still see their ads, some of which proclaimed their ability to provide a quality kerosene stove for the rural homemaker. I can also recall (not with particular pleasure) the smell which a kerosene stove generated in such a house. I would not care to have lived in such a place.

I wish I could say that the end of hostilities produced an immediate boom in ad business. One might think that this would have happened, but we have to remember that it took quite a while for American factories to convert from almost 100 percent war production to the making of civilian goods. But . . . this did occur, step by step. Meanwhile, my sales staff and I were back doing special "deals" similar to what had been used in the difficult Depression times. I should also mention another item out of the early 1930s . . . our use of the famed Blue Eagle for NRA (the National Recovery Act). NRA was a government tactic to try and get businesses to put supports under wages and prices. Federal propaganda urged customers to buy American from stores that displayed the Blue Eagle. We got into the act, making up ads which allowed businesses to become part of a large display of firms which were cooperating. The Blue Eagle didn't last long, for the Supreme Court declared NRA to be illegal, but I will say that we used the plan as well as anyone could have.

The post-war world was not exactly a shock to Pensacola, but it did cause us all to examine our future. There was a feeling in those days that some of the well-to-do in the city did not want "progress" if it meant changing the pleasant, slow-paced way of life the city enjoyed. Those critics said caustically that ". . . a few good funerals would put Pensacola into the twentieth century." I don't know about that, but I will say that our pace slowed once the Navy cut back its training activities, and the industrial plants had to beat the bushes for civilian contracts. But . . . things in general were good, and sometimes we were just plain lucky.

One of the delights which illustrated our lifestyle was breakfast at the Coffee Cup. The owners of this delightful Cervantes restaurant were Judge and Polly Cagle, and their place became the favored spot for a meal, any time of the day. It was almost like going to a party to go there, for one always found friends . . . and gossip. One morning I had stopped in to have a snack, and as I did so a man nearby began talking in a loud voice about how he was going to make a killing that day. He was going to buy a piece of land at a tax auction . . . and the land, he said, was right beside the *News-Journal*! My ears picked up. I listened to all he had to say . . . but said nothing myself.

My breakfast finished, I hurried to the office and called attorney Will Fisher, to see what was going on. Sure enough, there was to be a tax sale on the court house steps that morning . . . and the man was dead right on this one piece of property. I had to work fast. I rounded up several thousand dollars in cash and was on the court house steps when the auction began at noon. When the targeted parcel was offered the man I had overheard promptly bid five hundred dollars. I responded by doubling his bid. At this point he looked straight at me, with obvious recognition. He also saw the wad of bills in my hand. A scowl covered his face, he was about to speak again . . . but then thought better of it and bid no more. The bidding ended shortly at one thousand dollars, and I had gained control of the property for the paper. Later . . . when the *News-Journal*'s buildings were relocated, that piece of land became the site for the press room as it operates today.

I can't recall the exact year—but it was in the forties—that we began to be beset by special promotions in the entertainment field. Movies were going strong, and the city was playing host to circuses. Drive-in theaters were booming, thus the paper was getting a lot of advertising from that industry. We always maintained what we called an Amusement Rate, a rate much higher than conventional display advertising might command. This was so because we usually provided a story when a show came to town, and this required staff time and paper space. By this time some of the promotions being used by cinema people (and others too) were very unusual. I'll never forget one that helped boost interest in one of the Tarzan movies. The advance party for the picture had gotten hold of an ape costume, and they had this fellow go about, always with a "keeper" who had a leash. The whole business looked very real, and drew a crowd wherever the pair went.

One evening this duo had time to come to the paper to get a picture made, and a story done. But as they arrived the editorial room was empty . . . except for a man who was one of our faithful porters. The man was sweeping, and had bent over to pick up his sweepings with a dust pan when he felt a tap on his shoulder. He looked around, and came face to face with "the ape." Now, I won't say that this man turned pale, but his eyes suddenly doubled in size . . . he gulped twice and just took off running. The poor fellow was scared to death. I think the movie people apologized . . . but even if they didn't they had proven how effective their promotion was.

The *News Journal* frequently hosted figures of renown, even in the immediate post-war years, and I often had the pleasure (or the chore) of entertaining them. Most were fine people, and a joy to be with, and some left some unusual memories. One of the latter was the great rocket scientist Woerner Von Braun, who came to this country after the war to continue the work he had pioneered in Nazi Germany.

Mr. Von Braun was to be a participant in the paper's science fair, and he made a good impression. When his visit was over I drove him to the airport where his private plane was waiting. Being a convivial man he invited me to come on board for a little refreshment. I quickly learned that the onetime German scientist had become a lover of good Kentucky bourbon.

"What will you have?" he asked me, and I replied that bourbon would be just fine, and that I'd like just a splash of water. Then I noticed that my host poured his own generous portion straight . . . no water. "You are sure you want water?" he asked a little startled. I assured him that I liked it that way. "Ach," he continued, "never drink water. Fish swim in water, and they pee in the water. No, always take the whiskey by itself."

I understood, but I'm happy to say I remained unconvinced.

To this point I have said little about some of the key personalities who worked with me in Pensacola over many years and at different times, but several deserve recognition. In the forefront was Marion Gaines. Marion was a good deal older than I, and had come to Pensacola from a similar role at the *Mobile Press-Register.* He was our editor, and a good one. However, Marion was at opposite poles from me politically, thus we had many a "discussion" over the papers' positions regarding issues and candidates. He was also one of those people who like to do everything themselves . . . and in his case this meant handling the administration of the news department as well as its function. After a time Marion was just stretched so thin that I decided to give him some assistance. That was when Harold Stokes joined us. Harold was a very different kind of man, in temperament and style, but he was a good operator, and I made him executive editor, in charge of administration. Marion took some time to get used to the change. He didn't like giving up authority, and I suspect he always resented having to work under a young "whipper snapper" like me, who hadn't gone to journalism school.

Then there were Doc Coulter . . . and Don Hogan . . . and Charlie Somerby, who would later become a factor with the *Gulf Breeze Sentinel.* These were all fine newspapermen. Within the full staff at the time we had to face a little problem. A few of the men kept that "little flask" in a desk drawer, even though this was strictly against the paper's rules. However, that was one of those things which the publisher had to sort of turn his back on . . . for as long as the job got done those men were okay.

Another fixture over the years was Pat Lloyd. Pat was the daughter of funeral director T. M. Lloyd, who had come to this country from Wales. Pat had done some writing in high school, and she knew many people. She LOVED being involved in the society swim, and so she came on board to be one of our society editors, a person whose mission was to fill the paper with names. Pat did this well, as did her cohort Tani Sublette. Later, when our afternoon paper was beginning to slip (as were afternoon dailies everywhere) we decided to try a new trick to gain attention. This was to be a daily gossip column featuring people and current events. We chose Pat for the role of columnist, and then cast about for a name. At that time one of the big successes in national advertising was for the Toni Permanents . . . you may remember the key line: WHICH TWIN HAS THE TONI? Well, we changed the spelling a little and made it Tony . . . and then since this was to be a PM feature we chose as a second name NIGHT . . . except that we added a K and made it Knight. Thus Tony Knight was born . . . and became a successful feature for many years . . . as long as that paper survived. One other point about Pat: she had a marvelous and retentive memory so that she almost never had to take notes when doing a story. One time she interviewed the syndicated columnist Drew Pearson when he was visiting us. When the story came out that afternoon Pearson told me that he had never seen a reporter use that technique and still come forth with a quality article.

Still another stalwart was Earle Bowden. Earle was a West Florida man, from Altha, who joined the sports department after serving in the U.S. Air Force during the Korean Conflict. He was one of those fine newspaper men who was born with printer's ink in his veins, for he loved his work, all phases of it. Earle would serve the *News-Journal* in many phases . . . sports and news reporting, columnist and also editorial cartoonist, for which he developed a much-applauded talent. Later Earle would become the paper's executive editor, and as I write he is still holding forth under the Gannett publishers.

Then there was general manager, Julius Grice. I met Julius under the most surprising circumstances, in a way that violated all of the prescribed personnel hiring techniques. I was about to ride from Pensacola to Jacksonville aboard the L & N evening train and went into the downtown station to buy my ticket. There was a young man at the window, tall, slender, handsome, and as we talked I noticed that he wore the famous green eye shade which many railroad clerical personnel preferred. As the man wrote out my ticket in longhand I could not help notice how beautifully he scripted the words and few sentences. I had never seen handwriting so perfect. As we concluded our transaction I asked him if he was planning to make a career of work with the railroad. He said that he hoped for better things, and so I told him that if he were interested we just might find a post for him with the newspapers. A few days later Julius showed up to talk, and indeed we did find a spot for him. Quickly, I realized that I had made a wise move. Julius was intelligent, diplomatic, energetic, the kind of person a publisher needed for so many tasks. He literally became my right hand man, and in later years, as general manger, assisted me in financial, personnel and production operations.

In my entire career, I worked with just two secretaries, Beulah White Pinney, from whom Mr. Perry had originally purchased the *Panama City Herald*; and Dorothy Thomas, the sister-in-law of John D. Thomas, who had been my first Pensacola boss in advertising in the 1930s. Both of these ladies were superb, and as many people have said, a man's success can often be gauged by the secretaries he has. That's true.

These men and women were true professionals and very loyal. And they, like many of their co-workers, were extremely intelligent. (I have always said that I tried never to hire someone whom I did not think was smarter than I was . . . and I think that paid off!)

Many others shared in the success of my years.

One was Billy Cummins, who had been circulation manager in Panama City and who was promoted to the same role in Pensacola. Not only was

Billy wise in the ways of the trade in building circulation, but he also was a bird dog on cash flow, making sure that those who subscribed for papers paid on time. He and I maintained excellent records and had a very sharp follow-up system. If a subscriber became delinquent Billy knew how to collect the money. As a result, our records far outstripped those of most papers in this regard. In the 1940s and 1950s it would have been an extreme year when our losses for failure of payment exceeded sixty-four dollars for the whole year! Yes, Billy was a man to be treasured!

Still another who built a great reputation with us from the 1940s until 1971 was reporter Maurice (Moose) Harling. Moose came from Oak Park, Illinois, and was a graduate of the University of Illinois. He came well recommended at a time when I needed a good columnist and political writer, so I called him and invited him down. From the first, he was a success. Moose loved politics, he loved the community, and he loved to write. I suspect that in later years he might have become frustrated, for then reporters were not given the freedom to use great areas of space, but Moose loved to cover an event and then just let the words flow! People in Rotary, Kiwanis, JayCees and in politics loved him, for he was fair and honest and a fine writer. In the 1970s Moose agreed to join Reubin Askew in Tallahassee as a special advisor to Gov. Askew. At the end of his career Moose became a resident of the Azalea Trace Life Care Center.

Our longtime mechanical supervisor was Henry Chairsell. Henry was one of those men for whom anything mechanical was simple and a challenge. He could fix anything, and was a wonderful bird dog to sniff out the causes of mechanical trouble. He was a perfect fit in the organization of that time.

And then there was Lee Van Etten, press foreman. Like Henry Chairsell, Lee knew the mechanics of his presses like no one I ever saw—anywhere. He could sense a problem and anticipate it . . . or . . . if some breakdown should occur, he knew how to go about repairs quickly and effectively without starting a panic.

Yes . . . it was good to have these men and women about me.

With the coming of peace we were back in business with promotional tactics. First there was a church page, usually run on Saturdays, on which the various churches could be listed for a small sum, all appearing under some fancy canned art which encouraged families to attend the church of their choice. (That kind of promotion is still being used.) Then we moved into what I called Christmas cards. We would give our salesmen a 50 percent commission if they could sell a customer a display ad which offered holiday greetings to the public. That went over well, and in some years we had several pages of such greetings.

The idea of "specials" was always on our plate for sales, for if we would only keep our minds open there was almost always some kind of oncoming event that might lend itself to public celebration. In the 1940s the medical profession definitely did not advertise. It was almost as though Hippocrates had said "Thou shalt not . . ." But there were some opportunities, even so. During the war the health care professionals had been divided two ways. Many were called into active military duty, and those who remained at home were spread very thin. Some of these were older men, some had infirmities which prohibited military duty. But whatever their physical condition, these men had to cover the whole community, the hospital duties, even the traditional house calls at first, until things just became so tight that this form of care vanished for a time. As they went through the war, working eighteen-hour days sometimes, some fell ill themselves, men like Dr. Charlie Born, who suffered a severe heart attack and thereafter had to limit his practice to his office. He and most others had offices in the Brent, Blount or Theisen buildings. At war's end the community was truly grateful to these practitioners, and of course was glad to see the others return.

Shortly after that great day two things came to pass which allowed our papers to become involved in medicine. One was a campaign to transform the small TB sanitorium on Leonard Street into an acute general hospital owned and operated by the county. The Medical Society was behind the move, and with the aid of the governor's office and plenty of positive promotion on the paper's part this was accomplished.

Then, with Dr. Sid Kennedy, Dr. W. C. Payne, Dr. Bill Hixon and a few others in the vanguard, the city's physicians hosted a Gulf Coast medical symposium, to bring many regional physicians together to share recently gained wartime knowledge, and to plan for the future of the area's medical care.

That seemed like a great opportunity for all concerned, and so with the help of those key physicians, we began planning a massive special section which dealt with the local hospitals (including the Navy's), and the many services available here. With the aid of the Pensacola hospital and others we made contacts with suppliers of equipment and supply items, and got many of them to be advertisers. Other local firms, insurance agencies, ambulance services, equipment rentals and drug stores, came on board too . . . and so our section came together, guided throughout by advertising director Bob Rainey, who did a herculean job. This was one of the largest specials the papers had ever done to that time, and I'm still proud of the way it looked. The Escambia County Medical Society still has a full copy in its files.

One of the *News-Journal*'s major breakthroughs came in the late 1940s based on a plan hatched by Edward Ball and me. At that time there was no Jefferson Street north of Government to Garden Street. The area which the street would later occupy was covered with old, dirty and even unoccupied buildings. Some housed enterprises that were no credit to the city. Our own *News-Journal* building straddled what would become the Jefferson-Romana intersection.

Mr. Ball and I saw that there had been no progressive, major downtown changes in years; the city was in bad need of urban renewal, and the prospect of carving another street through north to south made sense. There were many property owners involved, including the operators of Pensacola Hardware, the Chamber of Commerce, the bus terminal, the newspaper and more. Mr. Ball had the idea that he would like to dismantle his ten-story Florida National Bank building and erect a new facility, facing Jefferson. Dominic Rand dreamed of building a huge store for Montgomery Ward, fronting on Garden Street. All of this would be accompanied by a parking garage. The entire arrangement was presented as a plan by architects, and pictures and story were presented in a *News-Journal* issue.

I wish I could tell you that everyone climbed on the band wagon. Some did not like the idea at all, including Bessie Lindenstruth, but parcel by parcel Mr. Ball literally bought up land and then proceeded to plan for demolition of the unwanted properties. The Chamber, whose building included a theater-style auditorium, wanted to proceed, but at first the leaders could not find clear title to their property.

I won't itemize all of the steps involved, and there were some of our dreams that never emerged from the drawing board. But, many good things did happen. The bank of course stayed in place, and Mr. Ball ended up with a block of property at Garden and Jefferson which together we would make the site of a new bank building in the 1960s. The *News-Journal* building itself was torn down and a fine new single-story, efficiently planned structure took its place. The architect for that property was Chip Roberts, of the firm of Roberts & Company, who had built some of the giant structures on Eglin Air Force Base. This was a small job for them, but they were friends of John Perry and that carried weight. On a Sunday evening we literally carried the press from the old to the new building, allowing us to make our move overnight. Then the old, rumbling three-story headquarters came down, at our expense.

There were many good features of what occurred. The Chamber used the money received for its building to erect a new headquarters on Romana, next to the new *News-Journal* building. They moved there in 1951, when Paul Damond was the manager. The paving of the new Jefferson Street by Noonan Construction Company worked out nicely. The city paid one-third of that cost, while the other two-thirds was shared by property owners along both sides. When the work was completed in 1950 most of us felt very good about what had been done, for it seemed to us that the city was now in a posture to renew itself. After all, we had found new uses for property where a carriage works had once stood, and the bulk of the disreputable enterprises and obsolete structures had disappeared.

There was one final tale which emerged from the Jefferson Street saga that drew a great belly laugh from Edward Ball, who enjoyed sagacious trading. As all of the land exchanges, condemnations, trades and purchases proceeded for the renewal project, there was one very odd piece of property more or less "left over." Jeweler and entrepreneur Albert Klein owned a large lot running north and south along what was to become the New Jefferson Street, and he now announced plans to erect a large building there which would house the Laritz Cafeteria. However, his property stopped five feet short of the Romana Street intersection. This meant that his new building would stop short of one street, an unusual situation, but a serious concern if the party owning the land chose to do something odd there. The *News-Journal* owned that small strip of land.

For some reason Mr. Klein thought that we were trying to hold him up on it, and yet there had never been a conversation over a possible exchange.

Thus he was quite taken aback one afternoon when I called on him and announced that I felt we should discuss the five-foot strip. Mr. Klein became very excited almost at once, and all but called Mr. Perry and me a pack of robbers, trying to hold him up. I calmed him down and said: "Now look, Mr. Klein, it doesn't make sense for us to hold onto that land. I'll tell you what: we'll sell you the strip for just $125."

Mr. Klein knew a bargain when he saw one. He walked—no, he ran—for his check book and I left his place of business with a check in hand and an agreement to sell. All was fine, and the deal was done.

Four weeks later Mr. Klein opened his mail and discovered a bill from the City of Pensacola. It was for $14,250 to cover his share of the cost of paving Romana Street! By getting the critical 5 by 125-foot strip he had become a fronting property owner on a street to be paved.

I'm not sure he was pleased.

Again considering the post-war world, I must mention a thing or two about my relationship with John Perry. In many ways he was the perfect employer. He left virtually all decisions to me, only reminding me, "You do what you think is best . . . but you'd better be right!" . . . and fortunately I usually was. Mr. Perry had met Theda before our marriage, and they hit if off right away. He truly approved of my marriage, I suspect believing that this might settle me down a little. And he was right there too. In the post-war years Mr. Perry would visit Pensacola periodically, though not often. Now, many people believed that with his growing number of papers and special publications (he acquired many struggling weeklies in the mid-1940s and converted them to successful daily operations) Mr. Perry was rolling in money. That wasn't really so, for he sagely reinvested his profits and thus was often glad to get a little ready cash that he hadn't planned for. Therefore I worked out a little scheme. Once our papers were doing well I would always have a package of cash for "the boss" when he came to our city. This would be, oh, maybe five hundred dollars, and this would enable him to be the host, the buyer of a drink, the entertainer . . . during his visit. He liked that.

One of my early public responsibilities in post-war Pensacola was a role on the newly formed Municipal Advertising Board. With this function Pensacola was ahead of the curve, for not too many municipalities had seized the opportunity to display their wares before the public in 1946. Our board was proud of its assignment, and used its modest budget well. Among our major projects was the preparation of a fine four-color brochure. In the 1990s such printing is taken for granted as state-of-the-art, but fifty years ago using full color was avant-garde. Our board purchased small space ads in big midwestern publications to note the brochure's availability, telling the public that they might avail themselves of this information by sending us one dollar. A surprising number did so, enough to more than offset our preparation costs. The active response in terms of visitors was good too.

However, within the year it appeared that our returns had been exhausted, yet we still had about five thousand copies remaining. Then providence walked in! In this case the role-model was Harris Mullen, the publisher of the recently started *Florida Trend* magazine. He was making a courtesy call, and as we talked about his magazine's mission and goals he told me of his disappointment that it was not yet financially feasible for the magazine to use color. At this statement a light went on in my head! I got out a copy of the Pensacola brochure and showed this publisher the careful technique we had used in assembling this material. It just so happened that our brochure would fit into his magazine as an insert! Now I suggested that we would furnish him with five thousand copies (about his total circulation) if he would fold our material into his. He got the message. At no cost to him he would gain several pages of good copy . . . and he would have first use of color inside. This might also trigger use of similar materials by other cities or Florida attractions.

We shook hands on the project, then and there. Pensacola had scored a breakthrough.

During this period our papers (and WCOA) had very little competition. Oh, there were two new local radio stations (WBSR and WEAR) but 'COA was far out in front in prestige and revenues. The paper had only competition from a few struggling weeklies that barely survived from month to month. These papers drew most of their revenues from legal ads, and from a very few "friends" who were merchants thinking they had gotten an advertising bargain, not recognizing the value of circulation. One of the competitors was Bill Healy, whose *Escambia County Herald* had such ad sales persons as Punch Newman and Mrs. Bessie Rosenau. I'm afraid that most of their sales techniques consisted of literally begging for business. They didn't trouble us much.

Then there was Edward Campbell Jones' weekly, the *Sun-Press*, which dabbled in county politics. Edward Campbell Jones, and then his son, would always hold a position of some kind with the local Democratic Party. I mustn't forget Barrow's Printing Company. The owners ran a small paper for a while too, but it died about 1950, I believe. Jones's paper went out of business after the founder's death.

In the politics of that day there is one feature that must be remembered. In the 1930s and into the 1950s Florida, and surely Pensacola, were one-party locations. For decades George Wentworth, a real estate and insurance agency owner, was the only Republican in the whole county! George was a curiosity, but he would often say to me: "You just wait, our day will come!" I'm sorry George didn't live to see that day.

It was just before the industrial boomlet of the 1950s that the Fiesta of Five Flags was born. I cannot claim to have been one of the planners, but we surely climbed on board to help promote the idea. Founding fathers there included Don Lynch, Holliday Veal, Carl Johnson, the Pace Brothers, Irving Welch, Justin Weddell, McHenry Jones, Bill Ray and others. Their ideas were sound. They felt that the area needed a festival to create an image that would help attract visitors and focus on the city's history. They also wanted this annual pageant to set the stage for a real bonanza in 1959, when Pensacola would celebrate the four hundredth anniversary of Don Tristan de Luna's Spanish colony, thus giving this area (and the state) the nation's first quadricentennial. The plans went forward, and the following June—1950—the first Fiesta was held. Carl Johnson became the organizational head, working out of his offices at Pensacola Greyhound Park. John Pace was the first reincarnation of De Luna, and that event set the stage for a long tradition, with beauty pageants, sports events, balls, parades and more. It was a grand success, with ten men and ten young women dressed in satin and sequins, costumes prepared by Dorothy Clemente who could make things look good if a little out of step with history.

As Fiesta was being developed there was still another major event occurring on the city's north side. In 1942 a group of Baptist laymen had conceived the idea of building a new, first class acute general hospital. The Pensacola Hospital (later Sacred Heart) was then more than a quarter century old; the town was growing, medical practice was changing, and these Baptist men felt that the city would not grow without better health provision. For the next eight years (slowed by the war, of course) these men campaigned, raised money, developed plans. In 1949, with the help of my old friend Dr. Walter Payne, the hospital's leaders, Earl Gaston, Dixie Beggs, Paul Caro, Dr. Sid Kennedy, Sim Davis and more, obtained one of Florida's first federal grants under the Hill-Burton Act. Raymond Dyson was named their contractor, and through 1950 and '51 construction continued. John Pace had been head of general fund raising, and our papers, in Pensacola and even in Panama City, helped promote the concept and raise dollars. In October 1951, the new one-hundred-bed Baptist Hospital opened. Our papers helped promote an open house a week before opening day, an event which drew an amazing twenty thousand visitors. Then, with Bob Rainey's leadership, we assembled a splendid special issue to highlight the actual opening. Pat Groner, the administrator, quickly became a community leader and my good friend.

The hospital enjoyed immediate success, but its presence also pointed up a community failing or two. One was that we had no blood bank, thus with Dr. Payne's urging, the paper helped promote the funding of such a service. The bank, administered by George Nicholson, was located in an old house on Palafox Street just north of Cervantes, where it prospered and served until a new structure was built on Ninth Avenue some years later.

A second problem related to ambulance service. By 1951 the city had several funeral homes—Fisher-Pou, Waters & Hibbart, McNeils, Benboe's, Joe Morris—and each had a hearse. The hearses—some of them World War I vintage relics—were our ambulances . . . and these funeral directors were "on call" from the police or others to hurry to an accident site to pick up a crash victim, or to go to a home to transport the sick to the hospital. Well, that sounds fine, except that competition set in. These firms wanted the business, because it paid a fee. There was many a story about these hearses racing through the streets to "beat the other guys," and that didn't stop until a serious crash demolished two of the vehicles. Then a new system evolved. The paper's role began with simply reporting the interesting events. But later we editorialized when the system became a public hazard.

As the calendar turned into the 1950s this entire area began to see major changes. The first came in August 1951, when the chamber hastily called an afternoon conference which met on the lawn of the Yacht Club. There the

Chamber president, Ralph Merrill, introduced two distinguished gentlemen representing Monsanto and the American Viscose Company. Roy Hemminghaus and Fred Gronemeyer were there to announce that those two companies, in concert with the duPont Company, were creating a new manufacturing company to produce nylon, and that the plant would be built on one thousand acres of land along the Escambia River. The arrangement had been made, they said, with the help of St. Regis Paper Company and the Pace brothers.

THAT was big news. Of course, in the next two years the giant plant would be built, to employ thousands of men and women in well-paid positions. You can be sure that we covered the story like a fog, and that when the plant opened, the *News-Journal* would have one of the best special sections ever.

I had a hand in the second big announcement.

The chamber had discovered that the American Cyanamid Company also was interested in locating a new plant near Pensacola, to produce a second synthetic fiber called Creslan. Our area was one of the several being considered, and the point man doing the investigating was named Red Loosli. Now Mr. Loosli was coming to the city to "look us over." With others I planned a party to which key figures from the city's hierarchy were invited. This was to be staged at Martine's. Then I discovered that Mr. Loosli was a Mormon. Out went a directive: that night no one was to smoke or drink, and language was to be "refined." As we made our presentation I made a speech in which I detailed what a great place this was to live and work, what wonderful people we had available for a workforce, and how the whole arrangement would fit into Mr. Loosli's own lifestyle.

I concluded by saying (in a carefully researched and practiced speech):

". . . and Mr. Loosli, like that great American Brigham Young, who reached a point of decision on the alkaline plains of Utah and then shouted 'This is it! This is the place for us . . . !' I am sure that this area will be The Place for your company. History has set a fitting precedent for what you do . . . !"

Well, the night seemed to go off just fine, and shortly the announcement was made that Cyanamid would locate in Santa Rosa County, near Milton. We were ecstatic! Soon after, Red Loosli returned, as he often would, and we had lunch together. In the course of that meeting he said to me: "Braden, I've never seen such a corny deal as you all pulled on me at Martine's. It was so phony that I almost burst out laughing . . . but I'm convinced that we made a good decision. Thanks a lot."

Obviously we became good friends.

Shortly thereafter the *News-Journal* paper played its part when the Escambia Bay Chemical Company and then the Columbia National Corporation announced the placement of plants also in Santa Rosa County. Things were going great. The area had never seen such a positive rain of new, quality operations.

The effect of having new manufacturers of size arrive in the area was not lost upon business leaders. Escambia and Santa Rosa counties began to surge forward economically. New subdivisions appeared, new home builders like Ouida Baggett Regan, Walter Dean, Jim Keltner and the Kelly brothers emerged, along with realtors such as the Baars family. Specialized employees poured in for the new plants, and with the onset of the Korean War the military bases peaked once more. All of this generated a need for more schools, and the Pensacola Junior College, which had opened in 1948, now began to mature. Yes . . . the area was flowering. The Quadricentennial celebration, which the Fiesta had helped to spawn, became a reality in 1959, with re-creation of an early village on the beach and scores of wonderful exhibits. Our editorial people worked hand in glove with J. McHenry Jones and John Appleyard in promoting these events, and wrote extensively when ambassadors arrived from several European countries for the grand historic climax in August of 1959. Yes . . . it looked as though—finally—Pensacola was going to live up to its promise.

Part of the prosperity which sprang from those days for our papers came from a source I'm afraid we had not anticipated. At the end of World War II just about every motorist was longing for a new car. There had not been new models available for the public since January of 1942, when wartime rationing began. Prior to that we had gone through a decade of the Depression during which auto production fell off sharply, for very few could afford new cars then. Thus by 1946 the market had been wide open. The auto makers responded by re-issuing the pre-war styled cars with a little new trim and bogus features, and dealers literally rationed. They put prospective buyers on waiting lists which they prioritized, and I'm afraid, in some cases used some unethical tricks to squeeze extra profits. Such things did not sit well with the public, and some dealers suffered loss of credibility which was slow to return.

But then something unusual happened. By 1949 the post-war sellers market had largely ended, and now some dealers, especially in smaller towns, could not sell all the cars they were required to take. Into that unusual situation stepped some non-franchised dealers who declared themselves to be "independents." These men would go from town to town in south Alabama, Mississippi and Georgia and develop links with the small franchised dealers there. When those men had excess inventory the Pensacola independents would pay them a few dollars over cost and then take the brand new car to Pensacola to be sold on the lot. This way they could undersell the asking price offered by the established dealer. Because they had little overhead these men could promote . . . and advertise heavily. As a result we sold page after page after page of ads, especially on Fridays and Saturdays, to people like Wendall Jarrard, Dave Trant and Jack Fiveash. The franchised dealers fumed, urging us to decline to carry such ads, saying they were illegal. We would not go along. Several of the franchises, men who were my friends, were very angry with me when I bought a Buick from Fiveash rather than Bill Lee. I did so because Bill could not (or would not) get me the car I wanted and Fiveash did. It was a steamy time, with many a conversation that was heated. But—the paper stuck to its guns, got full price for every advertising inch, and made lots of money for Mr. Perry. In 1958 Jarrard went a step farther. Sensing a trend to smaller cars he became a six-state distributor for foreign makes such as Peuget, Triumph and two German cars. He imported cars by the shipload and did very well indeed until, wisely, he sold the empire just before American manufacturers went into competitive small car production. Meanwhile, we had the advantage of carrying large ads—and stories—about the European cars.

As I've mentioned before, politics and electioneering have long been a personal interest if not a hobby, and since the morning paper had to be a conduit for results following an election we had to have a vote tallying system. I'm speaking now of times before the computer and even before the voting machine. In those days each precinct had a monitored tabulating system, and once the ballots were counted results would be called by telephone to a central headquarters. At the paper we maintained a line to that office so that we could tabulate on our own.

For election night we always sought the services of Tommy Johnson, a local businessman and friend of our editor Marion Gaines. Tommy had what today would be called a computer mind. Johnson could listen to incoming numbers and keep a running total in his head, race by race. When the contest was statewide he could link local numbers to those coming from the eastern time zone and thus could become our predictor. Johnson was uncanny, and people often wondered how the paper could be so accurate so quickly. He was one reason. Of course, to back his work we had trusty Moose Harling, our political writer, to produce the columns analyzing results and adding local color.

Then, in 1961, Pensacola's economic bubble began to leak.

Up to that time the local business district had remained centered downtown . . . along Palafox and Garden Streets principally. Then, out of city developers announced that they would construct a shopping mall, which they planned to call Town & Country Plaza. There were a few startled looks among our merchants, but there were few signs of reaction. Even the Chamber's officials shrugged the movement off. I can remember sitting in sessions next door at the chamber when this challenge was discussed, but most felt that one mall wouldn't hurt, especially since the buying population was growing so rapidly.

About the same time Sacred Heart Hospital announced that it would relocate to a new facility to be built along north Ninth Avenue, an area which then seemed to most to be in the wilderness.

I still retain one memory about the location used by the hospital that few know about. You see, the property where the hospital erected its initial buildings had in years past been one of the city's garbage dumps. This was back before there was any environmental science to such things, and people just came out to the area and dumped trash, as the city did garbage. This was one of those places where occasionally someone dumped fresh earth over the top and then people started dumping all over again. (I would add that across the country many fine buildings have been constructed atop such dumps.)

One day—I forget the date but it was back a good way—we had sent out a truck and three laborers to do what was done with some regularity—the burning of waste paper from our plant downtown. The workers liked this duty, for they were largely unsupervised, and would come out, dump part of their load and then start it burning. Meanwhile, until the second part of the load could be burned, they had no duties, and so usually would lie down under a nearby tree for a snooze.

On this one afternoon that's exactly what happened. The men burned paper, then napped . . . but as they did so the wind came up, and spread the flames beyond the usual area . . . right up to the *News-Journal* truck. As the men slept the blaze took hold . . . and when they finally awoke their vehicle was a torch!

Later the three embarrassed workers walked into town and, with heads hanging, admitted what had happened.

I must say that Pensacola was surprised by Sister Frances Michael's announcement for a new facility. She was administrator of the Sacred Heart Hospital. The hospital's Twelfth Avenue location had become outmoded, and by the early sixties the institution was being outdistanced by the work of Baptist Hospital. The sister held a press conference and a public meeting for the city's leaders to present her order's plans. These called for construction of a new hospital on North Ninth Avenue, just above Brent Lane. Many could hardly believe her! This seemed to be out in the country, far from population centers. But the sister's homework was good. The hospital was constructed and opened in 1964, and—sure enough—it proved to be a catalyst. Shortly plans were announced by an out-of-city firm to build a huge shopping mall just across the street, and before long that entire area was booming. The hospital's fortunes were reversed, and Sacred Heart moved ahead, building physician office buildings and more. Shortly thereafter Mr. Edward Ball and I encouraged the Carmelite Sisters to move their retirement center to the same general property area.

Thereafter, month by month, things changed. Our stories carried accounts of merchants announcing that they would either leave Palafox Street . . . or would open a branch in the new mall or in a similar strip mall being built to the north. Those who had felt that the public would not drive out to such centers discovered they were wrong. Now there were shopping areas where parking was close and easy, where air conditioning made stores more comfortable, and where stores seemed more "up to date."

At the same time the San Carlos Hotel began to suffer loss of patronage to motels with similar advantages. The Gray Lady of Palafox Street could not compete, especially when it came to parking for overnight guests. The fifty-year-old hotel was in trouble. So, too, were motion picture houses which now were feeling the brunt of the first big wave of television installations and the coming of better programming.

With the success of Baptist and Sacred Heart hospitals physicians began to change their practice methods too, and to move their offices away from the traditional Blount or Brent building locations. By 1964 chamber executive Waldo Carrell and his board realized that there was deep trouble downtown . . . and that remedies had to be found.

If downtown was suffering miseries in the early 1960s, the community as a whole had one major factor that helped balance the difficulties; that was the prospect of the University of West Florida. I, along with many others, had been working for a university in West Florida for many years, and now it appeared as though the time was right. John Pace was a member of the Florida Board of Regents and had gained the positive attention of other members. Gov. Farris Bryant was supportive too, in part because his cabinet member Wendall Jarrard was urging that a university be started here. The Chamber of Commerce was working hard for this, and Sen. Reubin Askew and Reps. George Stone and J. B. Hopkins were big proponents.

Finally, the state legislature gave its okay, and the Regents set priorities for the community. One debate was over whether the new university should be an extension of Pensacola Junior College; that was soon overruled. Then came the question of campus location.

The regents helped the community on this. They demanded that the site have at least one thousand acres, and that it be reasonably convenient for students in four West Florida counties. I was chosen as a member of the site selection committee. In their meetings committee members determined that this should be a totally open process and not a "good old boys network" affair which might be open to controversy bringing disfavor. We announced the guidelines and invited anyone to put land into consideration. Before the offerings were closed eight different plots were under consideration.

As a committee we pretty well had decided on several things before we looked at the properties personally. We meant to sustain the Regents' stipulation of a minimum of one thousand acres; and we felt that it made sense for this property to be east of Palafox Highway and north of the Nine Mile Road. This seemed by some to be too far from the center of the city. But we reasoned that such a place would be as close as possible to the eastern counties, and sufficiently removed from the center of Pensacola to have breathing room, room for other activities to grow up around the campus.

Once all of the statistics were on paper we arranged for a site selection tour. The visitation was to be by rented Greyhound bus, and it was agreed that we would begin by having an early morning breakfast at the Scenic Hills Country Club. It was summer time, and in considering a route I recalled an old story about land purchases told to me by my friend Edward Ball, who recounted a time when he got a good deal on property simply because he brought the seller into the woods at a time when it was hot, uncomfortable and gnat filled. I'll admit that I was prejudiced in the current selection, and so I proposed that as soon as breakfast was over we visit the nearest acreage, just a few minutes from the club. Thus in the cool of the morning we swept around and through the almost eleven hundred acres being offered by the Jones family of Atmore. We went, we looked, we walked about, we appraised the fine trees and the lovely rolling land, the almost eight miles of waterfront including the Escambia River, and the freedom from any objectionable neighbors. In that cool hour the men looked, calculated, compared what this property could be with the already lovely layout at the club we had just visited.

Then we were off through the day to see the other available tracts. Some of these were obviously too small; others were too far, or had poor road potentials; others were just not attractive property. As we viewed most of these the temperature climbed and our process became less comfortable. When the bus ride ended we journeyed back to my house at Woodbine Springs, and there the debate was carried on. It was not an argument. To a man the committee chose the Jones property. (It had paid to get the men there early, in the cool of the day.) And so the university was born.

In the years that followed I always remained close to UWF. My friend and fellow Rotarian Harold Crosby became the school's first president, and he frequently called upon me for counsel, or to share ideas. When the university created a foundation I was a charter board member, and became a Fellow a short time later. Then I managed to get Edward Ball to visit. He loved the UWF campus. He envisioned portions of this acreage as a wildlife retreat, and that is what it became. Mr. Ball and his associates arranged to feed the oversupply of wild water fowl that lived in the swamp which bordered the campus. Then he and his foundation built elevated walkways through the wilderness, creating a superb nature trail that is still enjoyed. The foundation even did the research needed to make a portion of the trail to accommodate the blind. When the Edward Ball Wildlife Foundation told its own story, Mr. Ball was always sure to add that the university's wildlife walk was part of the movement to protect sensitive acreages and creatures.

As the 1950s proceeded the Chamber's position became one of communication, and for this story I must turn the clock back just a few years to early 1957. With the town then seeming to be in upward mode, the chamber had needed to bring more business people together at all levels, to make everyone feel a part of the future. The result was what came to be known as The Gopher Club. I am proud to say that I was part of the committee which conceived GOPHER. Sam Love and I were the program's authors, and the term Gopher was part of the theme. Gopher meant that we would "go fer" anything good for the community. The idea was to stage a once per month morning coffee hour, to be held in the large Laritz Cafeteria downtown. At each meeting a sponsoring company would host a doughnuts-and-coffee breakfast, and would have ten minutes to tell about his or her own interests. Then, a speaker would be heard, detailing some topic related to the community's business future. Because we wanted to have commitment to regular attendance, and an easy method of interpersonal recognition, I suggested that we give each member a permanent, large, round card, with a gopher's picture and the member's name in the center. His attendance record could be noted around the edge.

We then convinced beer merchant Bob Box to become the permanent chairman of the club, the MC who would keep meetings moving and get people out in exactly fifty-nine and a half minutes. Bob, with his breezy style, was the perfect choice . . . and he went on to serve for over a decade.

Who attended? Business people at all levels, presidents of firms, ribbon clerks, secretaries . . . everyone. More than 150 would be present each month . . . and those meetings were a godsend in letting the chamber members know what was happening to their downtown.

Getting back to the invasion of the malls, one of the chamber's first attempted remedies was to dispatch our advertising manager, Bob Rainey, and others to Minneapolis-St. Paul where the local business community had already put in force some mall counter-measures which might be considered. Then Bob Box and others visited Milwaukee and other cities which were fighting battles much like Pensacola's. On our pages we tried to document what was happening, and to be fair. But month after month the situation continued to decline. Into the next decade it would worsen when additional malls were built, along Davis Highway and opposite the new Sacred Heart complex. More and more stores along Palafox became vacant, and offices too. Of course, the newspaper had to be impartial to the various changing interests. After all, advertising was our life's blood, and those new malls included large and larger stores whose ad budgets dwarfed anything we had ever experienced before. Even the trusty Sears and Penney stores were planning to leave downtown. It was a time of great difficulty for property owners such as my friends Tom, Bob and George Brent and their families, and for those who owned other major properties too.

However, the Chamber did not give up. To try and sustain momentum new bridges were built to the school system, and the paper helped promote such things as BUSINESS EDUCATION DAYS, farm tours and better links with the Navy. I had the privilege of working with an old friend, Adm. Jack Reeves, along with Adm. Macgruder (Tut) Tuttell, Capt. Porter Beddell, and Capt. Jim McCurtain in taking the first steps towards founding a museum to recognize the history of naval aviation. Our pages were filled too, with stories generated by a group which I had helped to found called PROJECT ALERT. This committee of business and professional people had become alarmed by the lack of understanding by the American public of the Cold War, and they proposed to provide background information to help citizens make good political decisions. Once they had passed a first plateau in such education the members switched emphasis and concentrated on education programs related to the American Heritage. Our editor and able cartoonist, Earle Bowden, helped with some of his drawings; meanwhile, our pages often carried special patriotic advertisements which the ALERT members generated to help celebrate patriotic holidays. The *News-Journal* itself won awards for this work from the Freedoms Foundation at Valley Forge.

Yes . . . the 1950s and 1960s produced some remarkable changes. Looking back, I'm proud of some of the roles we were allowed to play.

At this point it's appropriate to recall the origins of our Woodbine Springs property in Santa Rosa County. This all began at the Christmas season of 1949. I always had a personal policy of not accepting large gifts from customers, politicians, or even employee groups. Such things can lead to trouble. Occasionally, however, a group (even the unions) would bring me some little token, so small that no one could feel that I was being "bribed." Well, that Christmas the union boys gave me a gift certificate for fifteen dollars from Ordon's, and after the holidays I went in to see Harry and find what fifteen dollars might buy. He offered several choices, then brought out a wide-brimmed hat (a Stetson of the type President LBJ once wore), and it cost just fifteen dollars. I put the hat on, looked at myself in the mirror, and admitted that I was downright handsome in it. The hat was mine.

A few weeks later on a "prospecting trip" with Edward Ball to examine some land purchase opportunities for him in nearby counties. I was wearing my new hat, and he admired it. (Mr. Ball always wore a hat of some kind out-of-doors, and I made a quick mental note of his feelings. Soon thereafter I bought a Stetson for him.)

On this same trip Mr. Ball grinned at me and said, "You know, Braden, you look just like a rancher in that hat. You ought to get yourself a ranch."

I'll admit that I had harbored a few thoughts about buying some property, and after discussing the possibility with Theda, I consulted realtor Joe Burgess, whose work generally dealt with rural properties. Joe examined the availabilities, and first suggested a plot of about four thousand acres in the Mulat area at Avalon in Santa Rosa County. I went and looked. The price was right (about four dollars per acre) but the land was low, swampy and remote, without easy access. That wouldn't do, I told Joe. Then he came up with another possibility. This was in Santa Rosa County, bordering the unpaved road which led to Chumuckla. There were twelve hundred acres, though this was not a totally bounded piece; there was some seventy acres in small lots in and about the tract, each owned by individuals, to get full control we would have to find ways of acquiring those other ten-acre segments. Once again the price was right, and it turned out that the major piece of land was the property of one of my poker playing friends, C. W. Parker. I made the purchase.

For the many who later visited this property, which I named Woodbine

Springs after the onetime British officer and spy, I must record that when I made my purchase the land was just that—land. The property had been cut over for timber, leaving only a few scraggly pines and scrub oaks. There were some wild turkeys running about, and other birds too, but there were no lakes, no fences, no roads. There was one little old run-down house, and I did move it and put it to use, with considerable remodeling. There was a lot to do, and as Theda had warned me, it would become an expensive hobby for a time.

As I cruised the property I discovered that there was running water and the prospect of turning this into small lakes, which I proceeded to do, with plenty of professional help. The first lake was of ten acres, and the second was about fifty-five acres. The ten-acre lake became the site for the remodeled house, which we began to use as a summer place. I got some advice from the game and freshwater fish people, and stocked the new lakes with bass and bream. Then we began to replant trees, to re-establish the wooded look.

As the property developed there was an ongoing need to try to improve the grasslands, and I spent considerable time studying my options. I had learned much earlier to stay away from Bahia grass. It would cover quickly, but it also created many maintenance problems. St. Augustine looked good, but on the farm it would require too much upkeep. Centipede is a native grass to this area, and so this seemed the best option. However, sprigging and watering such grass to get it started would have been time consuming and very difficult. Then, just as I was facing the need to plant, agriculturalists came up with centipede seed. It looked as though I was home free.

But then I discovered that the seed cost about fifty dollars a pound, and was very difficult to broadcast evenly. The county agent had a suggestion. "I recommend mixing the grass seeds with grits, you know, regular grits like you eat with eggs. That way you not only have a good spreading mixture, you will also be able to see where you've spread your material," he said.

Great idea.

I went to the grocery store to buy enough grits to blend with about five pounds of seed. I figured that ten to one or thereabouts was a good ratio, so I got myself a grocery cart and picked up fifty pounds of grits, neatly bagged. Then I went to the check out counter.

I was dressed in work clothes and looked like a worker right off the farm.

Behind me was an old gentleman in overalls and a red shirt, with a two-day growth of beard. He was a nice old fellow, and quite talkative. We both had to wait for patrons ahead of us, and finally he said:

"Mister, you sure must like grits."

I replied that I did.

"How long's it gonna take you to eat all them there?" he asked.

I thought for a moment then said: "These aren't for eatin', I'm going to plant 'em." I should have known that this sounded a little odd, but it was out of my mouth before I could think.

The old-timer looked at me as though I'd been out in the sun far too long, and the check-out lady was shocked. She got wide-eyed, maybe thinking she ought to call the man in a white coat. Then he asked: "Pardon me for asking, brother, but would you mind telling me what you get when you put fifty pounds of grits in the ground?"

A fine crop of grass, I hope," I said. He must have guessed I was touched.

At that time (which was long before the building boom which is fast covering the area with houses, businesses and a golf course) Woodbine Springs was a remote place, with no telephone within miles. I needed a phone out there, so I worked through my friend in the Milton exchange and had a line put in which I shared with seven others, to give us the required eight-unit party line. However, that system, and running from Santa Rosa into Escambia County, meant a $1.50 toll call to get through to the *News-Journal* office. Thus I began to dicker with the man who was my friend and the phone company's regional manager. He said that if I could sign up the roughly one hundred homes in that entire region he would make us a sort of telephone district, and this would eliminate the toll charges. Thus I began my short career as a telephone service salesman. I met my new neighbors this way. That was productive, and surprisingly just about everyone opted to go along. We signed up the one hundred, and our service improved. Month by month Woodbine Springs became more of a place of beauty, away from everything, ultimately with several lakes, and opportunity for a little hunting and fishing and family fun. What more could a man want?

About this time I was invited to what the Chamber of Commerce called "a leadership retreat" that was held out near Carpenter's Creek. This was a combination informal get together in the out-of-doors, with brainstorming for the betterment of the Chamber and its services. There was good food, a little whiskey, plenty of fellowship . . . and I believe everyone saw benefit in this kind of gathering.

When I returned to my office I began thinking of how such a gathering might benefit the newspapers. After all, we had a growing number of good customers whom we'd like to entertain to show appreciation. Such a gathering might also let them get to know one another, along with perhaps some of the area's political leadership . . . and maybe even some big names from around the state. My friend Justice B. K. Roberts was one such name, and B. K. had often entertained me and others with his tales of "the good old days" in the rural parts of North Florida . . . stories about early politicians, outlaws, and the like. I talked to Justice Roberts, asking if he would be willing to be a speaker for an outdoor barbecue if I would put together an audience of about one hundred at my farm. He was delighted with the idea . . . and so our great plan took form.

Bob Rainey, Marion Gaines, Julius Grice and others on my staff helped develop an invitation list; and Judge Cagle, who was the operator of the Coffee Cup Restaurant, was engaged to provide some good food . . . an old fashioned barbecue. We had liquid refreshment, of course, and to make the afternoon more fun we provided some contests, shooting, horseshoes and golf. (You see, I had learned early that grown men, even those in high places, are like little boys when they go to an affair like this. Each has his forms of hobbies in the outdoors, and each liked to win prizes. So . . . we began by having a few such opportunities, and sure enough . . . that idea worked too.)

Well, I will tell you that the first Woodbine Springs barbecue was a howling success! My guests loved it, nature cooperated by providing a gorgeous fall afternoon, the food was first rate, Justice Roberts was entertaining . . . and when the visitors headed home the Thank You's were profuse. "We've never had anything like this in Pensacola," the men said, one after the other.

Monday morning our staff held a critique to see what the results might have been in practical terms . . . and all agreed that we had scored a winner. For the future this would become an ongoing event.

Year by year the numbers grew . . . two hundred . . . four hundred . . . one thousand. At the peak in its last year (1976) the event was attended by almost fourteen hundred people, who consumed copious quantities of good food and drink. Our games expanded too. We added basketball shooting, made the golf game a best approach shot sort of thing, and altered the turkey shoot so that instead of taking home a live bird the winners would have frozen Toms. We even provided a tent which would be the shelter for eating, in case of rain; but through all 19 years we were never inconvenienced by a downpour. Inside the tent we installed TV sets so the chairborne could watch their favorite football games. Sometimes we had a little band for music . . . and there was always a first-class speaker, sometimes local (such as Dave Johnson) sometimes from downstate. Edward Ball always came, and he told me time after time that this was his favorite outing of the year, every year. Others who came were MacGregor Smith and Bill Pauley, along with Lawrence Sheffey, who by then headed all of Southern Bell's operations for Florida. Lawrence and several others were invited from the Miami area, and flew up for the event. There were, on some occasions, other forms of special entertainment. I hired Odie Bell to have his two helicopters there to give people rides, and while he was in the state government, Wendall Jarrard flew in from Tallahassee and landed on our little air strip. Some of those who flew with Odie hit the ground saying that they had noticed that one of our lakes was in the shape of Florida . . . and had I known that? Indeed I had.

Many an amusing story came out of those many years of barbecues. One harkened back to one of the first years, when we were giving live turkeys as turkey-shoot prizes. On one occasion four men seemingly tied for the ownership of one bird. All had come together in one car, and as they started home they began to argue about which one actually had title to the bird. Finally, as they crossed the bridge across the river on Highway 90, the argument grew hot and so they proposed to settle it in a practical way. They got out took the turkey from the car trunk, and turned the startled bird loose. Then, each in turn was to have his shot at the bird, which by now recognized its opportunity and had begun to take off. One after another the hunters fired . . . and each one missed. To this day that turkey may still be inhabiting the nearby woods . . . for not one of those men scored a hit.

On another occasion one guest (who will remain nameless) won the live bird and took it home, planning to dispatch it the next day, for Thanksgiving. He put the bird in his basement and went about this business. Next day he got out his shotgun, and went outside and through the external entry to the basement. As he did so a neighbor happened to see him. Moments later a gun shot was heard and the neighbor, fearing that his friend had committed suicide, ran screaming into the basement to see if he could help. There were two rather surprised men (for different reasons), when my very much alive guest emerged carrying a dead turkey and ran into the arms of his almost hysterical neighbor. Needless to say that was the last turkey shot in that particular basement.

Year by year, as these outings grew, we expanded the roster of special guests. This was a fine way to encourage important people to come to Pensacola and to get acquainted; it was also good business for the *News-Journal*, for it generated news, and perhaps revenues too. For example, J. E. Davis, of Jacksonville and a top executive of Winn-Dixie stores out of Jacksonville, became a regular attendee, and he loved being here. His store's lineage with us was—well—very satisfying, though I wouldn't ever want to claim that his attendance at the farm in any way influenced what the chain spent. On one occasion, I forget the year, we had five men present from Miami, and by chance none of them knew the other. One of these men won a frozen turkey, and on the flight home as this man came on board my friend Lawrence Sheffey happened to sit behind him and noticed that this man was carrying an odd-shaped bundle which he handled very gingerly. This was a time when the country was very sensitive over hijacking and bomb threats, so immediately Lawrence was suspicious. Finally, he couldn't stand it any longer and began a conversation with the man, only to find that they had both attended my party. Lawrence's tension was decreased markedly by that conversation.

After a few years we began another tradition—presentation of the annual Page One Awards to outstanding Floridians, among them Dr. Ashton Graybiel, medical pioneer of the space program; MacGregor Smith, colorful president of Florida Power & Light; lawyer E. Dixie Beggs for his long community and legal career; Dr. Reed Bell, pioneer of the Children's Hospital at Sacred Heart; and the Rev. Van Davis, a popular church leader. In each instance we had a special picture story made up like the first page of the paper and made this presentation amidst much fanfare. This went over BIG!

Quality speakers were always a concern for me, as well as a sharp master of ceremonies who could move the program along. Up to this time I had known Fisher-Brown's Dave Johnson well, but we could hardly have been called close friends. Then, at a social function one day I happened to bump into

Dave's wife, Mary, who told me about his recent success as a speaker at a national insurance meeting. I made a mental note of this and soon thereafter asked Dave if he would be our speaker at the next session. He accepted with enthusiasm, and when he made his presentation he introduced a lot of fellow citizens to the fact that he was not only very articulate but also very funny. Thereafter Dave was almost always our MC.

As the number of attendees grew, the cost of those affairs skyrocketed too . . . but they were still considered very important to the paper. I checked our tax status on this with the proper people, and the tax officials encouraged having letters written to us that would document the interest and worth as considered by those in attendance. I received a huge volume of such mail—all of it highly complimentary—and I still treasure some of those letters.

Keeping the guest list current, and trying to eliminate gate crashers, was not easy. We discovered once, for example, that a few who had been invited were selling their invitations for as much as forty dollars. On one occasion we announced that—to keep our list current and be certain we had the proper mailing addresses—we wanted to have all present sign our guest book. That helped . . . but we never did solve the problems fully. We even had a carefully disguised female gate-crasher. My staff members worked hard at this, just as they did sending invitations, managing the parking, supervising the games and more. To this day I can see Pat Donnelley as a car park, and Buddy Sanchez trying to monitor the basketball shoot.

One other minor problem was theft. I soon learned to take the caps off liquor bottles so they could not easily be carried away. Some of the paid help had seemed to be helping themselves . . . and we wanted none of that.

The final barbecue was held in 1976, the year after my retirement from the Gannett organization. By then the inflation of the Carter years had begun, and Gannett felt that the time had come to end the event. I hated to see that, for our area has never had anything to equal it in terms of fellowship. More than twenty-five thousand men who had attended over the years expressed gratitude and sadness. But, there comes a time . . .

As publisher I was often the recipient of invitations to events which came about following local functions in which the newspaper had been helpful. Example: On one occasion we had been involved with a company which installed a new public water system for the city, and several of us were invited to a sort of "the job is finished" party. This was to be a duck hunt in rural Arkansas, near the city of Stuttgart. My trip to Arkansas was—well—somewhat eventful in that the Peabody Hotel in Memphis lost my overnight reservation and I spent several hours trying to snooze on an Army cot in the hotel's cavernous sample room. But, all's well that ends well, and I was in place when the hunt began.

For this event the hosts had arranged for the presence of "the world's greatest duck caller," and they had set up little stands covered by camouflage canvas, well out in the marsh. I will admit that I am not and never have been a very good shot where ducks are concerned, so they put me on the end in a row of seven blinds, facing across a marsh.

We took our places and the caller called, and I will say he lived up to his reputation. Within minutes the sky was growing black, clouded by a huge flock of excited birds seeking out the source of the call. I picked up my gun and was just getting ready to position myself to shoot when—to one side—I heard a strange padding sound, like some creature heading on the ground for my blind. I stopped what I was doing, bent down and parted the canvas. There, just below me and getting ready to try to enter my stand, was a very large skunk. I mean . . . a VERY large animal . . . and he was within seconds of becoming all too friendly with me. What to do?

At that moment good sense overcame reluctance. I raised my gun, pointed it towards the ground and the skunk, and fired. BAM!

Well . . . the results would have to be obvious to anyone. The skunk parted this world without doing his damage; but the ducks, thoroughly startled, were off in a flash, before another shot could be fired. That ended hunting for the day.

Now, I suspect that some would say that I used good judgement in that action. But, strangely, those nice people in Stuttgart have not to this day ever invited me back. I wonder why.

Thus far I've said very little about local politics in Escambia County. Someone who might read this fifty years from now might think that the area was lily white in its government, but that wasn't so. No, we had our share of rascals and thieves in public office, and I'll say that our paper tried hard to stand for what was good in government. We examined the backgrounds of candidates, and we were never afraid to recommend good ones.

At one time we even printed ballots on which we placed our stamp of approval of favored men and women, and then explained why we had made those choices. Sometimes this worked, sometimes it didn't, but generally our batting average was pretty fair. For a time, when our county system utilized specific districts for commissioners and some of those men began to build their districts as powerbases or fiefdoms, the paper, and others, mounted a campaign through the legislature and Supreme Court to change the system to have all commissioners elected at large. That went just fine until the mid-1950s, when the U. S. courts began to take such things into their own hands.

We got into other programs too that were partly governmental. For example, Earle Bowden suggested the concept of the Gulf Islands National Seashore and finally won a great victory, with a national park arrangement covering parts of three states. We were actively behind the group too, that began promoting restoration in the Seville Square district.

Another *News-Journal* objective was the expansion of the city limits, for it seemed obvious that progress was occurring under the city's rule but not necessarily outside. One of the geographic areas that really needed city help was Brownsville, which in the 1950s seemed to deteriorate more every year. I managed to call a group of Brownsville leaders together to try and promote the annexation issue, but I almost was run out of town on a rail! Those people would have no part of the plan. To try and promote the idea in a different way we started a small community newspaper for Brownsville, hoping that constant stories and editorials about the needs and the advantages of being in the city might make a difference in attitudes. W. G. (Bill) Champlin was our business manager, but the paper failed to win over the people.

Our successes in Santa Rosa County were more pronounced. When I acquired the Woodbine Springs property it fronted on an unpaved road, heading north towards Chumuckla. When the state began talking about paving that highway I stepped forward and gave property for the right of way. I repeat—I gave it—not sold it. There was even enough width in the land to allow four-laning of that road which I hope will be done some day.

In Milton we did not try to start a paper. The *News-Journal* circulation there was doing just fine, and so we just worked harder than ever to make the *News-Journal* their paper too.

Speaking of the politics of progress there are a few other tidbits to mention. When the State Road Board was considering the improvements to Highway 90 East, and a new bridge across the Escambia River, the initial plans called for a low-level Escambia River bridge. This didn't make sense to me, because Gulf Power already was considering the barging of coal to the Crist Steam Plant, and if any other industry should consider locating up the river and might need similar service, barges had to be able to go under the new bridge. I won't claim that the paper's position was all-powerful in the final decision, but the new bridge was built with an arch to accommodate industrial craft. Where would Monsanto have been if that had not been done?

We fought a similar battle to get a four-lane done on Highway 90 West. From the days when Edward Ball and others had fostered North Florida road building they had dreamed of a four-lane highway all the way from Jacksonville to San Diego . . . and in the 1930s several states and communities did get such work done. But the project came slowly in Escambia County. However, this was one of our projects, and as the 1950s passed, the paper pushed hard for such work. Finally, we got it.

One admission: a newspaper publisher gets many offers of special favors from special interest groups anxious to earn his support. One also gets similar opportunities when he sits on state and regional boards that deal with large sums of public money. I got such offers. But I will say this: I never . . . never . . . took advantage of a single one. When I was offered an opportunity to buy stock in WEAR-TV as it was being planned I had to decline with thanks. The TV station would be the paper's advertising competitor, and I could not be party to ownership under those conditions. The same was true of the Pensacola Greyhound Track. That was gambling, and I dared not become a target of criticism.

On another tack, some people have asked through the years why I did not serve more actively on more boards of organizations doing good for the community. Well, actually, I have been party to a good many, but in my role I had to devote a great deal of time and effort to the paper's day-to-day operations; I could not put myself in a place where I was going to have to give large blocks of time on a continuing basis. That just wouldn't work. I did encourage the paper's editor and key staff to be active, and I was surely part of many of the great programs of those years—the evolution of Community Chest into United Way—the development of the highly successful Debutante Charity Cotillion—the hospital boards—the various service agencies. Our papers tried to foster them, and to support such agencies as the Salvation Army in season. I had to put those accomplishments down as our contributions.

☞ ☞ ☞

I apologize if my tales of politics seem a bit disjointed . . . but in seeking only highlights that was inevitible. The two following incidents make the point.

On one occasion Theda and I were invited to a function at Pensacola Naval Air Station, to greet the Secretary of Defense, James Forrestal. Mr. Forrestal had made many headlines, and was perhaps the most famous man in the cabinet at this time. Thus we gladly accepted, but then something came up that made us late for the event. We rushed to the station and hurried to the Quarters house where this very large reception was taking place. But by the time we arrived the event was all but over, and as one of our friends told us as he exited, "Braden, you aren't the only one late; the guest of honor hasn't shown up either." By now it was at least ninety minutes past starting time, and the guests, many of whom had other commitments, were departing.

We went in, and already most rooms were all but empty. Theda went off to powder her nose, leaving me to myself. I stepped into the living room, which showed the effects of a large party. There was a profusion of used napkins in evidence, and on the large fireplace mantle stood a whole row of glasses, most of which had remains of drinks of many types. I was standing in a corner when a man entered. He didn't see me, and after a second look I realized that here was the guest of honor, Mr. Forrestal. Without hesitating, the secretary strode to the fireplace, and one after another downed the contents of those partly filled glasses. He never sniffed, he never looked at what he was attacking, though it was probable that some glasses also held remnants of cigarette butts as well as bourbon or scotch. He simply downed them all . . . then walked out. We never even got to shake his hand.

A week later, in New York, Mr. Forrestal leaped from a window in a tall office building far above the street. WHY he ended his life was never fully explained. But, his behavior at that reception could have been a signal that something was about to happen.

When the Presidential hopefuls began to line up for the 1964 campaign there was among them the rather liberal governor of New York, Nelson Rockefeller. As the primary in Florida neared Mr. Rockefeller was in the state for the National Governor's Conference in Miami. Newspaper publishers from across the state were urged to attend . . . and I did. As we entered Mr. Rockefeller was in a receiving line, flanked by aides who supposedly knew all of the guests who were advancing, one by one, to shake the candidate's hand. As I moved forward in the line I could hear Mr. Rockefeller say such things as "Oh, so nice to meet you Mr. Brown, we're counting on your help." As I came close I could not help overhearing an aide whisper to the host: "The next one is Braden Ball. He's publisher of the two Pensacola papers."

Others before me had been given a big smile and a cordial handshake. Theda and I, on the other hand, were seized by both hands, given the biggest, warmest welcome you ever saw by the governor and his wife, Happy, and about thirty seconds of warm conversation and greeting. Mr. Rockefeller proved in an instant what is meant by the "power of the press."

☞ ☞ ☞

It was in the mid-1960s that one of my most exciting hours came to pass in operating our newspapers. What developed had begun years earlier, when young John Perry, working for his father, had come into contact with the deep-seated feather-bedding by some of the unions that cost all publishers dearly. John Perry resolved then to do something about those practices which were time consuming, duplicative and very expensive.

In the late 1950s, when he and his father acquired a magazine operation in Palm Beach, John began experimenting with ways to eliminate the costly practices. They experimented with new presses made in Europe. They experimented with new methods of setting type that circumvented the traditional linotype and similar machines. They experimented with new headliners, and new ways of page makeup using cold type methods and photo composition which were fast and economical and which could be performed in many cases by skilled typists rather than union card holders sitting at large and slow machines. Going even beyond this John became one of the first industrial users of computers, finding ways through these machines to set, justify and hyphenate type . . . and then to send that material by means of telephone hookups from city to city. What was happening, you see, was that by using his non-union magazine as a research center, John (who incidentally got some very practical assistance from Cecil Kelley of Panama City, for Cecil was also a mechanical genius) was able to perfect a new method of publishing, step by step, and keep the information out of the hands of unionists who would try to stop him. It was interesting for me, in a way, as salesmen for newsprint and other supplies who observed John's experiments in south Florida would tell me what they had seen, and ask when we were going to introduce these changes. I always talked with them in a roundabout way, never disclosing what I knew about these projects.

Well, after a time the unions did discover what was going on, and in an effort to halt the progress they threatened to strike Mr. Perry's paper in Palm Beach and ours in Pensacola. Those were tense moments, for we had never had a strike here; but we were ready. We called their bluff, and union members walked out and began to picket. You know, it was wonderful how well the Perry group had done its homework! Our first edition done under the new system using the typesetting and preparation in Palm Beach and the telephone return to Pensacola, was just one hour late in putting papers on the street. After that things went so smoothly that one might have thought we had been using the methods for years.

The union members? They stayed on the street. It was funny, really. At Christmastime it had been our practice to give holiday turkeys to employees. This year, when the holiday approached the picketers were still on the street, and some called out to me and asked if they would receive their birds. My response was simple: "No workee . . . no turkey!"

The strike dragged on and on, with some of the strikers finding jobs with commercial printers, and others holding out, though after a time I'm sure they realized their cause was hopeless. Only a few ever came back to work with us. The strike was won . . . and from the moment the walkout began there was a parade of other publishers to the Perry plants to see how we had done it. Within a short time virtually every newspaper in the world had adopted John Perry's new methods, to the great benefit of the communications industry.

I have to admit to one of the more humorous aspects of the long strike. Unions, of course, often honor picket lines, and while we had no problem running or even circulating our papers, there was some difficulty with incoming trucks carrying supplies. Our syndicated Sunday comics were the best example.

The color comics were printed elsewhere and would arrive in the trailer of a big eighteen-wheeler. The driver would park his truck along the street. When the strike began drivers would not back the vehicle to the loading dock, for that would be crossing the line. And so Julius Grice and I had to take over and try to guide the monstrous truck into place. I tell you those episodes gave me new admiration for those who move such vehicles in and out of American businesses. Our movement had to be backward, off the street and through a narrow gate to where we could bring the back of the truck to the dock. Often I would be the guide and Julius the driver, though we both gave the two jobs a try. The strikers loved this! They would stand there and shout, "Just a little more to the left, Mr. Ball . . ." or "Guess you'll never be a trucker, Mr. Ball."

Actually, this was all done in good humor. The strikers and I were never in a mean-spirited exchange. Throughout the strike we treated one another with dignity, and there were no hard feelings that I know of. But even later, when the unpleasantness was long over one printer might come up to me and say: "You got a job driving over the road yet, Mr. Ball?"

The only sad note in all of this was that John Perry received very little recognition for his pioneering work. It was this, among other reasons, that encouraged him to sell his newspaper interests just a few years later. In 1994 I got John some help in writing a biographical account of how all of this had taken place.

In our plant, of course, we continued to make all kinds of improvements. We went from a tubular press to a four-unit Goss Headliner that could handle forty-eight pages at one run. There was even a new method of folding papers as they came off the line, and of course we made many experiments to further improve the quality of our product. The makeup areas were radically changed, for the old stereotypers were no longer needed. All sorts of clip art and then computer graphics came into play. Yes . . . these were exciting times to have been in the business, and with a good circulation team and a news nose for specials we continued to expand into other areas of Northwest Florida.

❧

CHAPTER FIVE
My Association with Edward Ball

I have mentioned my early meeting with Florida financier Edward Ball, at the time when we were attempting to assemble a special section of the *Panama City News-Herald* to celebrate the opening of the St. Joe Paper Company. From that point forward my contacts with him were infrequent for the next several years. We were both occupied with many projects—road building, the assembly of bonds purchased for acquisition of the Florida East Coast Railway and banking on his part; and of course running newspapers, doing war-related work and finally helping John Perry in the acquisition of additional papers for my part. Oh, we did have periodic contacts as our paths crossed through our various activities, but I cannot say that we became close friends until the mid-1940s. Then, by the happiest of chances, things changed.

The first incident came out of the blue. Theda was pregnant with Kirk, and I had elected to do a most un-husband-like thing: I went fishing at Lake Talquin. Of course I didn't just walk away at a time like that. When I got to Quincy I stopped at the hotel, told the managers where I would be on the lake, then asked that they be alert for a phone call. If the call came they were to engage a taxi and send the driver to the lake, where he was to honk his horn three times. Then I would come a-runnin'.

The fishing wasn't great that afternoon, but it was relaxing. I was having fun when—suddenly—there were the three blasts of a horn heard easily across the still water. I rowed ashore, paid the driver, then headed for the hotel. Surprisingly, the call was not a hurry-up from Theda but rather a message from Edward Ball. I could hardly believe it. However, I responded, and he quickly began talking about how good the fishing was at Southwood Farm, and that he hoped I would come over as his guest and wet a line. We had a fine chat, and I assured him that I would accept that kind invitation as soon as possible. And I did. Thus began a unique association, the most unusual one I would ever have with a human being.

One might think that Mr. Ball's message, coming as it did, and at such a location, was highly unusual. Not so. As years passed and I got to know him well I came to realize that he often had a notion to call someone on business or pleasure, on the spur of the moment. He would then tell his staff to get so-and-so on the phone . . . and old so-and-so might be anywhere, Chicago, London, Munich or Paris. Mr. Ball didn't care. He called with a reason . . . and the staff knew that they failed to make a connection at their own peril.

At this time Mr. Ball was in his fifties, and was already an extremely successful man. His sister had married Alfred duPont, and shortly thereafter Mr. Ball had been brought into the family camp as a sort of economic troubleshooter. He was so good at such work that when the duPonts chose to move from Wilmington to Florida Edward Ball was asked to come too. For the next nine years he helped his new employer lay the groundwork for a financial empire which at Mr. duPont's death included a million acres (plus or minus a few hundred thousand) of land in north Florida, a goodly portion of what became the forests for the St. Joe Paper Company. Together they began the assembly of what became the Florida National Banking group; and there were many individual real estate holdings, including the new duPont estate in Jacksonville, called Epping Forest. By the mid-1940s Mr. Ball was recognized as a catalyst who had initiated serious road building in North Florida; he was the kind of power behind the throne who made most ambitious political figures seek his backing. To be invited into a friendly gathering with this man—who by sheer coincidence shared the same last name—would prove a blessing for me.

What kind of relationship did we have? Well, I should begin by saying something about the character of this new friend. Mr. Ball had married in the 1930s, but the ten-year relationship did not come to be a happy one, and there were no children. Mr. Ball might have become a close family man, but I really doubt it. He was a workaholic. He loved what he did, and his thoughts remained driven in the pursuit of his many activities through most of his waking hours. He was a man with thousands of acquaintances but few really close friends. Yet he sought the companionship of that few to whom he could open his thoughts, and with whom he felt comfortable. I guess I just turned out to be such a person. As the years passed his little group expanded to perhaps a dozen or so, counting some wives of associates. Mr. Ball himself, after his divorce, enjoyed the company of lovely ladies, and he was forever the courtly gentleman whose birth and rearing in Tidewater, Virginia, showed through. As the years passed, his little circle came to include Florida Supreme Court Justice B. K. Roberts; power company executive MacGregor Smith, former ambassador William Pauley, B. J. Carter, Gilbert Smith and myself . . . plus a few others in and out, through the years.

I suspect that the call I had received on the lake came as a result of politics. I had recently been appointed to the state's first advertising board by Gov. Millard Caldwell, and Mr. Ball, hearing of this, may have figured some ways I might be helpful to him through that contact, and of course through the newspapers. By now the *News* and *Journal* were coming out of the period of wartime shortages and restrictions. And thus our meetings came into being.

Some of these sessions were very informal. Edward Ball loved to fish and to hunt, and he liked company, so there were frequent invitations to me to pick up rod or gun and join him at either Southwood, or later at Wakulla Springs, which he had acquired. Sometimes we were by ourselves, sometimes there were others present, but the out-of-doors was a passion with Mr. Ball, I suspect because his own boyhood had been spent in an area where the woods and waters were at hand.

As years passed Theda and the other wives were involved more often in our gatherings, sometimes at resorts, more often at the Edgewater Gulf Hotel Mr. Ball had purchased in a distress sale in Mississippi. The hotel was a lovely property, and frequently there would be group parties there, especially at Christmas time. During the holidays Mr. Ball would show his prowess as a master of beverages, preparing a fine eggnog. Now, in telling of my dealings with Edward Ball my timing may jump about a bit, for our activities were by no means conducted on a day-to-day basis. In fact, I suspect that one of my values to him was that I was never his employee, just his friend who could—and did—say what he thought when asked for comment or advice on projects.

Put another way, Mr. Ball knew that I would say what I really thought, not necessarily what I thought he wanted to hear. As time passed he included me as one of the intimates who might gain from some of his personal "deals." You see, Mr. Ball was always on the lookout for opportunities which might benefit the long-term development of the duPont Estate; but as he "prospected" he also might make some acquisitions of his own; often these might be shared with either employees of the St. Joe Paper Company or others, like myself.

The net result of this "prospecting" was that Mr. Ball and I often found ourselves riding together in some rural area, examining property. We sometimes rode in his big four-holer Buick, or on occasion we would go off on the train for some specific errand. These trips came in many shapes and flavors. One of the best remembered involved a castle in Ireland, at Ballynahinch. Mr. Ball had become very interested in Ireland, as a place to invest and possibly as a site to settle (this came at a time when he was very upset at what the Democratic Party was doing to the American tax system). In any event, one of our little group of intimates, Gilbert Smith, had heard Mr. Ball say that he surely would like to be the owner of a castle, and this man found one for sale. The purchase was made, with forty or fifty of us included as shareholders. Ballynahinch was a grand old place, and we all enjoyed visiting there; but later some of the investors felt that to keep pace with the times and to maximize opportunities the castle should be modernized and converted into a tourist hotel. This meant getting into some big bucks, and that was when I opted out. But . . . it was nice to be able to tell my friends (and show them pictures) of MY castle!

On one occasion Mr. Ball and I were traveling to his Mississippi hotel on the L & N Railroad's deluxe Jacksonville-to-New Orleans train, the Gulf Wind. We had reached the tiny station stop which had been installed for the convenience of hotel guests . . . but instead of coming to a proper stop the engineer permitted the train to drift almost half a mile farther down the track. Then we stopped, and the conductor invited Mr. Ball and me to detrain. We were the only passengers getting off there. Mr. Ball looked at our location and told the conductor that he would have to get the engineer to back up. The conductor allowed that this could not be done . . . we would have to depart or risk riding all the way to New Orleans. At that point Mr. Ball showed his mettle . . . and his knowledge of the law. He quoted chapter and verse of ICC statutes covering that state, which disclosed that a passenger had the right to demand that a train place him in a spot of convenience if he had requested a station stop. The conductor retreated, and shortly the train did indeed back up! Mr. Ball gave the man a very friendly smile as we departed. Edward Ball seldom acted unless he knew his facts . . . and if he did he would never back down.

I have many train stories involving Mr. Ball . . . stories of accidents and injuries he suffered, and of involving a potential heart attack . . . but I was not present for those. However, one where I was a party happened during those days when he was in a great struggle for control of the Florida East Coast Railroad. A public hearing was to be held in West Palm Beach. He asked me to join him, and I met him in Jacksonville the night before the meeting. Together we rode a standard FECRR pullman to the West Palm Beach station. There were other railroads contesting Mr. Ball's quest for control of the road, and executives of those companies had come to West Palm, too . . . on their plush private cars, at an obviously high cost. Now, at breakfast time, they were being served royally by white-coated busmen, and there were other conductors and porters bustling about in evidence. Their transport had obviously been expensive. Our train arrived and the two Mr. Balls alighted and walked across the station to a small public restaurant for a basic meal of some toast and tea. As we walked, Mr. Ball said to me: "You see why those companies are going broke? Here we are, riding a basic pullman car and eating at a small restaurant while they're burning up stockholder money riding in high fashion. There's a lesson to be learned there." Indeed there was. Soon afterward the courts awarded the contested railroad to Edward Ball and his associates . . . who proceeded to straighten out its financial woes.

I don't want to convey the thought that Mr. Ball was a penny-pincher. No such thing. In his way, and at appropriate times, he was very generous, to employees, to associates, and to the needy. But he knew how to save a penny, too. One example: Often Mr. Ball would drive all the way from Jacksonville to his hotel in Mississippi. It was not unusual for me to get a call from him at the office which might have gone something like this: "Braden . . . I'm just going through DeFuniak Springs. Why don't you meet me at the regular place and we'll have a nice lunch together?"

The nice place was a little general store on the highway six or seven miles from Pensacola, and at the appropriate moment I would hustle out there to meet him. There we would always have the same lunch . . . some peanut butter crackers and a Seven Up. Then we would play an Alphonse and Gaston game to determine who would pay for this expensive fare. He usually lost. This was ritual, you see . . . and we both came to enjoy it.

As years passed Mr. Ball often brought me into his circle of thoughts on political matters. He was surely no novice at this. Early in the 1930s he had spearheaded a movement to build roads across Florida, working as the outreach for the duPont interests. He was remarkably successful, too, and though some may have felt that this work was self-serving, since it did benefit the huge duPont land holdings, it also made it possible for thousands of small landowners to utilize their property, and for towns to become connected with the world. Some of this work involved influence in the governor's office, but much of it was at the local government level. That's why he liked to have my input. We newspaper people get to know local politicians, their wishes and their weaknesses; having that information could be very helpful. I will say this: I had the privilege of seeing Edward Ball work for many a fine cause, especially the one to which he ultimately willed his great fortune: the care of crippled children for whom real care meant legitimate hope. He was, in all of these things, a sound thinker and a humanitarian.

As years passed my contacts with Mr. Ball became increasingly numerous, and of deeper significance. In one, as the group's ownership and expansion of the Florida National Bank chain continued, Mr. Ball felt a need to have someone in whom he had confidence sit on the board of the bank in Pensacola. Consequently I became a board member, president, and ultimately chairman. In the course of that experience it was my privilege to help oversee the project which planned and then erected the new Florida National Bank Building at Garden and Jefferson streets. This was the culmination of an idea Mr. Ball had conceived during an earlier time when we had worked together to make Jefferson a thoroughfare. Then, he had hoped to raze the aging ten-story Florida Bank building which dated from 1910, to replace it with a more modern bank building. That move had not come to pass, but in the early 1960s a new four-story bank was built on that site.

There's one interesting sidelight to that project which virtually no one knew about. It seems that when Jefferson was continued from Government Street to Garden the intersection was not 100 percent plumb. That is, the angle of intersection was not 90 degrees. When the architect and engineers began to implement the bank plans they came to me and asked which street I wanted the bank flush with—Garden or Jefferson. I told them Jefferson, and so if a very precise individual went there today with calipers or transit he would find that very slight difference in alignment.

I enjoyed my time with the bank, and agonized with Mr. Ball in the late 1960s and into the 1970s when unions and leftist politicians combined to coerce the duPont estate into either divesting itself of its banks, or doing the same with other properties. Mr. Ball and others weighed the facts carefully and ultimately worked out a plan where up-front control of the statewide banking system was altered. When that occurred, my career as a bank director ended. It had not been a paying job, and it required considerable time. However, there is something nice about being able to say that one is chairman of the board of a prominent bank!

As the years passed Mr. Ball's interest in wildlife conservation continued to increase, with the result that in the 1960s he founded the Edward Ball Wildlife Foundation. Its directors included leaders in state and national wildlife activities, the Audubon Society and others. The foundation assembled under its wing several natural areas in which game and birds were protected. Keystone of the group was Wakulla Springs, where the Wakulla River, the deep spring, and hundreds of acres of unspoiled wilderness were carefully maintained. At one point I even helped with the making of a film which told the story of Wakulla, Southwood, the seventy-five hundred acre Box-R Ranch, and the wilderness trail the foundation had underwritten at the University of West Florida. For all of these activities our foundation board would meet periodically, develop policy and enjoy good fellowship. It was sad to see that when Mr. Ball passed on it was necessary to dismantle the foundation, and to almost literally give some of the properties, including Wakulla, to the state of Florida.

On the subject of Southwood Farm, Mr. Ball's retreat, there is one story that must be told. In the course of his divorce proceedings Mr. Ball made this house, not far from Tallahassee, his official residence, thus many of us would visit there regularly. Southwood Farm was a fine old home which originally had stood on other property but had been moved to a new site when the St. Joe Paper Company began to experiment a bit in cattle ranching. In any event, Mr. Ball had the place tastefully furnished in fine antiques, and he often entertained guests from far away places.

Now . . . one thing was unique about this house. It had a ghost! One bedroom in particular was visited by an apparition, who made odd overtures and used clammy fingers in the middle of the night. On two occasions when Theda and I stayed in that room we were visited by this spirit . . . and while many will say this is all nonsense, I can only repeat that we FELT and HEARD this visit. So did others, including some guests Mr. Ball had from England, where ghosts in old castles are a regular happening. The final appearance of this visitor came when several couples of us were being entertained at dinner and heard steps on the stairs. All of us heard the sounds, and all were at the table! There had been much talk about the ghost, so almost as one we leaped up and ran to see what we could see. The result? The Southwood Ghost had vanished once more.

Now . . . some people may not believe this story . . . but ask Theda! Her experiences in the night, waking with cold, clammy hands about her throat, made her a believer. Me? Well . . . I just take both sides . . . because I saw and heard this thing too. Mr. Ball? He would shake his head solemnly when the ghost story was addressed, and note that he was sure he had seen the vision, too.

As we grew older the little group of Mr. Ball's friends treasured its meetings more and more, and took opportunities to travel together. I have never particularly enjoyed flying, and Mr. Ball absolutely refused to get off the ground until quite late in life, when he realized that there were still many things he wanted to see, and that with any other mode of transport this wouldn't happen. His travels then took him—sometimes with me and with Theda—to Europe and other destinations. On one occasion—in Ireland—the three of us were to attend a reception given by our ambassador, and as we approached the receiving line Mr. Ball asked if I would trade places with him, and let him enter with Theda. That's what we did. The ambassador, who did not know us, was open-mouthed for a moment, surprised at Edward Ball's youthful wife, but he caught on and got a laugh with us.

On another occasion I was traveling with Mr. Ball and Jake Belin, the three of us heading for south Florida. We checked our bags, boarded our plane, sat quite awhile, and then were told by the captain that there was an equipment problem and that we'd have to deplane and be boarded on another flight. We were to claim and recheck our luggage. That went fine for two of us . . . but not for Mr. Ball. His bag was gone. "Well," he muttered, "I guess I'm the only man in history who tried to go by air then had the airline lose his luggage before he'd gone anywhere."

Late in his life Mr. Ball added still another kindness when he saw to it that I was named a member and later president of the board of the Alfred duPont Foundation, a Florida group which annually uses proceeds from a portion of the duPont Estate to assist worthy causes. I've been a member of that group for a long time now, and I will say that it has been a very pleasurable experience.

In his lifetime Mr. Ball suffered through a number of health problems, including several mild heart attacks. However, he never gave up his joy at having his nightly toddy of Old Forrester whiskey . . . and most of his cronies were glad to join him. He claimed that this tonic warded off pneumonia germs. However, at age ninety-three, there finally came a time when his body would not make that one extra effort, and using his phrase, he "crossed the creek."

Arrangements for his burial had been made well in advance through the good offices of Jake Belin. Following a memorial service in Jacksonville, many of his close friends boarded several private aircraft and flew to Wilmington, where he would be entombed with his sister and his friend, Alfred duPont. The plane I was on included as a passenger the prominent Jacksonville clergyman who had conducted the service there. (I cannot say that he was Mr. Ball's pastor . . . for Mr. Ball never formally belonged to a church. He had a very unusual relationship to religion . . . and I'll just leave the subject that way.) In any event, the plane had been well supplied with refreshments and spirits, but under the circumstances of the day—and with the presence of the good Baptist preacher—no one reached for a drink for some minutes. Finally, I decided to break the ice. I noted that throughout his days Mr. Ball had looked upon good whiskey as the elixir of life, and that if he had been in the cabin he would surely have been the first to suggest that we enjoy a draught. The clergyman grinned and said that he thought that was just right. Everyone but him joined in warding off the cold. Hours later my friend was put to his final rest. That was more than fifteen years ago. I have missed him very much, for in life (and then in death) he made arrangements to do so many good things for so many people.

CHAPTER SIX

Closing out a Career . . . The Good Life

I wasn't expecting the message I got from John Perry that day in 1969. John, like his father, was a newspaper owner who left his publishers alone so long as things were going well. And our papers had been doing extremely well throughout the decade, especially after we cut costs as a result of the new makeup processes.

John is a pretty direct person, and he began by saying that he had a message I might not like—and as it turned out he was right. "Braden," he said, "I'm thinking of selling off the papers. You know, I've made some noises about this before, but this time I really mean it."

Naturally I asked him what had brought this on, and he said:

"Well, you know, after a while anything gets a little stale. I've been working in newspapers since I was sixteen, and then I spent those years with eighteen-hour days perfecting the new technology . . ."

"Yes," I interrupted, "and look what you've done for every newspaper in the world. You brought us out of the dark ages."

"That may be true, all right," John continued, "but who knows about it? Has anyone, especially the big cats, been grateful? Have the *New York Times* or *Washington Post* ever run a feature and said 'Look What John Perry Did For Us'? Hell no! They made a lot of money and I hardly got an attaboy."

I could see that John was a little bit down, so I asked:

"But John, if you sell out, what will you do? You'll make a lot of money, and so will your stockholders . . . but then what'll you do? You're a young man ... you need to keep busy. You can't just quit."

John Perry let me know pretty quickly that he had no intention of quitting. "I'm going to expand my work with mini-submarines and other submersibles," he said. "And I've got a few other irons in the fire too."

Well, it didn't happen at once, but pretty soon I began to get calls from companies that were considering purchase of the *New Journal*. Down they came, to look into our files, evaluate our markets, examine our employees. I tried to be a good host, but often my heart wasn't in it.

Then, late that year, the people from Gannett, from Rochester, New York, announced that they were coming. Again, I put on our best face and I think did a good job of showing them the papers and Northwest Florida. They were impressed, and it wasn't long before I had another call from John to tell me the deal was done. Of course, he assured me that I was part of that arrangement, and that Gannett wanted me to stay on as their publisher. And, for five years I did. Those years were the first half of the 1970s.

One of the colorful events of that period came in the first campaign of Reubin Askew for governor. Reubin had been a local legislator and state senator beginning in the late 1950s, and the paper had generally supported his elections, though admittedly some of his financial positions were a bit more liberal than I preferred. However, in tandem with George Stone, Phil Ashler, Gordon Wells, and a few others, Reubin had been part of a delegation which did many good things for Escambia County. By now—the late 1960s and early 1970s—North Florida's political position in Tallahassee had been overridden by the growing voter strength in the southern part of the state. Our population was growing, but at nowhere near the pace that began to accompany the Disney World explosion, or the Cuban refugee situation in Miami and environs. So, often we felt that we were being left out where the appropriation of funds was concerned. For example, the interstate highway developments in the state mostly seemed to favor the peninsula; Interstate 10 construction had halted well to the east of us.

When the election plans for 1970 developed, many civic leaders and Democratic politicians favored Reubin; I must admit that I was lukewarm. Marion Gaines, of course, was strongly in his corner, and Askew ultimately surprised his doubters by winning. I will say that, slowly but surely, the interstate highway was extended, though I was disappointed in the path it took near Tallahassee. Local political pressures there set the route to the north of the city when logic (and the environment) dictated that it be to the south. North it was, with the result that the state ultimately paid dearly to correct drainage problems and other needs. Drivers, too, ended up going a good many extra miles as they went from Pensacola to Jacksonville.

This also was the period when pressures developed to improve Highway 29 north of Pensacola. For decades this had been the community's only route to the north, and its narrow two-lane construction was hazardous. One of the drawbacks to four-laning was the high cost of right of way, for there were homes and other structures along the obvious plan of construction. It was then that I proposed through the Chamber of Commerce that we simply abandon the old roadway just north of the city. We proposed establishing a new route which would allow Old Palafox Highway to continue to exist, but with a new Palafox being four-laned, through Ensley to the Nine Mile Road, and then beyond. People perked up and admitted that this made sense, for this route would bypass the costly procedures and eliminate inconvenience for many landholders. And so this process began, successfully. Pete Noonan's company won the contract to build the new highway. In like manner I succeeded in getting State Road Board member Billy Mayo to come to Pensacola and study the idea of making Nine Mile Road a four-lane divided highway from the initial university entrance to the junction with Palafox Highway. Billy liked the idea and pushed it. Much of the project was completed, to the delight of thousands of travelers.

However, there was one project on which I failed. I, and many others, recognized that the old route of the L & N Railroad along the Scenic Highway and the bayshore was inappropriate, and also that the railroad would one day have to build a new bridge and trestle across the bay. When planning began for Interstate 10, which of course required a bridge across the bay, we urged that the highway and railway passages be united at the same place. This would have made a major difference in rail traffic, though trains would have had to back in to the downtown station. The plan was given consideration and was approved by L&N officials, but not by the State Road Board. Later the railroad did build its new bridge, but quite a distance from the Interstate Ten structure. And the city continued to struggle with the delays forced by the ongoing rail route into the heart of the city.

It was also in the early 1970s that a new health care bombshell exploded. This came in an announcement by officers of the Medical Center Clinic that its members would build a new headquarters far north on Davis Highway, and that this would be done in a sort of partnership with Hospital Corporation of America. The news was a shock to the operators of the other hospitals, and to other physicians too, all of whom viewed the building of a third major hospital as a threat to their survival; and the fact that HCA was a for-profit entity made the situation even more tense. I was not involved in these changes, but the paper did follow the developments with care. First there was a contest over approval of a state-authored Certificate of Need to permit the construction of the new hospital. Then there was a considerable public relations effort by both interests, for some of the Medical Center's older physicians, anxious to sustain their image with old friends in the profession, maintained that even with a hospital on their new grounds they would continue to care for cases at Baptist and Sacred Heart. When the new facilities for clinic and hospital were occupied in 1975 the paper produced fine, large special editions, but we were not a party to the controversy.

There was a great temptation to add many personal items about my family in this account. I resisted . . . but there are a few which deserve mention.

A wise man once noted that it is a lucky man whose children wish to follow him into his chosen profession. In this as in many other things I have been triply blessed. My two sons, Kirk and Roger, each had an opportunity for part-time newspaper work early in their lives. Each began with a bag of newspapers over his shoulder, learning the fundamentals of salesmanship. Later, when he had finished school, Kirk became part of the news staff, and noted many times later that old school editor Doc Coulter was his mentor. Many years afterward, when he had become one of the heads of Fisher Brown Insurance, Kirk said: "I thought that I could write, but Doc would take my copy and just chew it up. It was mortifying . . . but he taught me how to write."

Roger followed a different path, into advertising sales and management, and he has made this his successful career for more than a quarter of a century as I write this.

Suzanne? Her path was somewhat different. She had majored in Spanish in college, lived in Spain for one year and then did her practice teaching in South Florida. But, in the 1960s I could foresee many negative factors beginning to have an impact on the teachers of that region. I began to urge her to come home and enter the newspaper business. "You could be a fine writer and a good addition here," I told her. Suzanne wasn't so sure. Finally she agreed, to a two week trial. Well, she came, and stayed as a reporter for twenty years. She was indeed a fine member of the staff, and it was always a mark of pride for me that I had all three of my children about me. Nepotism? So what.

As my children grew they became members of the Roman Catholic Church, following Theda, while I remained a religious outcast to them. However, the family had no hang-ups on that score. The boys and Suzanne always went to church, and when we were off together on trips I made sure they got there.

One weekend the boys and I were fishing in the Apalachicola River area and on Sunday morning we made the trip into town, and were among the later ones to enter that lovely old frame church. I went in first and sat down in the pew. Kirk and Roger followed, and automatically they slammed the kneeling bar into place and knelt down. Their action was very quick, and both the bar and weight of my two sons were promptly focused on my toes. My reaction was automatic: "Get off my damn toes!" I hissed . . . but at a level that had to be heard by almost everyone in the building. The boys reacted quickly, yet Kirk couldn't help hissing back.

"You were talking to God before we were!"

The congregation was convulsed.

It was in 1963 that my children and I went to New Orleans to the Sugar Bowl. Arkansas was one of the teams playing, and I'm afraid I can't remember the other. This was well before the Superdome, and the city's huge outdoor stadium was jammed. Our seats were in the first row of the second deck, and thus hung over a great part of the seating area.

Before we entered the stadium I was joking with the boys, for they had been impressed that this game would be one of the very first to be nationally televised, and that we might even show up on the TV screens at home. Then I had a brilliant idea.

"I'll bet I can get us on camera, and maybe even stop the game," I suggested.

"Aw, Dad, you're crazy," they replied.

I was undaunted. On the way in I stopped at a concession stand and changed a twenty dollar bill for twenty ones, asking for new bills if possible. The concessionaire was very obliging.

The game started, and things were going along nicely when I felt it was time to begin my act. I took out the bills, and carefully folded each one into one of those little paper airplanes that boys like to make. Then, as a particularly exciting play ended, I cocked my arm and sent the first bill into flight. There were plenty of air currents in that stadium, and as the bill floated and darted up and down over the heads of the spectators below several caught sight of it and quickly identified it. All began grabbing for the bill, which eluded many. As they did this others joined the fray. At that moment a second bill took flight . . . then a third . . . and a fourth. By now half the stands below were aware that "a Texas Oil Man in a big hat" was throwing money into the crowd. As the fourth bill fluttered down two collared clergymen immediately below tried to climb on each others shoulders to get above the crowd and make a catch. By the time the twentieth bill reached a landing hundreds, perhaps thousands, had ceased to watch play on the field and were competing for this floating money.

Did we stop the game? Well, not exactly, but we surely caught people's attention. However, I'm afraid we'll never know whether the cameras picked up our little escapade.

My friend Edward Ball had married once but was childless. As his years mounted it became obvious that he was uneasy around children. It wasn't that he disliked them; children just made Mr. Ball uncomfortable. I guess they're right when they say dogs and little children can detect such feelings. One day, when Roger was just a little fellow, we were together with Mr. Ball, scouting some property near Tallahassee. There was very little conversation between those two during the first hours, but then Roger suddenly looked up at Mr. Ball and asked:

"Mr. Ball, why don't you like little boys?"

My friend was a man of wit, and usually was well able to respond to questioning. This time he was speechless. He never did answer Roger, and I guess my son simply was confirmed in his suspicions.

One of the happy times in my life began when my daughter Suzanne took off for Spain to begin some post-graduate training in her college major of Spanish. Theda accompanied her on the trip over, and later the whole family visited Spain so that Suzanne might lead us in a tour of the highlights. We visited bull rings and cathedrals, ancient Moorish castles, and lovely monuments. Finally we arrived in Toledo and traveled by taxi to the cathedral where, in a sort of antechamber, they have hung one of the artist Goya's most famous paintings.

Now, I want you to understand that I like ancient castles and cathedrals as well as the next fellow, but in Spain these places were very old, and there was mold and dust everywhere. I have always been allergic to such things, so I did what I felt was the wise thing. I would go in, spend five minutes looking, and then retreat to sit in the cab. If the others wanted to sit for an hour's contemplation that was okay with me. But in Toledo the non-English speaking cabbie couldn't understand my actions. When Suzanne returned he asked her what was wrong, and why her father had shortchanged one of Spain's artistic treasures. Bless her heart, Suzanne tried to make the man understand that I did not mean to insult the Spanish culture . . . but that the dust in such places made me sneeze. She tried . . . but to this day I do not believe that this part of Spanish society has forgiven me.

When Roger was just a little shaver he became enthralled with horses. I guess it was the cowboy movies that did it, but whatever the cause he just pestered the daylights out of his parents to get him a horse. Well, we looked over the prospects and finally ended up with a beast named Baby. Baby was tall, solid, and sort of mean looking, but between those two it was love at first sight. Neither Kirk, Suzanne, Theda nor I could control the animal, but Roger, who was still so small that he would walk head high under the horse's belly, got along just fine as a rider. With Roger on his back Baby was gentle as a lamb.

One day my friend Dave Johnson came to Woodbine Springs with two of his children. As they arrived they could see Roger prancing back and forth on Baby's back. He really made it look easy. And so the Johnson kids pestered for a chance to ride too. I warned 'em, but Dave assured me that the two had been aboard horses many a time and were accomplished as riders for their ages. I nodded agreement. The two got on at once and I gave a soft command to Baby, who at once took off as though he was in the Kentucky Derby. Across the field he raced, with two terrified children shrieking commands and begging the animal to halt. When they had gone perhaps half a mile we could all see Baby make an abrupt turn, which propelled young Catherine Johnson through the air like a missile. Then Baby trotted on.

Happily Miss Johnson was not seriously injured, just shaken, but chagrined too. After that children had a new respect for what Roger could do with horses.

When my children were young I suspect that I overdid it in telling them stories of my childhood and how important salesmanship and selling can be to a career. All three of the kids got the message, but no one more than Roger. He took me up on my challenge. Next thing I knew he was selling little bags of the area's pure white sand to our neighbors, and at Christmas time he would locate discarded Christmas trees and drag them door to door, offering them for sale to family friends "at a very discounted price." It was amazing how understanding those good neighbors were. And—by the way—Roger obviously learned some lessons.

☞ ☞ ☞

One of the men I met early in my life in the eastern Panhandle was T. E. (Doc) Whitfield. Doc was what I must still call a real swamp rat. He had been brought up deep in the bayou country of Gulf County, where little streams and rivers flow together, and where the wildlife and fishing are outstanding.

Doc was as good a man in this regard as one will ever find. He was also smart as a whip, and a really smooth operator in selling backwater real estate. As years passed he was also elected several times as a county commissioner.

Along the way it seemed to me that Roger, who loved to fish, would profit from having a fishing lesson with Doc. It was arranged. They got into Doc's boat and started out. I stayed behind and did some paper°work. Two hours passed; then four. By then I was beginning to be concerned, so I decided to follow behind the pair, to determine what had happened. I found a suitable rowboat and, with a stout oar, I began my quest. I sculled along for half an hour . . . then an hour. Not a sound. Then I began to hear a soft noise, and so I turned in that direction, being careful not to be heard. Finally, Doc's voice could be plainly detected around a bend. A moment later Doc fairly shouted: "Damn it, you little SOB, you'll never catch anything or shoot anything lessen you can keep still in the boat." I couldn't see the pair, but I could imagine the expression on my son's face as he heard the outcry.

"He's getting some good lessons," I mused, and so I carefully removed myself from the scene.

The story had a fine ending. The pair returned to the pier with a handsome string of fish. Roger had learned to be still in the boat.

Often some members of our news department enjoyed playing pranks on older, more senior men who had grown a little more serious about life. Example: One time in the 1950s Pensacola was experiencing a hurricane, and everyone on the paper was straining to get an issue out. Several of the younger newsmen had pretty well finished their tasks. They were grateful that the day was over, for this had been one of those shifts when the phone rang every few seconds as citizens phoned in new storm details. The young men quietly left the department, leaving Doc Coulter behind, the lone man at the desk. Now, Doc was a journeyman, and he knew his stuff. He also recognized where a newsman's priorities were at a time like that.

With Doc remaining behind, the younger set crept into the nearby advertising department and began calling Doc Coulter's desk, one after the other. The more he tried to explain that he was alone and insisted they make calls quick, the more detailed the men became. One after another phones near Doc rang. Only after five minutes did he catch on, and realize that he was being tricked.

One night our family was enjoying a special occasion by dining out at Skopelo's Restaurant, the original location. It was a pleasant affair, and we were all very relaxed. At one point I leaned back in my chair, putting the top of the chair back against the restaurant wall. Thus I remained for a few moments, and then, with the conversation focused at the other end of the table, my chair suddenly began to slip. I didn't even have time to catch myself or ask for help. I simply went down . . . down . . . down . . . quietly ending up under the table.

Seconds later Kirk demanded: "Where's Dad?"

Now, I couldn't very well have walked out, for my place was blocked in. Then, a man at the next table noted what had happened and that I was pinned on the floor. Gallantly he and his tablemate rose, bent down and helped me up.

When my family caught on to what had happened they all burst out laughing. Somehow, I never found this so funny . . . especially since they didn't make the first move to get me on my feet.

Every man has his "happiest days" and his "saddest days," usually marked by something that happened within his family. I have not been an exception to that.

I think the saddest day of all occurred April 26, 1970. That was the day my son Kirk left Pensacola for his Army assignment at Ft. Lewis, Washington. He was en route to Viet Nam, and boarded ship on May 2. I know that countless parents face this kind of dating. Viet Nam was not a popular conflict, but it wasn't the politics that darkened my vision. The possibility that my older son might be lost in some remote, fever-ridden jungle was hardly a happy prospect. Theda and I worried every single day until we heard that Kirk had begun the long journey home. A happier date was October 23 of that same year. Soon he was back, having been met by his wife Colleen in New Orleans on October 25. Only then did the Ball family settle back to normal.

It was a far happier time when Suzanne departed for Spain and her graduate work. How can I say I was happy at seeing my only daughter take off for an extended period in Europe? Well, the background here was far different than it had been in Kirk's case. Suzanne was one student who truly loved her principal area of collegiate study, and for years she had dreamed of studying in the heart of the Spanish culture. Even being the Queen of the Fiesta of Five Flags celebration had not equalled her anticipation for the trip to Spain, and happily Suzanne's experiences lived up to her expectations.

I have to add one other anecdote that she shared later with the whole family. You see, Suzanne makes friends very easily, and while living in Spain she had a little apartment in a building whose concierge was a man who was a sort of block warden during the Francisco Franco regime. He was an older, kindly man, the sort who makes a fine local political contact, and he developed a sort of pseudo father-like relationship with my daughter. When the time came for her to leave, he was truly saddened, but finally he came to her and asked if he might accompany Suzanne to the Madrid airport. She was touched and quickly agreed.

Now, this elderly gentleman had lived in the large Spanish city all his life, but he had never been to the airport. He had no idea of how to get there. So, for several days prior to Suzanne's departure he began charting the course, going stage by stage on foot (returning by bus or taxi after each outing). Finally, he knew how to make the trip. On the morning of Suzanne's flight he escorted her to the cab, loaded her baggage, then knowingly directed the driver (who, of course, knew very well where he was going).

The pair arrived at the terminal, and the man seized Suzanne's bags and entered with my daughter. They walked a number of yards, then came to a mechanical monster which this fine old gentleman knew nothing about. To go up to the passenger check-in area one had to board an escalator. This the man had never seen before. As they approached the rising stairway he stopped, and just froze in place. Here was something foreign to his culture. Suzanne understood. On the spot she thanked him profusely for his kindness, then picked up the bags herself and boarded the conveyance. The man stood there and watched as she rose easily to the next landing.

She never saw him again, of course, but she remembered. So did we after we had all heard the touching tale.

Well, that's the way it happened, and that's the way we entered the 1970s. I've already commented on some of the local events of that period . . . Reubin Askew's election, the Hospital Corporation of America hospital, some new highway construction, the National Seashore. It was all interesting stuff. . . and so I kept my nose to the grindstone.

But, in the meantime Edward Ball had made me a member of the board of the Alfred I. duPont Foundation, and shortly thereafter I had become foundation president. That was a wonderful assignment, with some fine people, and it allowed me to be party to making bequests to many worthy causes in our end of the state. Then I was named to the Edward Ball Wildlife Foundation, and that was another opportunity to work for public good. As these things fell into place Mr. Ball, his own years growing on him, wanted to travel more, and he was kind enough to ask me—and often Theda—to accompany him to some wonderful places. Yes . . . these were good times.

In 1975, as I was approaching my sixty-fourth birthday, I began to talk with Theda about retiring. After all, I'd been working since I was eight, and the routine of the newspapers had been constant since I returned from Gainesville in 1931. She urged me to do it.

"After all, you've got a lot of property to manage out there," she pointed out, "and you've got some other land you and Mr. Ball have put together. Why not concentrate on that—and on ME?"

Who could refuse a suggestion like that?

In due course I gave notice to the Gannett people, thanked their leadership for their many courtesies and assured them that I would be available for help or consultation as needed. Then, as of October 1, 1976, I officially stepped out of my publisher's chair. That road had ended.

The twenty years since retirement have proceeded much as Theda had said they would. It has been a pleasure working with developers who purchased part of my Woodbine Springs property. They have done a quality job, and it's good to see this part of Santa Rosa County being made into a truly quality community, with a fine country club and all. And, of course, my own land, with a little par-three golf course and lakes that teem with fish, is a joy too.

The other property? I'll only mention one piece. It was along Perdido Bay, and I offered it to Dr. Arlin Horton, president of Pensacola Christian College. I'd heard him say that he was looking for a waterfront site for the college's recreational grounds that was also environmentally attractive. One day I took the good doctor and his wife to the site and asked what they thought. They were delighted. Now the Perdido land is the college's west campus and is a thing of beauty.

Who could have asked for a more fulfilling life? For fifty-seven years I've had a marvelous wife. We have a wonderful family, children and grandchildren, all of whom are a joy to me . . . and I've had the privilege of being a part of so many good things—newspapers, banking, radio stations, real estate and state government.

This story began with the Model T Ford and classic Hudson. Today it continues with travels across our acreage in a golf cart and over Northwest Florida's roads and highways in a well-worn Mercedes. But no matter which wheels are involved . . . it has been a grand ride.

Some years ago the actor Jimmy Stewart appeared in a movie called *It's a Wonderful Life*, a show that has become a Christmas classic. Well, the story of George Bailey in that film was great, but I wouldn't have traded with him. My eighty-five years have been wonderful too, and on these few pages I've really enjoyed sharing some highlights with you.